THE ART OF COOKING

CALIFORNIA STUDIES IN FOOD AND CULTURE

DARRA GOLDSTEIN, EDITOR

THE ART OF COOKING
THE FIRST MODERN COOKERY BOOK

COMPOSED BY THE EMINENT
MAESTRO MARTINO OF COMO,
A MOST PRUDENT EXPERT IN THIS ART,
ONCE COOK TO THE MOST REVEREND
CARDINAL TREVISAN,
PATRIARCH OF AQUILEIA

Edited and with an Introduction by Luigi Ballerini
Translated and Annotated by Jeremy Parzen
&
with Fifty Modernized Recipes by Stefania Barzini

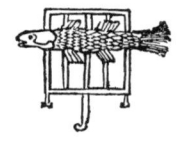

UNIVERSITY OF CALIFORNIA PRESS
BERKELEY   LOS ANGELES   LONDON

University of California Press
Berkeley and Los Angeles, California

University of California Press, Ltd.
London, England

© 2005 by the Regents of the University of California

Library of Congress Cataloging-in-Publication Data
Maestro Martino.
   [Libro de arte coquinaria. English]
   The art of cooking : the first modern cookery book / composed
by The Eminent Maestro Martino of Como ; edited and with an
introduction by Luigi Ballerini ; translated and annotated by Jeremy
Parzen ; and with fifty modernized recipes by Stefania Barzini.
      p.   cm.
   Includes bibliographical references and index.
   ISBN 0-520-23271-2 (cloth : alk. paper)
      1. Cookery, Italian—Early works to 1800.   2. Cookery—
Italy—Early works to 1800.   I. Ballerini, Luigi.   II. Parzen,
Jeremy.   III. Barzini, Stefania.   IV. Title.
   TX723.M3126513   2005
   641.5945—dc22   2004005160

Manufactured in Canada
14   13   12   11   10   09   08   07   06   05
10   9   8   7   6   5   4   3   2   1

The paper used in this publication meets the minimum requirements
of ANSI/NISO Z39.48–1992 (R 1997) (Permanence of Paper). ♾

CONTENTS

MAESTRO MARTINO

THE CARNEADES OF COOKS

Luigi Ballerini

Dear Reader: This is a cookbook—a historical cookery book. If you do not care to read about the world from which it grew (and it would be perfectly understandable if you didn't), skip the present introduction altogether. No need to feel guilty about it. Read it only if you are the type that does not mind a little suffering. I promise that, at the end, you will hasten to search for a great chef, either in the outside world or within yourself, to obtain from either of them (or from both) the culinary reward you undoubtedly deserve.

FOR A GOOD NUMBER OF YEARS, a few centuries in fact, the only known mention of Maestro Martino was to be found in the writings of the fifteenth-century Italian humanist Bartolomeo Sacchi, who was acquainted with him personally.

This means that the name of an unknown person was for a while on the lips and twice, at least, in the pen of a "reporter" who, in our day and age, is just as unknown as his "reportee." The muse of history contributed some humor of its own. So enchanted was Sacchi (who in his own time was actually famous enough to need no introduction) with Martino's gastronomic and rhetorical virtues that he did not hesitate to compare him to Carneades (213–129 B.C.E.), whom Sacchi's contemporaries would have immediately recognized as the illustrious philosopher who headed the New Platonic Academy in Athens, and whose subtle eloquence and argumentative dexterity, appreciated and praised during that rebirth of classical culture we know as the Renaissance, would eventually fall into the same oblivion that now surrounds the cook no less than the scholar.

There is more: ever since the hypertrophic question "Carneades, who was he now?" found its way into the pages of Alessandro Manzoni's *I promessi sposi* (*The Betrothed;* first published in 1827), only to be repeated, generation after generation, by legions of high school kids, Italians have adopted the name Carneades as the quintessential moniker of obscurity.[1]

Thus, to make sure that fame would not treat Martino unfairly, Bartolomeo Sacchi bestowed upon him the following encomium: "What a cook, O immortal gods, you bestowed in my friend Martino of Como, from whom I have received, in great part, the things of which I am writing. You would say he was another Carneades if you were to hear him eloquently speaking *ex tempore* about the matters described above."[2]

Luckily, by the time the events in this story began to unfold, the printing press had become a permanent feature of European cultural life, with the result that Sacchi's praise of Martino would be repeated a fair number of times, in the 1474 as well as in the numerous subsequent

editions of his treatise *De honesta voluptate et valetudine* (*On Right Pleasure and Good Health*). But Sacchi's treatise paid homage to Martino in a way that went beyond the exigency of a compliment, eventually yielding results that we are only beginning to appreciate more than five centuries later. By "lifting" the cook's recipes and translating them into Latin, Sacchi ensured that the highly original approach of Maestro Martino's *De arte coquinaria* (*The Art of Cooking*) would not remain confined to a few obscure manuscripts penned in the vernacular, but on the contrary would be disseminated throughout Renaissance Europe in the first cookbook deemed worthy of mechanical reproduction.[3]

To fully appreciate the novelty and impact of Martino's gastronomy, we must situate him in time and place, studying the changes in culinary practice that his example helped to usher in. Given the paucity of historical information available about Martino himself, our study must be necessarily oblique. We begin with the prologue-master, Sacchi, about whom much was known though little is now remembered, and proceed from there to the leading man, about whom we now know a little more than we did a few decades ago, although certainly not enough to satisfy our appetite. Along the way, we will season the plot with accounts of supporting actors and extras (Renaissance popes and cardinals, for the most part, but even a twentieth-century American gentleman), and with a register of motives that will surely pique the interest of those who love good food and the history and art of gastronomy.

Bartolomeo Sacchi is much more recognizable by his pseudonym, Platina (PLAH-tee-nah), a Latinization of Piadena, the name of the small township in which he was born in 1421, poised between Cremona and Mantua in the heart of the fertile, humid Padanian plains. We can only imagine that he couldn't wait to leave, as is the case for many even today. Remembering his birthplace whenever he appended his name at the bottom of an epistle or some official document must have seemed to him jingoistic enough.

Judging from his future career as a humanist, it is fair to surmise that he would have preferred to have been born in Greece, or at least to have perfected his competence in the language of literature, philosophy, and art by conversing with his peers in an appropriate academic garden or, lacking such a garden, under the roof of a well-constructed stoa.

But Platina had been born into a poor family that looked upon such Renaissance dreams as the ravings of a lunatic, and so he was forced to become a soldier of fortune. If Platina was present, as is highly probable, at the legendary Battle of Anghiari in 1440, in which Florence defeated Milan, he probably heard mention of Ludovico Trevisan—it is unlikely that he actually saw him on the battlefield. Trevisan, on orders from the Holy Church, had brought four thousand men to the site of the conflict, and some years later would be served by Maestro Martino in Rome.[4]

Quickly tiring, we presume, of both the art of war and the soldier's pay that came with it, Platina sought and obtained the protection of the Gonzaga family, the princely house that ruled Mantua. This enabled him to study with the famed humanist and preceptor Omnibonus Leonicenus, called by his friends Ognibene da Lonigo. When the latter, in turn, grew tired of instructing the Gonzagas' children, Platina was handpicked by him as his successor.

From the Mantua of the Gonzagas, Platina made his way to the Florence of the Medicis, which by then could claim to have become a New Athens, possibly the greatest center of that "renewal of learning" by which Italy has managed to capture and exploit the cultural attention of the modern and contemporary world. There he studied with Byzantine humanist John Argyropoulos (1415–87), who had arrived in Florence in 1456 after fleeing Constantinople (which fell to the Ottomans in 1453) and could boast of having as students the most illustrious scholars and poets of the time, such as Marsilio Ficino, Poggio Bracciolini, Cristoforo Landino, Giovanni Pico della Mirandola, and Politian.

Highly cultured and restless, Platina left Florence for Rome in 1461, following his student Francesco Gonzaga, who had been made cardinal—at the tender age of eighteen—by the "humanist pope" Pius II, Enea Silvio Piccolomini.[5] And in Rome he would remain, through good times and bad, until he died in 1481 from the plague and was buried in the glorious basilica of Santa Maria Maggiore, with funeral rites attended by a congregation of Roman literati.[6]

In the Eternal City, Platina sought fortune as obstinately as misfortune sought him, as we shall see.

After more than a hundred years of neglect on the part of her bishop and God-appointed master, the return of Pope Martin V, which concluded the so-called Avignon Exile or Babylonian Captivity (1309–1417), as well as the Great Schism (1378–1417), had engendered an explosion of creative activity that quickly dissipated the anxiety generated by the penurious squalor into which Rome had been precipitated.[7] Reflecting on those years, Platina himself commented that "Rome no longer looked like a city. . . . There was not even a trace of an urban reality."[8]

With the vigor and zeal allowed only to those who derive their power directly from God, Martin V cleaned the streets, restored the great landmarks, demolished dangerous illegal constructions, and had criminals decapitated. In just a few years, his improvements to the city were so great that, in the *Diarium urbis Romae (Diary of the City of Rome),* Stefano Infessura would recount how Paolo di Benedetto di Cola allowed himself to be won over with enthusiasm for the renewed urban life, and wrote that a man could travel undisturbed for miles and miles, night and day, throughout the Roman countryside, with his money in the palm of his hand.[9]

Once again you could breathe in Rome, both physically and metaphorically: the city had transformed itself from mephitic village to capital of the High Renaissance. Fledgling patronage attracted some of the greatest humanists to Rome, like Lorenzo Valla and Leonardo Bruni.[10] These and others came to work in the papal chancellery. And though it did not take long for their passion in *humanae litterae* and their fundamental admiration of pagan culture to turn into (or merely be mistaken for) manifestations of immorality, Pope Martin V preferred to turn a blind eye to such calumnies and misunderstandings.

In its rebirth, Rome also attracted the most famous artists of the day: there was no lack of commissions or money to pay for them. For the frescoes (later destroyed by humidity) in the church of San Giovanni Laterano, Gentile da Fabriano received an annual compensation of three hundred florins during this period. Even the great Masaccio was drawn there, only to die of the

plague at the unacceptably early age of twenty-seven. So compelling was the allure of Rome reborn that the temptation to go there could not be resisted by Pisanello, Fra Angelico, and Flemish painter Rogier van der Weyden, among many others. Even though Florence retained its cultural supremacy for a while longer, Rome was rapidly coming into its own as a formidable contender.

In undertaking this renovation, of course, the pope received considerable help. He soon realized that for his restoration project—one of the greatest the world has ever known—to succeed, the pride and the purse of the prelates and cardinals who had returned to Rome, each with his retinue of secretaries, chamberlains, pages, and most importantly (as far as we are concerned) cooks, had to be properly massaged and squeezed. His tactic was extraordinarily astute. After spending the astronomical sum of fifty thousand florins to refurbish the roof and portico of St. Peter's, he obliged all the "princes of the church" to restore their titular churches, expecting of course that each of them would try to outdo the others.[11] Once this was under way, there was no stopping the competition, nor was there anyone who was interested in doing so. In just a few decades, the courts of the Roman cardinals began to rival that of the Vicar of Christ. Any trace of asceticism vanished: the cardinals' hedonistic dispositions often blurred the line between their own lives and the kind of life they recommended for good Christians, a discrepancy that would in short time fuel the reformist zeal of Martin Luther. They excelled in the patronage of architecture, entertainments, and of course gastronomy, or rather the art of throwing banquets.[12]

It is in this context that the momentous and critical contributions of Maestro Martino and Platina become discernible, for their gastronomic approach stood in stark contrast to the practices of Renaissance conviviality in which eating and feasting assumed primarily a political function.

To illustrate the pomp and circumstance of the banquet tradition, let us turn to the Renaissance chronicler Bernardino Corio (1459–1519?), who in his *Historia di Milano* described in great detail a fabulous feast held in Rome in 1473.[13] It was a true feat of gastronomic delirium prepared for the guests of Pietro Riario, cardinal of San Sisto, "who could himself be called a true pope" (the host was *not* his uncle, Pope Sixtus IV, as is sometimes reported).[14] The banquet was held in honor of Leonora, daughter of Ferdinand I of Aragon, king of Naples, who was passing through Rome on her way from Naples to Ferrara, where she was to meet her future husband, Ercole I d'Este.

Writing in the service of the Sforzas, who were involved with the cardinal in dubious political machinations, Corio had to persuade his readers that the pope was an easily expendable character, ready to abdicate and leave the Holy See to his nephew Riario. The Sforzas went out of their way to divulge this "secret" piece of information, which, however false it may have been, did not do them any good: the cardinal died in 1474, probably poisoned, and Galeazzo Maria Sforza was murdered on December 26, 1476, by three young men who dreamed of freeing Milan from the tyranny of the Sforzas as Brutus and Cassius had done for Rome when they assassinated Caesar.

The combined display of theatrical pomp and culinary extravagance spells out in no uncertain terms the amphitryon's plan to outshine whatever splendor the pope might have been capable of mustering. Since we cannot possibly recount in every detail this truly sumptuous event, in which admiration for food was more important than its consumption, let us resort to an abridged description of the banquet by Claudio Benporat, the brevity of which doesn't lessen the visual, auditory, and even gustatory experience of the original:

> The banquet . . . took place in a great hall [in the cardinal's residence at Piazza Santi Apostoli] where there was a sideboard with twelve shelves on which gem-studded trays of silver and gold were featured. Two tables covered by four tablecloths were prepared in the middle of the hall: the first was for the seven nobles of the highest station while the other table was for the lesser among them.
>
> In accordance with the custom in usage since the beginning of the century, the guests were still standing when they were served a meal that included trays of candied fruit covered with gold leaves and accompanied by painted glasses of malvasia. Once the guests were seated, musicians with horns and pipes announced the next dishes, which were divided into four services in correspondence with the four tablecloths that covered the tables.
>
> The first service combined pork livers, blancmange, meats with relish, tortes and pies, salt-cured pork loin and sausage, roast veal, kid, squab, chicken, rabbit . . . whole roasted large game, and fowl dressed in their skin or feathers. Next came golden tortes and muscat pears in cups.[15]

And this was just the first service! At the risk of causing the reader stomachic discomfort, the following is an unexpurgated list of the foods brought forth in the remaining three services (at the end of each the tablecloth would be removed, and the guests washed their hands because they served themselves from communal trays and forks were not in use): fried dough shaped like pine cones, smothered with honey and rose water; silver-wrapped lemons in sugary syrup; relishes; pies; sturgeon and lamprey; aspics; more tortes; junket drowning in white wine; Catalan-style chicken; green blancmange; stewed veal; mutton and roebuck; suckling pig; capon; and duck and black and sour cherries macerated in Tyrian wine. And *dulcis in fundo*: ices, almonds, coriander seeds, anise seeds, cinnamon, and pine nuts.

But the best gauge of the feast's unparalleled choreography is Corio's own mouthwatering description. He devoted great attention to the *coperti,* or "covers": that is, the buns distributed throughout the table and wrapped in gold and silver leaves featuring the coats of arms of the host and guest families (but also that of the Sforzas). And he concluded his portrait of the *convivium* with the following flourish:

> [There were brought forth] confectionery victuals, three of the Labors of Hercules, that is, the Lion, the Boar, and the Bull, and each one of them was in the shape of a common man. But first Hercules, nude, with the skin of a Nemean lion and with stars on his shoulder to signify holding up the Sky; and following the labors of Hercules, grand confectionery castles were brought forth complete with towers and fortifications inside, and an infinite num-

> ber of confectioneries in all different manners; and these castles with confectioneries were
> plundered and tossed down from the tribunal into the square to impress those present; and
> it seemed a great storm. Then there was brought forth a large confectionery serpent on a
> mountain, very lifelike. And then a dish of wild men. Afterward, perhaps ten great ships with
> sails and ropes, all of them confectioneries and filled with nuggets of sugar. While still eat-
> ing, there was also brought forth a Mountain, from which a man jumped out, who acted very
> impressed with the banquet, and he said some words, but not everyone understood them.[16]

Of course, the serpent on the mountain is an allusion to the Sforza family (this image had
appeared in the Milanese coat of arms from the times of the Visconti family). There is also a
transparent homage to the house of Este, whose future was in the hands of Leonora's husband,
Ercole (Hercules) I.

To conclude, let's quote again from Benporat's description of the interludes between services:

> In perfect harmony with the humanist culture of the century, the performance [reflects]
> the event to be celebrated, the riches of the guests, and the foods served to the dining com-
> panions. The scenes are inspired thus . . . by ancient Greek figures of mythology and the use
> of the myths and stories of Atlas, Hippomenes, Perseus, Orpheus, Hercules with Deianira,
> Jason with Medea, the battle between Hercules and the centaurs, the loves of Bacchus and
> Ariadne. And all of it was enhanced with songs and music, and by the best wines served in
> golden cups.[17]

But not all of the princes of the Church, who had been honing their social skills (not to mention their aesthetic and sybaritic inclinations) in Rome for fifty years, were as ambitious as Riario.
Their titles were often acquired through the ready money of their families for purely political
motives. The power conferred upon them by their cardinal's hat must have been an abundant
source of gratification. The ample margin of tolerance they enjoyed went hand in hand with
their opportunity to ask for and obtain favors from a pontiff, who, ruling over them like a feu-
dal lord, might need their support (and their resources) at any given moment. This fact clearly
made the pope sensitive and vulnerable to their requests. In the final analysis, and no matter
what the specific circumstances, their exchanges were the object of a refined semiosis that went
far beyond the moralistically defined margins of adulation. Cardinals could even convince the
pope to close an eye when it came to questions of religious orthodoxy. No matter how grandiose
these feasts may have been, they were often deplorably unsuited for the political ends intended
by their architects.

Well aware of this, many of them preferred the company of a small number of carefully
chosen souls inclined exclusively to refined entertainment. In fact, their mode of conviviality
marked a fundamental break from the art of the banquet in previous generations. As food historian Massimo Montanari has shown, the traditional notion of the banquet called for victuals to be displayed before being served: the spectacle of the meal as an outward expression of

power was the primary motive of the banquet. And in some cases, Montanari goes on to explain, the hosts did not even consume the foods they showed off. For the emerging generation food was instead an opportunity to explore the depths of one's own culture and imagination. The new ecclesiastical gourmet was undoubtedly aware that excellence was by no means a right, but rather a privilege attained by guiding desire through the solitary and harsh fields of critical awareness.

The markedly ostentatious character of banquets, writes Montanari, exemplifying his assessment with the description of the Pantagruelian meal served in Bologna in 1487 by Giovanni II Bentivoglio (to celebrate the marriage of his son Annibale to Lucrezia d'Este), reveals the "progressive introspection and closure of the dominant classes. . . . The table was no longer a place of social cohesion centered on the leader, but rather one of separation and exclusion: a few were invited to participate; the rest were left to watch."[18] It is equally clear that the point was not so much to show the plebs the insurmountable distance separating them from the rich and powerful (an unfortunate given of the times), but rather to humiliate somewhat their equals: individuals, families, and clans who were also rich and powerful but not quite so much as the hosting party was or pretended to be.

By contrast, for Platina and his circle of associates and patrons, intimate gatherings were de rigueur, and the cooks they employed, chief among them Maestro Martino, were meant to prepare real food for real people.[19] On the one hand, Platina was a Humanist (with a capital *H*), envisioning every aspect of his life as an expression of Renaissance ideals, including the manner in which he dined, the persons with whom he broke bread, and the foods that were prepared. No dish was served at his table casually: each recipe and formula had a unique place in the humanist culinary hierarchy. Some foods had symbolic meaning; others were intended to balance the humors of his fellow revelers, and, indeed, as is clear from even a cursory reading of his *On Right Pleasure and Good Health,* Platina was keenly aware of his companions' physical condition as well as their personal likes and dislikes.

On the other hand, Platina was shrewd at political jockeying. Perhaps by pure instinct, perhaps through keen observation of the world around him, he chose the horses that he would ride through his tumultuous life and career with judicious skill, although not with unerring acumen. In addition to his renown as a humanist, his culinary expertise must have helped to open the doors of the illustrious and powerful who sought to surround themselves with the greatest artists, thinkers, conversationalists, and gourmets of their day.

Platina's association with Cardinal Francesco Gonzaga was typical in this respect. It's not unreasonable to suppose that it was typical also of his relationship with other cardinals, such as Giovanni Bessarione (1402–72; a Greek humanist who attempted to reconcile Platonism and Aristotelianism). It was through Bessarione's mediation that Platina was able to obtain a coveted seat in the College of Abbreviators, a prestigious appointment that lifted him from his chronic state of penury.[20] Platina also believed (wrongly, as we shall see) that his powerful friends would shield him from the ill will of Pius II's successor, Paul II (Venetian Cardinal Pietro Barbo,

elected in 1464), who despised humanist culture and ultimately abolished the College: in his opinion, the Platinas of the world were nothing but reborn pagans and moral degenerates.

But Platina's most significant protector remained Cardinal Gonzaga, through whom he was introduced to the legendary household of the famous and powerful Cardinal Ludovico Trevisan, patriarch of Aquileia and employer—as previously mentioned—of Maestro Martino. It is highly probable that Platina was a member of Cardinal Gonzaga's entourage when the latter stayed with Trevisan in Albano (just south of Rome) in June 1463. This summer month of *ricreatione* may have been the occasion on which Platina obtained his copy of Martino's book.[21]

Born in Venice and educated in medicine at the University of Padua, Ludovico Trevisan (1402–65) was the son of a medical doctor. He became physician to Cardinal Condulmer, who would later, as Pope Eugenius IV, appoint him patriarch of Aquileia (where he would set foot only briefly, if at all) and titular cardinal of San Lorenzo in Damaso, where he built his legendary residence.[22] It was through excellent military service (like his presence at Anghiari) and his Machiavellian ruthlessness that he rose to power.[23] After the feared Cardinal Giovanni Vitelleschi was jailed and subsequently died in the Castel Sant'Angelo, Trevisan was charged with collecting the spoils from the former's loyalists: the fulfillment of this perilous duty was fundamental in the restoration of papal authority in Rome, and it brought him immense notoriety.[24] By 1455, he had been appointed admiral of the Papal Fleet by Calixtus III, and he was the mastermind of a crucial victory over the Turks at Mytilene in 1457. At the Congress of Mantua in 1459, he opposed Pius II's plans for a crusade against the Turks, and he would also be remembered for his vehement—if not self-serving—opposition to the expansion of the number of cardinals.[25] The election of Venetian Cardinal Pietro Barbo, his archrival, as Pope Paul II in 1464 is generally believed to have accelerated Trevisan's death the following year.[26]

But the brilliance of his political career did not in any way efface his fame as an epicure. Indeed, his love for the good life earned him the title "Cardinal Lucullus."[27] Trevisan was very well known and admired for his love of entertaining. His home in San Lorenzo in Damaso was the San Simeon of his day: there he collected unusual animals—like white asses, Indian hens, lapdogs, and goldfinches—and cultivated rare varietals of fruit that he obtained from his friends and from purveyors of foods.[28]

Trevisan's earthly splendor transpires indirectly in David Chambers's essay "The Housing Problems of Cardinal Francesco Gonzaga," wherein he examines the young cardinal's difficulty in procuring suitable housing for himself and his entourage:

> Cardinals in the fifteenth century were expected to live in a style of magnificence tempered by decorum. It was not a simple formula to put into practice even at the mundane level of setting up a house, finding a seemly place of residence in Rome.... For just a moderate magnificence, to maintain a household of the minimum numbers which propriety demanded, accommodation could be expensive, but there was no regular system which provided cardinals with palaces or apartments in Rome as of right.[29]

Seeking to associate her cardinal son with a great personage of the Curia, Barbara of Brandenburg wrote in 1461 to the Mantuan ambassador in Rome, Bartolomeo Bonatto, that "it would be beneficial for Francesco to live near to Cardinal Ludovico Trevisan . . . , Apostolic Chamberlain."[30]

A prominent member of Francesco's escort, Guido dei Nerli, wrote to Barbara, insinuating that the young prelate should indeed set his sights on the palace of Cardinal Ludovico Trevisan: "My most illustrious Lady," wrote dei Nerli, "the Patriarch wears the crown in all things. His house truly seems like Paradise."[31] It would not be until 1467 (two years after Trevisan's death), following many mishaps (including several plague scares), that Francesco would finally obtain the house he so coveted.[32]

We know with relative certainty that Trevisan "took a paternal interest in Francesco Gonzaga after the latter's arrival in Rome" and that Trevisan was "among those exciting Francesco to Christian belligerency."[33] Along with the many exotic gifts he bestowed on Francesco, Trevisan must have exhorted him to cultivate his skills in entertaining and to excel in his hospitality when charged with papal visits.

So obsessed was Trevisan with obtaining the finest and most unusual foods and wines for his guests that his requests for certain delicacies could easily take precedence over discussing politics in his correspondence—even when the very balance of power in Italy was at stake. After no less than three missives to his friend and putative son Onorato Caetani, lord of Sermoneta, in which he requests fish—the "finest possible"—for a dinner he will host on the occasion of Pope Nicholas V's visit to San Lorenzo in Damaso, Trevisan mentions almost as an afterthought a political event of epochal importance:

> As of this day, we have written three letters to your Magnificence, which we have scribed with our own hands and which were delivered to you by your own secretary who was here. Strangely, we have had no response from you. Now, for this reason, we are writing you again and imploring you to provide us, by way of your fishmongers, with two portions of the finest sea fish possible, and we would prefer that all of it arrive by next Monday because the seventeenth day of the month, which will be a Tuesday, is the day of the visit [of the pope] to San Lorenzo in Damaso. So we are imploring you, if possible, to serve us with these two portions of fish and we will certainly pay the fishmongers however you advise us. And may it please you that you respond by the same messenger to this letter. We believe that you have heard how Francesco [Sforza] has obtained Milan. Otherwise, no news. *Rome, March 10, 1450.*[34]

In light of the fact that Francesco Sforza's conquest of Milan was one of the great turning points in the balance of power in northern Italy, and that a mercenary like Sforza had transformed his career as soldier into that of one of the most sophisticated rulers of the Renaissance, the fish must have been very good indeed. According to Gelasio Caetani, annotator of the letters and descendant of the correspondent, they are supposed to have come from the famous fisheries of Fogliano in Friuli.[35]

It's no wonder, then, that Trevisan also sought the services of the greatest cook of his times,

Maestro Martino. But in order for us also to find Martino, we must return—albeit briefly—to our Platina.

Profoundly wounded in his pride as both a humanist and a consumer of fine foods by the sudden loss of his gainful employment as a papal abbreviator and his subsequent return to the poverty he thought he had escaped once and for all, Platina reacted so intensely that the man who had made him redundant, Pope Paul II, thought it best to lock him up in the recently renovated Castel Sant'Angelo.[36] There was nothing Platina's friends could do to avert the lightning of the pope's fury—except to help him lick his wounds when, upon his release, he "threatened" to leave Rome, never to return. Nor was his ill fortune over just yet. He had hardly begun to savor his newly acquired freedom when the rumor spread that members of the Roman Academy, of which he was a leading figure, and its founder, Giulio Pomponio Leto,[37] were conspiring to assassinate the reigning Vicar of Christ, whom they regarded as the principal obstacle to the realization of their republican program.

Platina would soon be arrested again, and he was tried together with a number of his fellow academicians. They were all turned loose eventually, thanks to a long display of the legal ingenuity of their counselors and Platina's writing of a number of epistles—not exactly the most dignified examples of apologetic literature—in which he asked the Holy Father's forgiveness, not because he had actually attempted to harm him in any way, as it were, but merely for not having done enough to shield His Holiness from his enemies.[38]

Platina had fallen from grace as many times as he would rise back up: in the end Paul II granted clemency to nearly all the members of the Roman Academy. Three more years would elapse before this pope could join his predecessors in their eternal reward, during which time Platina stayed in Rome and enjoyed a sort of guarded freedom. But then Sixtus IV was elected pope in 1471: a spendthrift, an incorrigible nepotist, but also a wholehearted admirer of antiquity, the discovery of which, as well as the cult attached to it, was proving to be more and more exciting and had in fact reached the point of no return. Platina thus thought it advisable to dedicate to the new pope his *Lives of the Popes,* the first systematic survey of the papacy.[39] This good deed landed him a remarkable job and the privilege of painterly immortality: he would be portrayed by Renaissance master Melozzo da Forlì (1438–94) in a fresco that can still be viewed today in the Pinacoteca Vaticana.[40]

But what made Platina a citizen of high stature in the republic of gastronomy was his *On Right Pleasure and Good Health,* a text that outright cannibalized Maestro Martino's *Art of Cooking.* Not only does this text shed light on the history of Renaissance nourishment and dietary habits, but it is also an indispensable tool for learning about the "card-carrying" members of what the author liked to refer to as the *contubernium pomponianum* (the group of humanists who gathered around Pomponio Leto and his Roman Academy), in terms of both their cultural formation and their guiding philosophies.[41] By reading Platina's pages, for instance, we become aware of the novel attention that this fellowship (young prelates, scribes and secretaries, papal abbreviators,

etc.) paid to the figure of the cook, who, if possible, "should be completely like the man from Como [Martino], the prince of cooks of our age, from whom I have learned the art of cooking food."[42]

Inscribed to Cardinal Bartolomeo Roverella, title of San Clemente in Rome and archbishop of Ravenna (1445–76), whose powerful patronage of Platina helped to make *On Right Pleasure and Good Health* the first gastronomic treatise ever printed, the book was begun sometime before the author's incarceration in Castel Sant'Angelo in 1464, as Platina himself declares in an undated (and most revealing) letter to Cardinal Giacomo Ammannati Piccolomini:

> Before my [first] prison term I wrote this little book, *On Right Pleasure and Good Health,* which I commend to your generosity, striving eagerly to win a patron for it.
>
> As you are aware, it deals with the business of all the food merchants, and creeps through the taverns, and is, therefore *a greasy and sordid* [emphasis added] subject. But he who is versed in cookery is not far removed from genius, since the meals that are to be concocted are largely a matter of ingenious composition, and, therefore, he must be proficient in it; he who takes upon himself this work as a profession must inform himself. Of course in the last analysis, it appears to me a dry and unpolished subject, and therefore, *I am cleaning it of imperfections* [emphasis added] which, I have recognized, must be eliminated without fail. Surely, because good judgment in these matters will mostly benefit the superiors, I place this book, however dreadful (it certainly takes a chance with inspiring the ingenious ones, if you like) in your hands for your kind consideration and criticism, hesitatingly and also conditionally.[43]

There is no known response from Piccolomini, but it is fair to surmise that the project—which Platina perversely called "greasy and sordid" and "unpolished"—may not have appealed to him. Yet the idea, epitomized by the perfect title, *On Right Pleasure and Good Health,* is nothing short of a stroke of genius. We must assume that Roverella's intellectual acumen was, at least in this case, a tad sharper than Piccolomini's.

Although it is customary to translate *honesta* (as in *De honesta voluptate*) as "right," a more accurate rendering of the original might be "permissible,"[44] that is, *On Permissible Pleasure and Good Health,* since the term challenged the ascetic prohibitions that for so long and under so many circumstances had doomed attempts to expand the notion of food beyond mere necessary sustenance.

The reorientation of the cultural axis that was taking place in Platina's times, on the other hand, enabled him to approach his topic from a philosophical angle, and to record his findings under a rubric combining hedonism with health, a locus of the mind where Epicurus (no longer humiliated by medieval hearsay knowledge of his writings) and archmedical doctor Hippocrates could be seen eating at the same table.[45] It is thus crucial to emphasize the dietetic concerns illustrated by the second segment of the title (*et valetudine*).

High-ranking officers of the Church, who were supposed to frown on culturally sanctioned pleasures that enhanced the well-being of the body, were among the first to welcome the new perspective introduced by Platina. The moral issues were nullified by the medical concerns, and no one would ever object to remedies that, frankly, had never tasted better.[46] A savory, well-

balanced meal could then be regarded as preliminary to a fine practice of intellectual pursuits. Openly contradicting the gargantuan extravaganzas of the guzzlers, gluttons, and profligates that ecclesiastical agencies had successfully dismissed for centuries, this notion canceled out the de facto connection between bodily pleasure and sin, introducing the far more sophisticated belief that culinary pleasure, on a par with pleasures of all kinds, was the ultimate goal of artistic research. Culinary application, in other words, could be placed alongside architecture, conversation, music, war, diplomacy, politics, painting, pottery making, wood carving . . . and whatever else you might want to add to the list. *On Right Pleasure and Good Health,* writes Emilio Faccioli in the introduction to a recent Italian edition, is not

> a simple manual, nor is it a compendium . . . but rather a systematic treatment of the art of cooking, dietetics, culinary hygiene, the ethics of eating, the pleasures of the table—all things that had been substantively illustrated in writings of previous eras, although in singular instances. . . . It is a treatment organized according to a criterion that alternated technical prescriptions with moral ones relative to nutrition . . . together with observations on the nature of various foods, their nutritional and curative properties, as well as their use and their side effects.[47]

Notwithstanding his great familiarity with the culture of the classical world and the superb ability displayed by the author in quoting from its literature (see, for instance, his comparison of the ripening of a mulberry to the blushing of the Egyptian girl Thisbe, delicately lifted from Ovid's *Metamorphoses*),[48] the fact that a humanist, and a famous one at that, spent time writing about food raised more than eyebrows. Such mundane musings by a prominent man of letters were sure to inspire some more or less malicious epigrams, like the following one by Jacopo Sannazaro:

> On the character, customs, life and death of the popes;
> You used to write. A sharp history lesson it was.
> Now, Platina, you write tractates on cooking millet
> For the popes themselves to eat.[49]

Nor were Platina's critics confined to the Renaissance. More than a century later, in his *Ragguagli di Parnaso (Advertisements from Parnassus),* Traiano Boccalini imagined that the philosopher Agostino Nifo da Sessa entered a shop where Platina was rolling pie dough and wrested the rolling pin from his hand to beat him with it.[50] This act, as da Sessa later recounts to Apollo, was a way to avenge himself for Platina's slandering of da Sessa as "one of those useless persons, who delighting in gluttony, study nothing but how to eat well." Despite Platina's apology and attempt to clear himself (from what he considers a false accusation), Apollo reprimands the humanist, telling him also how shameful it is for a philosopher to be caught visiting a food shop, "for the arms of men of honour, and of such a philosopher as is my beloved Nifo, ought to be seen in libraries, not in cooks-shops, where none but those of smell-feasts ought to hang; for, there is no fouler defect nor vice, than to study how to please the palate, and to make the base and shameful profession to hunt after good victuals."[51]

Like Traiano Boccalini, other detractors of Platina persisted in decrying him as a glutton. But their allegations would not have held up in a court of law. In fact, even a cursory reading of *On Right Pleasure and Good Health* reveals how, in the intimate relationship between "pleasure" and "health," the compass leans more toward medicine than toward crapulence. But most of all, the interrelationship between these two concepts provided a perspective by which the Renaissance man could see himself in a positive light, fully the peer of the ancients, in his radical return to Epicureanism. It was perhaps Platina himself who, in his dedicatory letter to Roverella, best expressed the Renaissance gourmet's *excusatio,* responding to his accusers and perfectly illustrating his *ratio scribendi:*

> [Some] upbraid me about food as if I were a gluttonous and greedy man and as if I were proffering instruments of lust and, as it were, spurs to intemperate and wicked people. Would that they, like Platina, would use moderation and frugality either by nature or instruction; we would not see today so many so-called cooks in the city, so many gluttons, so many dandies, so many parasites, so many most diligent cultivators of hidden lusts and recruiting officers for gluttony and greed.
>
> I have written about food in imitation of that excellent man, Cato, of Varro, the most learned of all, of Columella, of C. Matius, and of Caelius Apicius.[52] I would not encourage my readers to extravagance, those whom I have always in my writing deterred from vice. I have written to help any citizen seeking health, moderation, and elegance of food rather than debauchery, and have also shown to posterity that in this age of ours men had the talents at least to imitate, if not to equal, our ancestors in any kind of [writing].[53]

Although he shows some humility—or is it false modesty?—in sizing himself up in relation to classical culture in the last sentence above, when it comes to gastronomy he does not hesitate to pass a verdict in favor of the moderns. Indeed, on the subject of blancmange, a recipe that he lifted nearly verbatim from Martino, Platina clearly states his preference for this dish over any proposed by Apicius: "Even if we are surpassed by [the ancients] in nearly all arts, nevertheless in taste alone we are not vanquished."[54]

Judging from the frenzy of reprints that immediately followed the *editio princeps,* there is no doubt that the book struck a chord at the right time: it was reprinted in Venice in 1475, 1498, 1503, and 1517; in Louvain and Cividale del Friuli, 1480; in Bologna, 1499; in Strasbourg, 1517; in Cologne, 1529, 1537; in Paris, 1530; in Lyon and in Basel, 1541.

Of course Platina, just like his fellow humanists, wrote in Latin, a language in which, I am sure, they also dreamed. But a good number of readers trained in the redignified profession of cooking needed some help in deciphering his text. As a consequence, the book prolonged its life and success in an equally frantic series of translations: into Italian: 1487, 1494, 1508, and 1516; into German: 1530, 1533, 1536, and 1542; and into French: Lyon, 1505, 1528, 1548, and 1571, and Paris, 1509, 1539, 1559, and 1567. The extremely wide diffusion of the work into the major languages of Europe is testimony to the primacy of the Italian culinary canon throughout the sixteenth century. Consequently, the myriad translations into French (the language that would

definitively replace Italian as the European koine by the eighteenth century) played a clear role in the future Francophilia of European cuisine.[55] Undoubtedly, Caterina de' Medici's presence in France, as well as that of her cooks with their advanced technique, also reinvigorated French cuisine with an infusion of Italian know-how and tastes around the same time that Platina's book was becoming the first best seller in cookery book history.[56]

Perilously balanced between gustatory enthusiasm and his claims of Franciscan sobriety, Platina sought to demonstrate that he truly practiced what he preached, maintaining that his friends—Pomponio Leto, above all—were people who shunned the idea of gulping down peacocks and pheasants, "dishes of distinguished people, and especially of those whom not virtue and hard work but fortune and the rashness of men [had] raised, by luck alone, from the depths."[57] They were perfectly content to dine on a few meager vegetables. Whether or not these observations are an echo of the theory whereby different social categories are endowed with varying degrees of digestive and metabolic capabilities is a matter of pure speculation: can it not be proven that there are noble and rich stomachs suited for beef steak, while there are poor stomachs at best able to digest beans, as asserted in certain socially questionable *regimina sanitatis* of the Middle Ages and in the fourteenth-century *De sanitatis custodia*, a dietary guide scribed by the renowned doctor Giacomo Albini?[58] Speculative as this might be, Platina's unbridled fondness for vegetables is attested to by at least two witnesses, one of them rather conspicuous.

The first was Platina's detractor Giovanni Antonio Campano, from whom we learn that our author was unable to sing because his mouth was full of leeks and his breath reeked of onions: "Calvus, aricini sordent qui prandia porri / Laetum nec bulbos ore obulente carit."[59]

The second was no less a charismatic personage than Leonardo da Vinci. Among the many curious aspects of Leonardo's personality was the fact that he did not eat meat. This was so remarkable for the times that Florentine traveler Andrea Corsali related in a letter to Duke Giuliano de' Medici, "Certain infidels called Guzzarati [Hindus] . . . do not feed upon anything that contains blood, nor do they permit among them any injury be done to any living thing, like our Leonardo da Vinci."[60] (Aesthetic considerations aside, might it be inferred that the protracted execution of the fresco at Santa Maria delle Grazie [1495–98] could be attributed to the artist's embarrassment before the spectacle of saints dining on lamb's flesh?) Indeed, for Leonardo, meat eaters were on a par with cannibals: man, he wrote, was not the king of animals but rather the king of beasts, whose gullet was the "tomb for all animals." In a direct appeal to humankind, he asks, "Does not nature bring forth a sufficiency of simple things to produce satiety? Or if you cannot content yourself with simple things can you not by blending these together make an infinite number of compounds as did Platina and other authors who have written for epicures?"[61]

It is perfectly legitimate to surmise that Pomponian suppers comprised more than just arugula and chicory. The "permissible" pleasures that they pursued included, besides chicken in verjuice, roast suckling pig, ground liver balls, sausages, partridge, veal's brain, and kid in garlic.[62] At any rate, there are a great number of purely vegetarian dishes in Platina's recipe collection. And this, in and of itself, was an entirely novel concept. In the Middle Ages it was the poor who

ate vegetables exclusively, mostly in the form of sops. Now, instead, the dietetic benefits of eating vegetables came to the foreground. Vegetables were recommended for those who wished to keep their minds free by not overburdening the stomach. But it was not just a select group of humanists for whom vegetables were a central part of the diet. With their cult of chard, parsnips, and parsley, grains, legumes, and sweet fruits prepared in savory dishes, the Italians caught all of Europe by surprise, overturning the old medieval preconception of meat for the rich and cabbage for the poor. As late as the end of the sixteenth century, English traveler Robert Dallington would write:

> Concerning herbage, I shall not need to speake, but that it is the most general food of the Tuscan, at whose table Sallet is as ordinary, as salt at ours; for being eaten of all sorts of persons and at all times of the yeare: of the riche because they have to spare; of the poor, because they cannot choose; of many religious because of their vow, of most others because of their want.[63]

Nor should we neglect the writings of Giacomo Castelvetro, who after fleeing to England to escape "the furious bite of the cruel and pitiless Roman Inquisition," decided to teach his hosts the virtues of the many greens that were consumed in Italy. The English had actually begun to appreciate them in limited numbers, but often only as means "to beautify their gardens." Castelvetro's *Brieve racconto di tutte le radici di tutte l'erbe e di tutti i frutti che crudi o cotti in Italia si mangiano* (*Brief Account of All Tubers, Greens, and Fruits That Are Eaten Raw or Cooked in Italy*) is not only a small literary gem, but also a precious sign confirming the influence exerted by Platina's work on the dietetic customs of Europe more than a hundred years after its initial publication.[64]

Before taking leave of Platina and giving in to the allure of Maestro Martino himself, it is important to note that the Cremonese humanist was unable to accomplish in Latin what his source had triumphantly achieved in the vernacular tongue. Platina's humanist Latin lacked the lexical flexibility inaugurated by Martino. For example, where the latter discusses distinct types of cherries—for example, cornel cherry (*cornioli*), black cherry (*cerase negre*), and sour cherry (*visciole*)—the former is forced to subsume all kinds under one heading, *cerasia*, specifying that "some are tart, some sour, some sweet."[65] Indeed, the all-encompassing (and still unfinished) *Grande dizionario della lingua italiana* (the equivalent of the *Oxford English Dictionary*) cites Martino's text, for example, as the first registered appearance of the term *rosselli*, or rose apples (see the recipe for rose-apple sauce, on page 79).

Of course, "linguistic innovator" is only one of the many titles accumulated by the Carneades and prince of cooks, who, after such a long excursus (from the restoration of Rome to popes, humanist and not; from cardinals with big ideas to jailed abbreviators), finally takes center stage.

The extraordinary importance of Maestro Martino's *Art of Cooking* becomes crystal clear when his text is viewed as the cornerstone of the culinary edifice built by Platina. To begin with, all but 10 of the 250 recipes in Platina's book (books 6–10) belong to Maestro Martino. They are

often listed in the same order in which they originally appeared and are nothing more than verbatim translations. An example of this is the recipe for red chickpea torte (see page 86). In Martino, the recipe reads as follows:

> Cook a libra of red chickpeas, crush well, and together with their broth pass through a very thick stamine; and take a libra of well-peeled, blanched almonds that have been very well crushed, because they should not be passed through a stamine; and together with the almonds, crush two ounces of raisins and three or four dried figs; likewise an ounce and a half of slightly crushed pine nuts, not ground, adding some sugar, rose water, cinnamon, and ginger, mixing all these things together well. To make it thicken, incorporate some fine starch or some pike roe, as above, and cook it with a crust on the bottom; and when it appears to you to be nearly done cooking, top with some sugar and some rose water, and apply heat again from above from a high flame. Note that this torte should be short.

In Platina, as such:

> Crush red chick-peas, well cooked in their own juice and with a bit of rose water. When they are crushed, pass through a sieve into a bowl. Add to this and mix a pound of almonds so ground up that it is no task to pass them through a sieve, two ounces of raisins, three or four figs crushed at the same time, besides an ounce of semipounded pine nuts, as much sugar and rose water as is enough, and the same amount of cinnamon and ginger. When they are mixed, spread in a well-oiled pan with a lower crust. Some add starch or pike eggs so that this pie becomes firmer. When it is almost cooked, you will make it browner by putting fire above it. It should be thin and covered with sugar and rose water. *This food helps only the liver and stomach* [emphasis added].[66]

Platina's only contribution here is the medical advice added at the end of the recipe.[67]

The modern revival of interest in Maestro Martino and his relationship to Platina began in 1927, when Joseph Dommers Vehling (1879–1950), American chef and hotelier, gentleman, scholar, and bibliophile, purchased a copy of Martino's manuscript from an Italian antiquarian. In the October 1932 issue of *Hotel Bulletin and the Nation's Chefs,* of which he was editor, he published a notice of his discovery that the author was indeed the very same Martino whom Platina had acknowledged as his source. He would later develop this piece, "Martino and Platina: Exponents of Renaissance Cookery," into his major oeuvre, *Platina and the Rebirth of Man* (1941).

The manuscript, which for many years was the only known text attributed to the Renaissance cook, was eventually donated to the Library of Congress (where it still is kept) in 1941. In the 1930s, Vehling lectured on ancient and Renaissance cookery at Cornell University (in 1936, he published the first English translation of Apicius's *De re coquinaria,* which, together with his *Platina and the Rebirth of Man,* represents a great contribution to the study of historical gastronomy). Scholars and food historians are greatly indebted to the enthusiasm and entrepreneurship of Mr. Vehling, who nearly singlehandedly restored Platina's name to the annals of food scholarship and history after centuries of denigration and neglect. His library of rare culi-

nary tractates, which comprises more than four hundred titles, including two editions of *On Right Pleasure and Good Health* (one of them, the first printing, from 1494, and a later 1516 edition), is housed at the Kroch Library at Cornell.

As to the specific circumstances under which Platina and Maestro Martino may have turned a casual acquaintance into a fruitful friendship, it is not implausible to surmise that the cook was himself a member of the Roman Academy, as Claudio Benporat has boldly suggested—if not a full member, then at least a prominent fellow traveler. From a letter sent to the duke of Milan, Galeazzo Sforza, by the duke's ambassador to the Roman Curia, Augustinus de Rubeis (Agostino de Rossi), we are given to understand that the society was, in the sender's opinion, nothing but a den of iniquity: "They [the Pomponians] are of the opinion that there is no other world than that in which we live; they believe that once the body dies so does the soul and that nothing has any value except the enjoyment of all kinds of pleasure and delight." The academy was made up of "scholars, youths, poets, and philosophers . . . including Calimacho from Venice, secretary to the most reverend cardinal of Ravenna; Glaucho Condulmero, also from Venice; Petreo, secretary to the most reverend cardinal of Pavia," and many others. And it did not discourage socially less powerful individuals from increasing its ranks, which "grew with persons of every station, and for the most part, with servants of cardinals and prelates."[68]

Given Platina's expressions of enthusiasm for the exceptional culinary dexterity and artistic genius of Maestro Martino, it is also plausible to allow not only that he may have occasionally shared with him the sobriety of the Pomponian table, but also that he had ample opportunity to enjoy the lavish meals that Martino prepared for his master and his master's friends (we know of at least one occasion, as we've noted above, when they spent up to a month together).

Much more elusive is the question of where, when, and how Maestro Martino was first engaged by Cardinal Trevisan. No document thus far has emerged that defines the temporal contours of their association. The matter is further complicated by the epithet on the title page of the Riva del Garda manuscript (see Jeremy Parzen's textual note at the end of this volume), which declares "the Eminent Master Martino di Rossi" to be a native of "the Milanese Valley of Bregna [Blenio]" and not of Como, as Platina wrote, "born to the House [Monastery] of San Martino Viduale" and "cook to the Illustrious Seigneur Gian Giacomo Trivulzio."[69]

This has given rise (but little credit) to the conjecture—a term its supporters would find terribly restrictive—that there must have been two Martinos: one, the Maestro Martino from Como employed by Trevisan, and the other, the Maestro Martino de Rossi, or de Rubeis, from Blenio, employed by Trivulzio.[70]

The general uncertainty shadowing Maestro Martino's biography is barely sufficient to induce a smile at the acrobatic efforts made by Aldo Bertoluzza, in his edition of the Riva del Garda manuscript, to certify the existence of a doppelganger.[71] Bertoluzza pays no attention to the affinities of the codices and handles "his" document as if it were an autograph rather than a copy, which, as such, was inevitably subject to manipulation (see the textual note). Had Bertoluzza proceeded more prudently, he would have realized that the Riva del Garda man-

uscript is a composite of recipes taken from the tradition represented by the Library of Congress and Vatican collections, with other recipes gleaned from an unknown source outside the Maestro Martino tradition.

The area of influence of this rather desperate belief does not extend much beyond a gastronomic community bent on the understandable but nonetheless problematic exploitation of a jewel miraculously mounted in an otherwise anodyne crown: the Municipal Library of Riva del Garda. Regrettably, it would seem that among their ranks we might also find Giuseppe Chiesi, whose well-documented contribution, "Martino Rossi un cuoco bleniese alla Corte Ducale" (Martino Rossi, a Cook from Blenio at the Ducal Court), outlines Martino's years of culinary apprenticeship at the rectory of San Martino Viduale.[72] It also establishes the cook's later presence in Milan as one of many "Swiss" cooks who had traditionally migrated to the centripetal residence of the Viscontis, and later of the Sforzas, one of the greatest cultural—culinary and otherwise—centers of Renaissance Italy.[73]

Naturally, these laborers were Swiss only in an incipient manner, hailing as they did from very distinct areas of the canton Ticino, whose cultural profile has always been much influenced by its geographical and linguistic proximity to Milan. At the time of Maestro Martino, the valleys of both Blenio and Leventina "belonged" to the canons of the Duomo of Milan and were governed by Milanese rulers. After reversals of fortune, the political ties with the Lombard capital were definitively severed by Ludovico the Moor's downfall during the last year of the fifteenth century,[74] brought about largely by Gian Giacomo Trivulzio, who fought against him on behalf of the French king after having valiantly served under Ludovico's father, the great Francesco Sforza himself.

The gastronomic splendor that peaked in Milan under Ludovico the Moor, together with a number of other Renaissance splendors in the fields of music, painting, architecture, engineering, and classical studies,[75] had not been neglected by his predecessors, as can be inferred from the documents of the "Fondo Sforzesco," preserved in the Archivio di Stato di Milano, and in part published recently by Grazia Rossanigo and Pier Luigi Muggiati in their hastily compiled *Amandole e malvasia per uso di corte* (*Almonds and Malvasia Used at Court*). Among these documents, fragments of letters, lists of supplies, recipes (from Maestro Martino), and dietetic observations are mysteriously juxtaposed.[76] None of the Sforzas, however, relied as much—politically speaking—on entertainment and conviviality as Ludovico the Moor. Ludovico's amphitryonic inclination was so great that in 1492 he put up some Venetian ambassadors (who were passing through Milan on their way back from a visit to the emperor) at the Tre Re, the very best hotel in town.[77]

While information abounds about the rich and famous, we are not totally ignorant of what was likely to be considered a good meal by a solid bourgeois of the time. If a *sonetto caudato* (a "tailed" sonnet, i.e., a sonnet with two quatrains and as many tercets as desired, commonly used in fifteenth- and sixteenth-century satirical poetry) can be treated as a bona fide source of historical knowledge, this is what we learn about such a meal from Antonio Cammelli (better known

as "il Pistoia"), who, for as long as he found it convenient, devoted much time and energy to singing the virtues "beyond compare" of Ludovico the Moor:

> When I dined with Marco Nigrisollo,
> the tablecloth was as white as snow.
> The first serving was a mug
> of sweet Malvasia and candied fried dough.
>
> Then arrived the son of Tereus stuffed and roasted [i.e., fowl],
> the Argus pheasant, the partridge and the quail,
> and she [i.e., the sheep] who defecates the immaculate [lamb] on the hay,
> and the brother with his testicles removed [mutton].
>
> The poor souls snared in the net [more fowl]
> were there, just as she who no longer washes
> her muzzle in the clear water once her consort has died [the goat].
>
> The child of the sow was also at court,
> fatty in its broth, cheese, and pastry [a veal pie]
> and seeds in their shells who had died in their prison [beans],
>
> Bacchus of a thousand sorts [wines]
> now flowing to the west, now to the east,
> to some he seemed a dwarf, to others a giant.
>
> Gorgeous white Ceres
> was there, as was the white juice
> from a sow's teat on the aspic fronds.
>
> Melon seeds planted in
> sugar from Messina [marzipan]
> were the last victuals served us.
>
> And when the conversation was over,
> The body satiated, the soul consoled,
> we washed our hands in rose water.[78]

Pertinent information about bourgeois and aristocratic culinary practices and nutritional concerns can of course be gleaned more profitably by analyzing—as we shall soon do—the book of recipes ascribed to Maestro Martino, whose presence in Milan is confirmed by written documents.

On June 27, 1457, Francesco Sforza granted his cook permission to return to his native valley, provided that he speedily returned to the city of Milan: "Permission is granted to Maestro Martino, cook at this court, to go to the valley of Blenio for the time specified herein and then to make his return to this city."[79]

Many of the briefs mentioning Martino's family name are available, but caution is recommended in assuming that the "Rubeus de Blegnio" (cited in a *littera passus,* June 11, 1458, and a *mandatum,* January 8, 1461, signed by the duchess) and the Rosso addressed in the briefs written by the duke to his vicar at Blenio (November 6 and 7, 1460; June 18, November 9, 1461;[80] November 2, 1462)[81] are one and the same as our Maestro Martino: the names Rossi, Rosso, Rubeus de Rubeis (depending on whether the document is written in Italian or in Latin) were and still are rather frequent in those parts. Furthermore, in at least one case (November 6, 1460), the "Rubeus from this valley of ours" is explicitly called Petrus, and in yet others his professional qualification is that of a mere *famiglio* (servant), not that of *coquus* (cook).

Whether Martin or Peter, cook or lackey, they all seem to be as keen to visit their native village for the purpose of collecting monies owed to them as the duke is to have them back in the kitchen: "Rosso, our servant, carrier of this brief, is here to solicit payment of some credits of his, as well as to attend to some business which he says he has with his brother. As he cannot be away too long, I am asking you to assist him in carrying out his affairs as quickly as possible, so that he will not be detained there."[82]

Assuming that the hypothetical existence of a doppelganger has been successfully brushed aside, we can now quickly address, and just as quickly dispose of, a second hypothesis, which not even its principal proponent held for very long: that Martino was first cook to Condottiere Gian Giacomo Trivulzio, and later to Patriarch Ludovico Trevisan.[83] This sensational change in scene (from Milan to Rome) on the part of Martino is supposedly reported in the *Hermaphroditus,* a work by the celebrated and licentious poet Antonio Beccadelli, better known as the Panormite (i.e., "of Palermo," from the Greek name of the Sicilian city, Panormos). Beccadelli writes that an "outstanding" cook (named Martino and nicknamed "Polyphemus" due to his portly stature) laments that his former master Matesilano (yet another Carneades?) has decided to avenge himself for the loss of his services: the cook's inhumation will be carried out during a starless night and without allowing so much as a single candle to be lit, despite the fact that he was one of the greatest vivandiers of all times and that he showed love and appreciation for "young men keen on study."[84] It would be difficult to find a portrait of Maestro Martino's Roman life and deeds more fitting than the one provided by Beccadelli, yet treating this document as a reliable source of identification may be ill-advised.

To begin with, the text was composed in 1425 (or early 1426), when Trivulzio was not even a glimmer in his father's eye (he was born around 1441).[85] It assumes, moreover, a degree of fame that Maestro Martino could not have achieved by that time, unless of course he was blessed with an extraordinary and quite implausible longevity. Thus while a defection by a cook named Martino may have inspired Beccadelli, the assumption that his Martino and Maestro Martino are one and the same could be proven only with biographical evidence that we simply do not possess.

If Gian Giacomo could not be counted upon as the man behind Martino's incipient success, the problem of how and where Martino's reputation was established remains a haunting one.[86]

In this respect, it may not be inappropriate to lend a favorable ear to Emilio Montorfano's speculative but hardly far-fetched reconstruction of the cook's early career.

Uncertain, as he confesses to be, about Martino's age "at the time of his leaving his valley" and suggesting, however, that "it may have occurred, quite plausibly, when he was in his 'advanced teens,'" Montorfano suggests that his tenure with Trevisan might date as far back as 1439, when the latter was made patriarch of Aquileia. And the prospect of a transfer to Rome must have worked wonders to persuade the cook to accept the offer. As to the intermediate phase (Martino's presence in Udine, which was in fact the official residence of the patriarch of Aquileia), this is what Montorfano has to say:

> It is more than likely that he [Martino] may have accompanied a prelate from Como to Udine. Ever since the so-called Schism [Controversy] of the Three Chapters (in 543 C.E.?), the two cities had maintained close and very special ties predicated on their adoption of analogous rituals of public worship.[87] This entailed the presence in Udine of members of the clergy from Como. . . . Some have even suggested that as a member of a high prelate's retinue Martino himself may have been a man of the cloth. The fact that, in times of widespread illiteracy, he knew how to write and did so with some refinement would seem to support this hypothesis. . . . The image of a monastic Martino is not in harmony, however, with Platina's description of their lively gastronomic exchanges.[88]

But we are confronted by a deplorable lack of foolproof documents, and it may be safer to assume that the hiring occurred in Rome—where, by the way, Trivulzio also resided occasionally, discharging a number of diplomatic functions on behalf of Francesco Sforza.

Claudio Benporat has proposed a sojourn of Martino, in Naples and other southern Italian locations, between 1458 and 1467.[89] If these dates seem to conflict with the cook's presence in Rome (but accompanying one's own master on a trip or a mission cannot be considered an insurmountable obstacle), they could hardly be more fitting for the grooming of Trivulzio as a "magnifico," and thus as a worthy employer of a celebrated cook, whose movements after Trevisan's demise cannot be imagined with the slightest degree of certainty. So here they are, in all their puzzling splendor: the tantalizing tidbits of an impossible quest.

We have even less information regarding when the first and most significant (for reasons that we shall soon make clear) cook of Renaissance Italy may have reached his final destination—the locus, that is, where the torments awaiting the followers of Epicurus were tempered by the epiphanies brought about by exquisite flavors and aromas. The same thick clouds obscuring Martino's life have for some time "protected" Martino's text. To begin with, because of the wide and multifarious diffusion of *On Right Pleasure and Good Health,* the pages penned by the Swiss-Lombard cook remained exactly where he had put them: in the drawer of his kitchen writing desk.

Later on, plagiarized and expanded versions of *The Art of Cooking* transmitted Martino's work into the seventeenth century. In the end these too vanished and no more news was heard of

Martino until Vehling recovered the text upo
the textual note), identifying its author as P.
Nic[c]olò Zopino and Vincenzo Compagni, pr
tled *Epulario,* by a certain Giovanni de Rosselli (
which is nothing more than a nefarious compilatic
with enormous success and was reprinted seventee
glish translation appeared as early as 1598, publishe
other recipes as well: *Epulario, or, the Italian banquet: wh*
all kind of flesh, foules or fishes: as also to make sauces, tartes, pies,
of many other profitable and necessary things, translated out of 1
produced yet another reprint of Rosselli's work, thus
This edition, however, is barely legible and once again r
the mendacious profile of Rosselli looms that of the pat
Como.[90]

Having perhaps said enough, and hopefully no more than r
ment that gave rise to *The Art of Cooking,* all we have to do no
(though unfortunately not *ad potum*) is to highlight briefly t
essential pivot in the structure of Western gastronomy, one t
into two distinct epochs: before Martino and after Martino.

To begin with, however, it is necessary to warn against the f   un
neous, hypothesis that Martino was influenced by Apicius. W   th   Apicius
during the Renaissance elicited a lively discussion among philol   work had little if any
impact on the philosophy of gastronomy and culinary practices of Martino, or on the writers
inspired by his example.[91] Whereas Apicius declares triumphantly that with his treatment "no
one at the table will recognize what he is eating," Martino makes an effort, as we shall see below,
to maintain or even enhance the unique flavor of each ingredient, applying seasonings sparingly
and with great care.[92]

Far from being a mere list of recipes, as was the custom of culinary manuals at the time, *The
Art of Cooking* is a veritable treatise, which not only diligently divides various types of food into
separate chapters (meats, broths, soups, pastas, sauces and seasonings, tortes, eggs and omelets,
fish), but also reveals the secrets of the art itself, seeking to disseminate the tricks of the trade.
The book identifies the number of persons that a given recipe will serve, the quantity and kinds
of ingredients required, the proper method of cooking (such as whether to boil or roast), the
most suitable cookware to achieve the desired results, and the time required to cook the dish.[93]
In short, the book describes each and every phase of the culinary process in some detail, such
that it can be utilized by anyone capable of following instructions. Since instructions of this
sort are standard in the cookbooks of today, it is perhaps difficult to appreciate fully the novelty of Martino's contribution and the impression that it made on his contemporaries. *The Art*

of Cooking is to the Renaissance what Auguste Escoffier's *Le guide culinaire* (1903) is to contemporary French cuisine.[94]

Prior to Martino, detailed specifications were not a feature of culinary manuals, since they were not aimed at persuading as many readers as possible of the convenience or superiority of a given cooking style. In fact, just the opposite was true: food writers wrote primarily for themselves, and what they jotted down was intended merely to remind themselves how to produce a desired effect given a list of ingredients. And good practitioners, when confronted with formulas that were not their own, would know the right proportions and suitable procedures to execute the dish.

But there is perhaps another, more caustic explanation for the scantiness of information contained in culinary manuals prior to Martino: the desire not to divulge professional secrets. Like chemists, doctors, dowsers, soothsayers, wood carvers, painters, silk dyers, and so on, cooks were quick to realize that their prestige (and compensation) would increase in proportion to their bravura—if, that is, it did not become an easily accessible commodity. Unlike the purported individualism of today's consumer capitalism, which boils down to the persistent push to keep up with the Joneses, Renaissance individualism was largely the outcome of a search for distinction. This did not mean acquiring what everyone else was induced to own, but possessing what no one else had yet discovered. Even books, one of the earliest artifacts to be reproduced mechanically, were at times printed in such a way as to seem unique. Think, for example, of Aldo Manuzio's creation of the italic typeface, an innovation that indelibly changed printing and script and created a new standard for excellence in typography.[95] In any activity, cooking included, where excellence depends on a special technique of execution, "only the favorite apprentice would be made heir or shareholder," Vehling writes in his book on Platina, "after his worthiness has been demonstrated to the master's satisfaction—usually by the payment of a tidy sum of money, apprentice's pay."[96]

With *The Art of Cooking* by Maestro Martino, and even more so with Platina's *On Right Pleasure and Good Health,* which carried its wisdom and flavors to the four corners of the known universe, this ceased to be the case. In an age of general prosperity, at least among a wide stratum of the population in many Renaissance urban centers, the happy few were growing in number and in their aspirations. This occurred, quite simply, because the merchant class that replaced the medieval aristocracy (or compelled the latter to adapt to new political, economic, social, and military imperatives) had a cultural project of its own, which was predicated upon the idea that wealth (and patronage) were no longer to be measured against land and privileges inherited from God, but in terms of work done and credit extended. This meant personally accounting for one's own deeds, which is in stark contrast with the abnegation of responsibility typical of today's affluent society.

Seeking excellence in all fields of activity, under the pretense of "imitating" classical antiquity, was by far more rewarding to a Renaissance man than the inert archaeological protection of cultural artifacts that underpins today's notions of sophistication. And the notion of imita-

tion, in any event, did not preclude the enthusiastic adoption of new technologies. Taking advantage of the printing press to disseminate how-to books (and treating both classical and contemporary texts as instructional material) can be seen, for instance, as an anticipation of the modern "cybernetic" concept of "distant learning."[97] If a would-be chef could not learn from Maestro Martino as an apprentice, he could at least learn how to please his employer by studying the maestro's treatise.[98]

Martino's aim, however, was not only to compile and organize a set of specific instructions, the absence of which could (and in fact did) lead to deplorable results.[99] His method was that of an innovative synthesis based as much on his firm confidence as on his matchless practical knowledge. The opening paragraphs of his book have the stylistic poise of a writer who has analyzed his subject and its every implication, and who can write about it with that lapidary simplicity that is ultimately the best *captatio benevolentiae*—similar to the opening lines of Machiavelli's most famous treatise, *Il principe (The Prince)* ("How many kinds of principalities there are and how they are acquired . . . Concerning Hereditary Principalities . . . Concerning Mixed Principalities . . . and so on"):

> The fatty meat of oxen and that of beef should be boiled, the loin should be roasted, and the haunch made into cutlets.
>
> All the meat of mutton is good boiled, except for the shoulder, which is good roasted, as is the haunch.
>
> Although pork meat is not healthful—no matter how you cook it—the chine should be roasted with onions, and when roasted, pork meat should be salted to taste.
>
> All the meat of kid is good roasted or boiled, but the hindquarters are best roasted. The same holds for lamb.

Nor should Martino's writing style be viewed exclusively as an example of consummate rhetoric. Rather, his most meaningful and lasting contribution was the establishment of a clear and reliable gastronomic lexicon. This becomes apparent when we note that his task was not simply to transliterate foreign terms into a highly specialized jargon—as is the case with *bianco mangiare* (blancmange), from the French *blanc manger*, or *mirause* to the Catalan *mig-raust* (Provençal, *mieg-raust*), meaning "half-cooked" or "half-roasted." Martino's semiotic concerns are visible in the linguistic clarifications he offers his readers, as in the case of *pitartima* as a common name for coriander, or *cannella* as an alternate name for cinnamon.

To appreciate how "thorny" the problem of lexical norms is, consider the example of fish. While the name of any particular fish is the same in ichthyological manuals throughout the world, their commonly used names may vary from restaurant to restaurant. This normative aspect of Martino's text, which I would argue is a sign of his socio-linguistic commitment, is summarily dismissed by Bruno Laurioux as merely the by-product of his professional service or the adoption of local customs. Thus, according to Laurioux, the fusion of Venetian linguistic elements with typically Roman denominations in the classification of fish can be explained as follows:

In the former we detect the need to accommodate the whims of the [Venetian] patriarch of Aquileia, while the latter can be explained quite obviously by the influence of the environment in which Martino worked for some time. Having been at the service of personalities as diverse as Francesco Sforza, Lodovico Trevisan, and Gian Giacomo Trivulzio must have enriched the experiences of the cook, making the various versions of his work both a veritable repertory of Italian cooking at the time and a perfect example of the culinary cosmopolitanism of the end of the Quattrocento.[100]

If Laurioux underestimates Martino's taxonomic contribution, he truly ignores the value of Martino's linguistic inventiveness. Take, for example, the case of *rape armate* (garnished or "armored" turnips, page 91). Had Martino not given an intriguing name to what are essentially turnips, a description of the ingredients of the dish alone would probably evoke an impression of poverty and be shunned by most food devotees. Nor does Laurioux's assessment capture the intensity of the travail gastronomy had been undergoing for quite some time in the search for a semantic tranquillity of its own. Before Martino's *Art of Cooking,* even a seemingly innocuous term such as *macaroni* would cause a great deal of referential perplexity.

Many point to Boccaccio's *Decameron* as one of the earliest places where the term *macaroni* appears. In the third story of the eighth day, in fact, Calandrino, whose gullibility knows no bounds, overhears a conversation (held for his benefit) in which a Florentine gentleman, Maso, maintains that certain miraculous stones (among them, one that grants invisibility to those who carry it in their pocket) are abundant in "Berlinzone, a city of the Basques, in a country called Bengodi, where the vines are tied up with sausages and a goose can be had for a farthing, with a gosling thrown into the bargain." Moreover, Maso tells Calandrino,

> in those parts [Cornucopia] there was a mountain made entirely of grated Parmesan cheese, on whose slopes there were people who spent their whole time making macaroni and ravioli, which they cooked in chicken broth and then cast it to the four winds, and the faster you could pick it up, the more you got of it. . . .
>
> Seeing that Maso was saying this with a completely straight face, the simple-minded Calandrino took every word of it as gospel, and he said: "It's too far away for me, then; but if it were nearer, I can assure you that one of these days I'd come with you, so as to see all that macaroni tumbling down, and feed my face on it."[101]

Some debates have arisen over the nature of the mythical food macaroni, and culinary historians, as well as philologists, have offered evidence that it may not have been macaroni at all. It seems safe to assume that in the language spoken in Florence at the time of the great storyteller and shortly after, during the Renaissance, *macaroni* meant *gnocchi,* or "dumplings." This theory is supported by descriptions that suggest small lumps of pasta are *maccat,* that is, pressed against a cheese grater. The fact that they tumble headlong down a hill of cheese suggests an indisputably round, dumplinglike shape. Macaroni—in the modern and Martinian sense of the word—would fail to roll and would simply get stuck.

By contrast, when Martino speaks of "Sicilian macaroni," he describes unequivocally a type of pasta that is obtained by rolling sheets of dough around a narrow rod, leaving no doubt about the object to which the term refers: Martino's macaroni are quite similar to today's Neapolitan fusilli. What sets them apart is the use of egg in the present-day version, absent in the dough used to make Martino's Sicilian version.

An early and peculiar event in the life of Martino's book sheds light on the beleaguered process of lexical sedimentation that he endeavored to bring about. When the terms that Platina had lifted from Martino's *Art of Cooking* were "translated" into Italian by translators who had scant knowledge of gastronomic secrets and jargon, the results were patently absurd. While Martino's original *maccaroni* becomes *isicium frumentum* in Platina's Latin translation (Platina's Latin was not Cicero's, for that matter), the Italian "translation" of Platina proffers *exitio frumentino,* a food that no Italian, then or now, would recognize as edible. And Platina's *cibarium album,* which is his candid translation of Martino's *bianco mangiare,* rather than being "Italianized" is Hellenized as *leucofago,* a word more reminiscent of an incurable disease than of a food.[102]

Finally, Martino formulated many neologisms that have since taken root in the "official" language and entered, as such, into ordinary linguistic usage (not to mention the Italian dictionary). So although Martino's name is not explicitly connected to literature, which furnishes the lion's share of new terms, it certainly belongs on the list of authors whose work left a mark on the particular definition or understanding of a given term. As we noted above regarding *rosselli,* or rose apples, Martino's text is cited as the first instance for a number of terms in the *Grande dizionario della lingua italiana.*

Despite Maestro Martino's monumental effort to promote a modicum of terminological standardization, a full consciousness of the necessity of a univocal gastronomic lexicon would not dawn until several centuries later. In fact, a high degree of terminological clarity was achieved only after the unification of Italy, with the publication, over many decades, of Pellegrino Artusi's *Scienza in cucina e l'arte di mangiar bene (Science in the Kitchen and the Art of Eating Well).*[103] In the meantime, a number of problems remained unresolved. *Ravioli* is a case in point, appearing in twenty-seven recipes (Library of Congress manuscript; see the textual note), whether named explicitly or referred to by way of analogy.

As Odile Redon and Bruno Laurioux have correctly observed:

> The content of the recipes throws doubt on the unified nature of the terms. Certain recipes stay on course: a thin dough envelops a stuffing of cheese, herbs, and chopped meat. These ravioli, the size of chestnuts, cooked in broth and served sprinkled with spices and grated cheese, are close to the classic ravioli of contemporary Italian cuisine. However, the term *ravioli* is also used to define foods covered with dough of smaller dimensions, such as "eggs in the form of ravioli," and it can even extend to dishes formed into little balls or rolls without the envelope of dough, simply rolled in flour (*ravioli bianchi* Bühler [the Neapolitan Recipe Collection]).[104] Often, they must be fried in oil or lard, thus making it difficult to differentiate them from *beignets* or *frittelle.* One can say as much of tortelli.[105]

It is an exceptional resource for lexicographical studies, but the full impact of Maestro Martino's *Art of Cooking* cannot be assessed without considering at least some of the many practical suggestions and techniques that constitute his culinary art. These include not only cooking methods and procedures, but the various ways of displaying dishes, and novelties in the selection of ingredients and seasonings. In this regard, the book reflects the radical transformation of medieval dietary and convivial customs (of which a few significant traces remain, to be sure) during the Renaissance, an era in which the rich "pretend" to eat, the bourgeois eat and become *grassi,* or "fat," and the cooks of sophisticated prelates are encouraged to view the food restrictions their masters had the audacity to impose on the famished and destitute lower classes as wonderful opportunities to indulge the holiness of their own palates.

Consider, for example, the following recipe for Lenten imitation eggs (see page 113), where rich pike broth, starch, and almonds make for a "fat" dish for "lean" times:

> Take some cleaned almonds that have been blanched as much as possible and crush well, moistening them with a little rose water so that they do not purge their oil. Thin with cooled, good, fatty, and rich pike broth; pass through a stamine, turning it into milk; take a half libra of rice that has been cleaned and washed, or more or less, as needed; cook it well in half of the above almond milk, and also take three ounces of the best and whitest starch you can get, and add it to the remaining milk until you see that the starch is fully dissolved; then boil this milk and starch together for a half-quarter of an hour, stirring continuously with a spoon, and make sure that it does not burn. Once this has been done, take the rice with all the milk and pass together through a stamine by the force of your hand; the thicker the mixture, the better it will be, and do not forget to add a generous amount of sugar. At your discretion, take the quantity or part of this mixture that you think is sufficient, make it yellow with saffron, and shape it into small round balls like egg yolks; then take two wooden molds shaped like eggs; and if you do not have the molds, you can use two egg shells in their place; put the white mixture beneath and above and all around the egg yolks, thus making it look like eggs. And one by one, arrange them on a dish, and they will appear to be hard-boiled eggs that have been peeled. Thin and make liquid a bit of the white composition with rose water and sugar, hot or cold as you wish, and you can use it to top the eggs and it will appear to be milk. If you like them dry, leave them as they are without topping with this liquid, but in its place top with fine, powdered sugar.

The end result is imitation eggs (today's imitation eggs are made from egg whites with the yolks discarded) that have an uncanny resemblance to the real thing but have an entirely different (yet delicious) taste.

The above recipe is a leftover from the Middle Ages, when extravagant recipes were developed over hundreds of years to address the many fast days in the Catholic calendar. There are at least two other traces of medieval cookery in Martino's book: recipes that hark back to the Catalan tradition and the satisfaction derived from a conspicuous desire for visual gratification (a dish was greatly appreciated if it tasted good, but when presented in an unusual manner, it

was astoundingly good). The fact that a certain number of Martino's recipes are accompanied by the qualifier "Catalan" (like that for *mirause*, partridges, squash, etc.) or the fact that blanc-mange, a common dish in Catalan cuisine, is dealt with obsessively in Martino is a reflection of Catalan dominance in the culinary arts of that period (just as, after Martino up until the time of Marie de France, it would be Italian, and then French; and today: who knows?).

As far as visual gratification is concerned, albeit less theatrical and phantasmagorical than in the Middle Ages (or in Roman times: who can forget Trimalchio's dinner party, in Petronius's *Satyricon?*), there are some extraordinary examples of *mirabilia gulae* (culinary wonders; *sotiltees* or subtleties, as they were known in Renaissance England) in Martino, like the recipe for "how to dress a peacock with all its feathers, so that when cooked, it appears to be alive and spews fire from its beak" (see page 54), where the "special effect" is easily obtained by stuffing the bird's mouth with cotton soaked in alcohol and then lighting it on fire. Even more "special" are those for the "flying pie" (the closing recipe in the Library of Congress and Vatican manuscripts) and "how to make aspic in a carafe with a live fish inside," which appears only in the Riva del Garda manuscript and could very well be a subsequent addition to the Martinian tradition.

In the case of the first formula, live birds are placed into an already baked pie, in which an-other "real" (and smaller) pie has been placed. Once the crust is removed, the little birds take flight, eliciting "oohs" and "ahs" from onlookers. In the second, little fish are made to slide through a pitcher with a spout. Inside the pitcher a chamber of water has been created with gelatin above and below. Satisfied with this ingenious formula, Martino, or perhaps a scribe who may have added the recipe to the collection later on, writes, "send it as a gift to anyone you wish" (see page 125).

While Martino's approach to cooking is somewhat influenced by the tradition of the ban-quet-as-spectacle, as well as by the nearly dominant *modus coquinandi* derived from Arabic cul-ture, it is not the product of thoughtless observation and mechanical repetition. Martino's habit of sprinkling victuals with sugar and spices, as well as the idea of flavoring sauces with raisins, prunes, and grapes, undoubtedly reflects practices fundamental to Arabic cooking. The same can be said about the employment of such staples as rice, dates, pomegranates, and bitter or-anges—the availability of which goes back to the Arabic occupation of Spain. First introduced by the Arabs to the island of Cyprus, the subsequent presence of sugar cane in Sicily, on the other hand, accounts for the passion Italians developed for sweets in the thirteenth century. As Anne Willan notes, "Martino is one of the first cooks to use sugar in large quantities to make dishes that are specifically sweet, such as fritters, almond paste cookies, and sugared apples, rather than treating it as a seasoning like salt, in the medieval manner."[106]

But Martino's most remarkable talent lies in his subtle ability to combine old and new in-gredients. It is perhaps the most salient aspect of his art—a trait which makes him the first in-carnation of a modern cook. For it is a mark of sophisticated artistry to know, for example, when one drop of oil adds flavor but two ruin a dish, or to appreciate that different cuts of meat man-ifest textural differences that require specific methods of cooking. It is also worth noting the care with which Martino specifies that, while an ingredient must be *well crushed* in a mortar and

passed through a ubiquitous stamine, it is sufficient for others to be *roughly* or *finely chopped*.[107] The allure of Martino's *Art of Cooking,* which is at once a culinary decalogue, a compendium, and a memoir, can be understood only when one keenly observes such small but essential gestures, the rigorous alchemical subtleties woven throughout the text, and, lastly, the author's trust in his own imagination.

Other verbs complement this mosaic of gestures: *dilute, chop, mince,* and so on. None of these procedures were required or advocated by medieval gastronomy, which revolved around the spit and the cauldron, cookery staples which of course did not disappear in Maestro Martino's time. But we know, thanks to him, that the success and taste of a dish cooked with these utensils depends on how one stirs or turns the skewers. In short, we know that rhythm is no less important to successful cooking than invention.

With regard to ingredients, Martino (and his "disciple" Platina, even more so) advises his readers that proximity to regional sources is often synonymous with quality. When in Rome, he writes, cook the unusual varietal of Roman broccoli; when in Lombardy, the unique species of pike found in Lake Garda. But even the right provenance in ingredients is no guarantee for success in cooking. Staples and condiments must be combined in such a way that they render more flavor than when they were in their natural state. This aspiration, of course, is an ancient one, but it has often created more frustration than satisfaction. With Maestro Martino, its fulfillment is the outcome no longer merely of chance but of conscious effort and calculation. In a departure from past practices, in which meats, fish, cabbage, and eggs were assaulted from the outside and drowned in spices or sauces, Martino stipulates that the ingredients employed to enhance the flavor of foods should be sought by keeping in mind the nature of the staples themselves. In some sense, condiments, sauces, flavorings, and the like should be seen as extensions of what is being cooked. It is as if the ingredients of a dish "required" one specific treatment rather than another. This is what contemporary Italians refer to as *la morte* (the death) of any given food, curiously lending to the expression a positive value: if lard is better than any other agent to enhance the flavor of fried meat, then lard becomes its death. The smart cook is thus he who draws pleasure in conjuring up the verdict, the outcome of which will be a mouth-watering execution.[108]

The development of new culinary habits, furthermore, did not depend at all on the discovery of new ingredients. Long before corn, potatoes, and tomatoes brought from America revolutionized the diets of Europeans (although for centuries they responded to these enticements with contempt), a systematic interest in wheat flour and common backyard vegetables (such as carrots, celery, and onions) and herbs enabled the formation of a radically new diet that only recently has been dubbed "Mediterranean" by shrewd mass-media publicists.[109]

Typically, flour led to pasta (although the name *pasta* referred to a host of products made with lesser grains, such as barley, spelt, and millet). In his book *The Culture of Food,* Massimo Montanari has convincingly argued that ever since pasta began to be dried and thus preserved in the twelfth and thirteenth centuries, it might have been a popular food in those areas where it was produced.[110] If eaten fresh, on the other hand, it bore the connotation of luxury and gluttony.

Eating food that could spoil gave the consumer an enhanced social status. This is indeed the image of "*maccheroni* or *lasagne* that we can glean from books of 'high cuisine' where such dishes are depicted as richly buttered, smothered in cheese, and dusted with sugar and sweet spices."[111] Martino devotes much attention and space to *pasta in brodo* (pasta in broth), and, as in the above-mentioned case of ravioli, to pasta filled with meat, cheese, or vegetables. He devotes an equal amount of space and attention to fava beans, peas, chickpeas, squash, cauliflower, elderberry, fennel, eggplants, and still other vegetables. Thanks to Martino, vegetable dishes that had been the hallmark of the pauper's diet for centuries shed their demure aspect and found a dignified place next to the roast and brined fish on the tables of the rich.[112]

Above and beyond this rehabilitation of vegetables, Maestro Martino turned his ingenuity toward assigning new functions to onions, dill, parsley, celery, and carrots (which, oddly enough, were not orange, but purple)—functions quite similar to those Italians ascribe to them even to-day. It is hard to say whether these preparations were a full-fledged anticipation of today's house-hold *battuto* (the common chopped onion, carrot, celery, and parsley base that would become a staple of Italian cuisine from the nineteenth century onward), but they surely came close.

To be sure, radical changes in culinary habits in this period were in large part forced on the "consumer" by dramatic political changes occurring in vast areas of the eastern Mediterranean basin, which had fallen under the control of the Ottoman empire. With trade routes virtually cut off or made wildly circuitous, traditional foodstuffs and spices imported from the East—first among them pepper—became extremely scarce.[113] Although their dietetic value was insig-nificant, no ancient or medieval gourmet would have done without them.

It is a well-known story that reaches its climax with the fall of Constantinople in 1453. The ships of the Most Serene Republic of Venice returned from the East with half-empty hulls. The prices of the spices escalated to an unsustainable level that even the wealthiest could no longer afford. Before solutions could be devised to avoid an economic disaster (for the Republic of Venice, anyway)—that is, before a catastrophe could be turned into a new *incipit*—people who paid no attention to Martino's *battuto* (and consequently no attention to the possibility of di-minishing their reliance on spices that had become impossible to obtain) began to promise mon-archs and potentates that they had envisaged new routes to reach the old supply centers.[114] Among them, a Genovese licensed to navigate on behalf of the Spaniards fixated (against the better judgment of his peers versed in science) on the idea of *buscar el levante por el ponente* (seeking the East by voyaging westward). True, he did not quite succeed in doing so, but only because of an inconvenient "new world" that he stumbled upon halfway between Spain and Cathay. And to add insult to injury, this new mysterious land was not half as rich in spices as the territories were supposed to be that he had promised his sponsors he could reach.

So it became necessary to make the best of an unfavorable situation: to seek refuge not along sea routes, but in the kitchen. Much less heroic, certainly, than the idea of smothering food with pepper, the modest proposal suggested by Maestro Martino was accepted as a compromise and temporary solution. To be absolutely preposterous, we could even say that because of this sud-

den paucity in the supply of spices, and because of the colossal geographical trompe l'oeil, the Italian way of cooking—that is, Martino's way—was able to invade continental Europe (putting an end to the exaggerated use of pepper, which may not be so healthy anyway). This invasion was short-lived, as quite soon the *grande cuisine* of the Italians' cousins beyond the Alps erased even the faintest trace of Martino's teachings. More recently, of course, events have taken yet another turn: there has been a worldwide renaissance of Italian cuisine, and Italians have become vociferous in flaunting their culinary pedigree. More preposterous still, a claim could be made that had Maestro Martino's *battuto* taken root more rapidly and widely in daily culinary practice, the "discovery of America," as a by-product of the mad and obsessive search for pepper, could have been postponed for who knows how long.

NOTES

1. See Alessandro Manzoni, *The Betrothed,* trans. with an introduction by Bruce Penman (London: Penguin, 1972), p. 143.

2. Platina, *On Right Pleasure and Good Health,* a critical edition and translation of *De honesta voluptate et valetudine,* ed. and trans. Mary Ella Milham (Tempe, Ariz.: Medieval and Renaissance Texts and Studies, 1998), p. 293.

3. The incunabulum saw the light at the shop of Ulrich Han, better known as Gallus, who had arrived in Rome with his printing equipment in 1467.

4. The battle was depicted by Leonardo da Vinci in a fresco in the Salone dei Cinquecento in the Palazzo della Signoria in Florence. Although the work was ruined before being finished (and ultimately was covered by a painting executed by Giorgio Vasari), traces of Leonardo's dizzying fray of horses and men have survived in the many copies and engravings made from the original (notably Rubens's *Battle of the Standard*). In 1976, ultrasonic tests were performed in an unsuccessful attempt to recover the Leonardo original.

5. Born in Pienza, one of Tuscany's most beautiful Renaissance towns and home to some of the best pecorino (sheep's milk cheese) and *porchetta* (roast suckling pig), Piccolomini (1405–64) had become one of the greatest humanist writers of his time, reigning as pope from 1458 to 1464.

6. See Milham's description of the services in the introduction to *On Right Pleasure and Good Health,* pp. 43 ff. The inscription on the tomb shared by Platina and his brother reads as follows:

XYSTI IIII

PONT. MAX. / AN. VIII

STEPHANO QVI

VIXIT AN. XXVII / MEN. VIII

PLATYNA FRATRI

BENE MERENTI

POSVIT

SIBI QVE AC POSTERIS

QVIS QVIS ES SI PIVS PLATYNAM

ET SVOS NE VEXES ANGVSTE

IACENT ET SOLI VOLVNT ESSE

ΘΑΡΣΟΝ ΑΔΕΛΦΕ ΚΑΔΩΣ

ΘΝΗΣΚΩΝ ΠΑΔΙΝ ΦΥΕΤΑΙ

7. For an efficacious description of the deplorable conditions into which Rome had fallen and of Martin V's campaign to restore its glory, see Ludwig Freiherr von Pastor, *The History of the Popes*, vol. 1 (London: Routledge and Kegan Paul, 1949; reprint, Nendeln: Kraus Reprint, 1969), pp. 214–19.

8. "Nulla urbis facies . . . nullum urbanitatis indicium in ea videbatur." This famous epithet comes from Platina's best-known work, *Liber de vita Christi et Omnium Pontificum,* composed between 1471 and 1475. For an English translation, see Platina, *The Lives of the Popes, from the Time of Our Saviour Jesus Christ, to the Reign of Sixtus IV,* trans. Sir Paul Rycaut (London: Wilkinson, 1688). Except for a brief intermission, nine popes, Clement V to Benedict XIII, inclusive, took up residence in Avignon, which was a town of no great importance at the beginning of the fourteenth century, and they developed it into a major center of Western culture. Administrative tasks in Rome were carried out by papal vicars, who let the situation there deteriorate to an unimaginable degree. At one point during the Great Schism, no less than three popes contended for St. Peter's legacy, including Benedict XIII, who fled to Spain with the papal tiara after being deposed by the Council of Constance in 1417. Martin V, who had been legitimately elected by the council, was unable to secure the tiara's return and was forced to commission a new one by the great Lorenzo Ghiberti. But even the new tiara did not survive the fury of the times and curial debts.

9. Pastor, *The History of the Popes,* vol. 1, p. 223.

10. Lorenzo Valla (1407–57): author of the great Renaissance Latin grammar the *Elegantiae,* and of the famed *Declamatio,* in which he proved that the Donation of Constantine, the document upon which the Roman Church had built its temporal power, was a forgery; Leonardo Bruni (1370–1444): author of numerous Latin translations of classical Greek works, including Plato, Aristotle, and Plutarch.

11. This was not the St. Peter's that we know today, which was built during the sixteenth century.

12. The art of banqueting, in fact, goes back to Roman times and remained prominent throughout the Middle Ages. But in those days, the hosts were princes, kings, dukes, counts, and *condottieri* (military leaders) — in a word, lay persons. Ostensibly, the Church thundered against the sin of gluttony and imposed strict fasting and levied fines for transgressions. But in Renaissance gastronomy, besides these amphytrionic feats executed at the instigation of prelates, much ingenuity was devoted — as Maestro Martino bears witness — to transforming lean fast days into very elaborate "lean" feast days.

13. Anna Morisi Guerra has edited a two-volume modern edition of *Historia di Milano* (Turin: UTET, 1985); the description of the banquet fills pages 1385 to 1392 of volume 2. The Turkish occupation of Asia Minor, by contrast, is allowed a mere line and a half. Understandably so: this is a history of Milan, not of the world. Corio, born in 1459, became chamberlain to Duke Galeazzo Sforza at a very early age and was with him when the duke was assassinated. The date of Corio's death is uncertain.

14. Corio, *Historia di Milano,* vol. 2, p. 1386 (unless indicated otherwise, all translations are by Jeremy Parzen). "The ostentation of Cardinal [Pietro] Riario," said a contemporary, "surpassed anything that our children will be able to credit or that our fathers can remember" (Pastor, *The History of the Popes,* vol. 4, p. 239). Son of Pope Sixtus IV's sister, Pietro Riario was born in 1445 and was made cardinal in 1471 at the age of twenty-five. Pietro was a true papal "nephew," in all senses of the word. Before his death, he had accumulated numerous bishoprics (Mende, Treviso, and others) and abbacies, and by all accounts he enjoyed an extremely lavish lifestyle. He died in Rome in 1474 upon his return from northern Italy, where he had attempted to secure support for his papal aspirations. The banquet is also described in Pastor, *The History of the Popes,* vol. 4, pp. 243–45: "The splendid reception of the Neapolitan Princess had, in part, a political object; it was intended to make an alliance between the Pope and Ferrante [the king of Naples] evident to the world."

15. See Claudio Benporat's *Storia della gastronomia italiana (History of Italian Gastronomy)* (Milan: Mursia, 1990), pp. 74–75.

16. Corio, *Historia di Milano*, vol. 2, p. 1391; Benporat, *Storia della gastronomia italiana*, p. 75.

17. Benporat, *Storia della gastronomia italiana*, p. 75.

18. Massimo Montanari, *The Culture of Food* (Oxford: Blackwell, 1994), p. 92.

19. The differences between the convivial gatherings of the Roman Academy, to which Platina belonged and of which he was a leading member (see below), and the various banqueting traditions that had reached the modern age from Roman times could not be more distinct. The dinners attended by Pomponians (so named after the founder of the academy, Giulio Pomponio Leto) were also notably different from the feasts of the so-called *brigate spenderecce,* or spendthrift clubs, of the thirteenth century, where young people purposely wasted their fortunes on the most lavish banquets they could conceive. A celebrated *brigata spendereccia* was the one described by Dante in *Inferno* 13.118–23 and *Inferno* 29.125–32. The father of the Italian language attributed to one of its members, Niccolò, the first gastronomic usage of cloves: "and Niccolò, the first to make men see / that cloves can serve as luxury (such seed, / in gardens where it suits, can take fast root)"; *Inferno* 29.127–29. Moreover, they stand apart from their contemporary culinary societies of aesthetically inclined friends such as the Brigata del Paiuolo, or Cooking Pot Club, in Florence, wherein twelve artists (apostles?), including Andrea del Sarto, were each required to bring a dish of his own whimsical invention to the home of their "lord," Giovan Francesco Rustici, who would punish those who brought identical dishes and who would then distribute all the victuals in such a manner that each participant could taste the others' (certainly wreaking havoc on the palates of all). For a true magisterial analysis of these societies, we enthusiastically recommend Lauro Martines's essay (entitled "Who Does He Think He Is? The Fat Woodcarver") on Antonio Manetti's novella of "the Fat Woodcarver," written in the 1480s. See *Italian Renaissance Sextet,* ed. Lauro Martines (Toronto: University of Toronto Press, 2004).

Only a few such fantastical creations are mentioned in Platina's book, and each is borrowed from Martino's repertoire. Even fewer mentions are made of true *mirabilia gulae,* or culinary wonders, in which a recipe incorporates a transformation of the ostensible object. This quasiomission is yet another indication of the waning of the Middle Ages and the dawn of the modern age, an epoch in which the number of dinner guests decreases together with the number of dishes served.

Such an admixture of formulas consumed simultaneously would be sure to irritate the taste buds of current gastronomers. But such "confusion" of flavors was already present in individual preparations that incorporated many disparate elements, like that of Andrea del Sarto, who

> presented an octagonal temple, similar to that of San Giovanni [the Baptistery of Florence], but raised on columns. The pavement was a vast plate of jelly, with a pattern of mosaic in various colours; the columns, which had the appearance of porphyry, were sausages, long and thick; the socles and capitals were of Parmesan cheese; the cornices of sugar, and the tribune was made of sections of marchpane [marzipan]. In the centre was a choir-desk made of cold veal, with a book of lasagne [long broad noodles] that had the letters and notes of the music made of pepper-corns; and the singers at the desk were cooked thrushes standing with their beaks open, and with certain little shirts after the manner of surplices, made of fine cauls of pigs, and behind them, for the basses, were two fat young pigeons, with six ortolans that sang the soprano.

"The Life of Giovan Francesco Rustici," in Giorgio Vasari, *Lives of the Most Eminent Painters, Sculptors, and Architects,* trans. Gaston Du C. de Vere (London: Warner, 1912–15), p. 120.

20. Platina was appointed to the Abbreviators of the Upper Bar *(de parco majoris)*, who examined and abridged solicitations and drafted the Apostolic response.

21. As suggested by Milham in her introduction to Platina's *On Right Pleasure and Good Health,* p. 12. See also David Chambers, *A Renaissance Cardinal and His Worldly Goods: The Will and Inventory of Francesco Gonzaga (1444–1483)* (London: Warburg Institute of London, 1992), p. 65; and David Chambers, "The Housing Problems of Cardinal Francesco Gonzaga," in Chambers, *Renaissance Cardinals and Their Worldly Problems* (Brookfield, Mass.: Variorum, 1996), p. 33.

22. Before this time (1439), he had been bishop of Trau (1435) and archbishop of Florence (1437). Trevisan is often referred to—erroneously—as Scarampo or Mezzarota-Scarampo. See Pio Paschini, "La famiglia di Lodovico cardinal camerlengo," in *L'Arcadia* 5 (1926): 91 ff. See also Pio Paschini, *Lodovico Cardinal Camerlengo* (Rome: Facultas Theologica Pontificii Athenaei Lateranensis, 1939), p. 7.

23. On Trevisan's presence at Anghiari, see Paschini, *Lodovico Cardinal Camerlengo,* pp. 47 ff.

24. Ibid., pp. 30–46.

25. For his speech, see Pope Pius II, *Commentarii rerum memorabilium (The Commentaries of Pius II)* (Northampton, Mass.: Department of History of Smith College, 1942).

26. Trevisan was described by one Renaissance chronicler as a "small, dark man, hairy, very proud and stern" (Andrea Schivenoglia, *Cronaca di Mantova dal 1445 al 1484* [Mantua: Baldus, 1976], pp. 135–37). In contrast with Schivenoglia's account, the celebrated portrait of Trevisan by Andrea Mantegna depicts the cardinal in an imperial pose and is among the most important representations of power in Renaissance portraiture (it is at the Berlin-Dahlem Staatliche Museen). See R. W. Lightbown, *Mantegna: With a Complete Catalogue of Paintings, Drawings, and Prints* (Berkeley: University of California Press, 1986), pp. 408–10; and Keith Christiansen, "Cardinal Ludovico Trevisan [Portrait]," in *Andrea Mantegna* (London: Royal Academy of Arts; New York: Metropolitan Museum of Art, 1992), pp. 333–35. Christiansen wrote of this painting, which marked the introduction of classical elements into Renaissance portraiture:

> Apart from being the touchstone for Mantegna's work as a portrait painter, this is one of the landmarks of Italian portraiture. Only Andrea del Castagno's *Portrait of a Man* (National Gallery of Art, Washington), of about 1450–57, certainly precedes it in profile. . . . Mantegna's depiction, with the shoulders firmly anchored by the heavy folds of the cloak and the head turned at an angle that emphasizes its volume, is also indebted chiefly to portrait busts, though to ancient rather than contemporary ones. (pp. 333–35)

27. Lucius Licinius Lucullus (ca. 117–58/56? B.C.E.), Roman consul and general known for his military and financial skills, as well as for his lavish banquets that made his name synonymous with culinary extravagance. The moniker "Lucullus" was applied to Trevisan by Paolo Cortesi in his *De cardinalatu libri* (in Castro Cortesio, Quos Symeon Nicolai Nardi senensis, alias Rufus Calchographus, imprimebat, Die decimaquinta Nouembris M.CCCCCX [November 15, 1510, i.e., 1513?], vol. 3, p. 67), where he wrote that Trevisan was "accused" of holding "sybaritic" feasts, spending "twenty ducats daily for his repast." Following his example, "no one in Rome dined frugally anymore." See also Raffaele Maffei (*Commentarii urbani* [Basilea [Basel]: n.p., 1543], p. 528), who wrote that "forgetting his origins, [Trevisan] took on such airs that he was the first among the cardinals to raise dogs and horses, and he introduced a magnificence in his sumptuous banquets and in his household furnishings that were well above his station." See also Paschini, *Lodovico Cardinal Camerlengo,* pp. 216 ff.

28. Francesco Gonzaga and his mother, Barbara of Brandenburg, received numerous gifts from Tre-

visan's residence. David Chambers documents this in his meticulous reading of the Gonzaga correspondence (see Chambers, *A Renaissance Cardinal and His Worldly Goods,* p. 78). Trevisan's luxuries are documented in his constant correspondence with Onorato Gaetani, seigneur of Sermoneta, whom he advised and protected, and by whom he was provided with the "best fish possible," buffaloes for grazing his lands, and poultry, as well as the local *pomaranzi,* or orange trees of Sermoneta, which he then planted in his famous garden. See, for example, letter 1451.4.1, in *Epistolarium Honorati Caietani, lettere familiari del Cardinale Scarampo,* ed. Gelasio Benedetto Anatolio Caetani (Sancasciano Val di Pesa: Stianti, 1926), p. 8.

29. Chambers, "Housing Problems," p. 21.

30. Ibid., p. 23.

31. Ibid., pp. 25, 43.

32. Ibid., pp. 37–38:

> Francesco's final house removal in Rome took him to the house formerly inhabited by Cardinal Ludovico Trevisan, the house at San Lorenzo in Damaso.... Cardinal Ludovico had died in April 1465, but any slight hopes Francesco had then of Paul II making good his promise of a house and granting him this one were dashed by his bestowing it up on the Spanish Cardinal Mella, Bishop of Zamora. After Cardinal Mella's death on 12 October 1467, Paul II showed that he still had a bad conscience by conferring the house up on Francesco three days later: then he suddenly changed his mind again and suspended the bull. Arrivabene wrote on 17 October that the pope had decided to reserve the house for his own use, at least while building works were going on at San Marco.... Paul continued to waver, three days later offering to release the bull but only on condition that Francesco did not move in without his license.... [It] was not until the middle of March 1468 that the way cleared at last for him to move to San Lorenzo in Damaso.... [Francesco's mother] Barbara ... commented that he would have to move in haste in case the pope changed his mind again. Francesco was certainly in residence before Ascension Day, for Paul II then came to stay as his guest. After six years, Francesco could now be considered a well-housed cardinal.

33. David Chambers, "Virtù militare del cardinale Francesco Gonzaga," in Chambers, *Renaissance Cardinals and Their Worldly Problems,* "Additions and Corrections," p. 6.

34. *Epistolarium Honorati Caietani,* p. 4.

35. This claim is not substantiated, but it would seem reliable considering that he must have had access to the entire archive and was a well-informed redactor of his ancestor's letters. For a classic biography of Sforza, see Eugenio Garin's profile in *Renaissance Characters* (Chicago: University of Chicago Press, 1991). Even a cursory glance at this collection of letters reveals how fixated Trevisan was with hosting banquets and obtaining the highest quality in victuals. Besides the documents cited here, there is also ample correspondence among Trevisan, Caetani's wife, Caterina Orsini, and their son, Niccolò, in which he discusses the procurement of fowl and other foodstuffs.

36. On October 15, 1464, G. P. Arrivabene, bishop of Treviso, charged with the task of "handling" Platina, wrote Marchioness Barbara of Brandenburg to inform her that "Bartolomeo [Platina] had been called to the palace and he arrived infuriated. And the more the bishop reproached him, the angrier he became, and thus, he was sent to the castle [the jail in Castel Sant'Angelo]." Archivio di Stato Mantova, Sezione Gonzaga, E.25.3. Platina was released a few months later, in 1465.

37. In 1450, humanist Giulio Pomponio Leto (in Latin, Julius Pomponius Laetus; 1428–97) came to Rome, and only seven years later he succeeded Lorenzo Valla as professor of rhetoric at the university in Rome, La Sapienza. He was an editor and commentator of classical texts (although many modern schol-

ars have discounted his contributions for his lack of rigor), and he published many *editiones príncipes,* including Curtius and Varro, as well as a compendium of Roman and Byzantine emperors (printed posthumously in 1499). He was an organizer of literary gatherings and founder of the Roman Academy (Accademia Romana or Accademia Pomponiana, so named for its leader). In 1468, Pope Paul II condemned Pomponio Leto and his fellow members of the academy, including Platina, for their materialistic vision of the world and their interest in pagan ritual. He was released a year later by an act of clemency, but it was not until Sixtus IV succeeded Paul II in 1471 that his professorship would be restored and the academy would be allowed to meet again.

In the name of classicist ideals, and even to the point of renewed pagan ritual, the Roman Academy had begun to meet, probably as early as 1466, at the home of Pomponio Leto, where he and fellow members would discuss literary and archeological subjects and debate Neoplatonic philosophy. These meetings were also social occasions, and the members of the academy (Platina among them) took pagan names and indulged in Roman rituals, comestible and otherwise. Indeed, their paganish engagements in the catacombs of Rome were probably occasion for indulgence of the flesh as well.

At least one such meeting was noted by the nineteenth-century recorder of Renaissance inscriptions, Rodolfo Amedeo Lanciani, in his *Ancient Rome in the Light of Recent Discoveries* (Boston: Houghton, Mifflin, and Company, 1898):

> It is, no doubt, exceedingly remarkable that the evidence against these men, sought in vain by Paul II and his judges, should have come to light only a few years ago [1852] . . . in the remotest part of that subterranean labyrinth which had been used by Pomponio's brotherhood as a secret place of meeting. On the white plaster of the ceiling the following inscription had been written with the smoke of a tallow candle: "January 16, 1475. Pantagathus, Mammeius, Papyrius, Minicinus, Aemilius, Minucius, all of them admirers and investigators of antiquities, and the delight of the Roman dissolute women, [have met here] under the reign of Pomponius, supreme pontiff." . . . Pomponio and his colleagues were very wise in confiding their secret to the deepest and most impenetrable recesses of the Roman catacombs. (pp. 11–12)

See also Joseph Dommers Vehling, *Platina and the Rebirth of Man* (Chicago: W. M. Hill, 1941), pp. 51–52. Both Lanciani and Vehling misidentify Platina as "Pantagathus," and Lanciani erroneously cites Platina as a "cardinal." In fact, "Pantagathus" was Marco Romano Asclepiade, while Platina was "Calvus," Latin for "bald." It has been suggested that Platina's nickname derived from a play on words: in Italian the expression *essere in piazza,* or to be out in the town square, means to have a bald patch; the Italian word *piazza* is derived from the same Greek root, *plateia* (meaning broad and flat), that gave Sacchi's birthplace its name (Piadena), from which he drew his own name, Platina (see above, in the introduction). It is highly improbable, however, that the expression *essere in piazza* circulated in Platina's times. And it is thus far more likely that his nickname was nothing but an ironical antiphrasis alluding to his beautiful mane, as can be clearly seen in the Melozzo da Forlì fresco at the Vatican (see note 40). See also G. B. de Rossi, "L'accademia di P. Leto e le sue memorie scritte sulle pareti delle catacombe romane" (The Academy of P. Leto and Its Memories Written on the Walls of the Roman Catacombs), in *Bollettino di Archeologia Cristiana,* 5th series, 1 (1890): 81–94; and *Dizionario critico della letteratura italiana* (Critical Dictionary of Italian Literature), vol. 4 (Turin: UTET, 1994), s.v. "Umanistiche, Accademie," p. 353. For a complete account of the Roman Academy and the persecution by Paul II, see P. Medioli Masotti, "L'Accademia Romana e la congiura del 1468" (The Roman Academy and the Conspiracy of 1468), in *Italia medioevale e umanistica* (Medieval and Humanist Italy) 25 (1982).

38. "If you will free me and my companions," wrote Platina, laying it on rather thick, "if you will relieve us from indigence, I promise (invoking God and all the Saints as my witnesses) that we will be your most humble servants and we will sing your praises tirelessly. In prose and in poetry, we will celebrate the golden age of your most happy reign." This prompted Cremonese writer Agostino Cavalcabò, from whom we have gleaned this quotation, to remark, "He probably would not have written this had he been free" ("Platina, maestro nell'arte culinaria," *Cremona* 7, no. 7 [1935]: 391).

39. *Vitæ Pontificum Platinæ historici liber de vita Christi ac omnium pontificum qui hactenus ducenti fuere et XX,* first printed in Venice in 1479. Platina wrote it as a direct attack on Paul II, on the advice of Francesco della Rovere (later Pope Sixtus IV, to whom the work would be dedicated). Although lacking in rigor, it is an excellent history of the popes, indeed the first ever, and some have speculated that Sixtus IV would not have accepted the dedication had he read the book's contents. It even includes an account of Popess Joan, although Platina himself questions the authenticity of the tale (see www.newadvent.org/cathen/08407a.htm).

40. The fresco (executed in 1477) depicts the inauguration of the library (1475). Platina, its first preceptor in the modern era, kneels before Pope Sixtus IV; beside him is Giuliano della Rovere (the future Pope Julius II); standing beside the pope is Protonotary Apostolic Raffaello Riario; behind Platina are Girolamo Riario and Giovanni della Rovere.

Replacing Antonio Bossi di Vigevano, Platina heralded the rebirth of the immense library by reorganizing the collection. He was paid ten ducats a month, plus provisions and a horse. He would die only six years later, in which time he managed to construct a fine house on the Quirinal in Rome, willed to his friend Giulio Pomponio Leto (see note 37).

41. *Contubernium:* from the jargon of the Roman military, where it meant a group of ten soldiers occupying a tent together, literally a mess or squad (see note 37).

42. Platina, *On Right Pleasure and Good Health,* p. 119.

43. Vehling, *Platina and the Rebirth of Man,* pp. 74–75. The original of this letter was published in *Epistulae et commentarii Jacobi Piccolomini* (Mediolanum [Milan]: apud Alexandrum Minuzianum [Minutianum], 1506). Giacomo Ammannati Piccolomini (1422–79) was made cardinal in 1461 by Pope Pius II, who greatly appreciated his scholarly and military accomplishments. He was a close friend of Platina, and the fact that two of his relatives were charged along with Platina by Paul II is perhaps an indication of his own involvement in the conspiracy against the pope. Perhaps his greatest work was his *Commentarii,* which represented a continuation of his protector Pope Pius II's own work.

44. I owe this insight and much more to Joseph Dommers Vehling, in whose essential book *Platina and the Rebirth of Man* the connection between Platina and Maestro Martino was outlined for the first time.

45. The link between eating and good health is what permitted the birth of medicine in the first place. In his *Hippocrates* (Baltimore: Johns Hopkins University Press, 1999), Jacques Jouanna sums it all up: "Endowed with too frail a constitution to partake of the same diet as animals without suffering harm, man was forced to discover an art for modifying natural foods in order to adapt them to his nature. Humanism, it may therefore be said, was born with cooking." And bearing more specifically on the topic of his own dissertation:

> To this discovery relating to the diet of persons in good health a second one came to be added that
> extended and perfected the first: the discovery of the diet best suited to sick persons ... medicine
> was therefore a sort of customized cuisine. More than this, it was the sign of a superior degree of
> humanism in which not all men shared. Incidentally the author of *Ancient Medicine* mentions in his

description of the second discovery that medicine was unknown to barbarians. Consequently if cooking represented the highest degree of a humanism that included foreigners as well as Greeks, medicine corresponded to the most evolved form of humanism—Hellenism. Despite his attempt to conceive of humanity in general terms, the Hippocratic physician was unable wholly to free himself from a characteristic kind of Hellenocentrism. (pp. 234–35)

What could be more enticing, for a humanist of the fifteenth century drenched with Hellenistic aspiration, than to go the way of medicine to justify cooking?

46. For an excellent survey of eating habits and dietary guides in the Renaissance, see Ken Albala, *Eating Right in the Renaissance* (Berkeley: University of California Press, 2002).

47. Platina, *Del piacere onesto,* ed. Emilio Faccioli (Turin: Einaudi, 1985), p. xxi.

48. Platina, *On Right Pleasure and Good Health,* p. 125. See also Vehling, *Platina and the Rebirth of Man,* p. 78, who remarks on Platina's simile, perhaps unaware that it is drawn from Ovid (*Metamorphoses* 4.55 ff.).

49. "Ingenia, et mores, vitasque, obitusque notasse / Pontificum, argutae lex fuit historiae. / Tu tamen hinc lautae tractas pulmenta culinae: / Hoc, Platina, est ipsos pascere Pontifices" (Epigram 1.23) (Jacopo Sannazaro, *Opera,* Amstelaedami: apud Gerardi Onder de Linden, 1728, p. 195). Jacopo Sannazaro (or Sannazzaro) (1456–1530), a Neapolitan and author of the first pastoral romance in Italian (*Arcadia,* a partly autobiographical allegory consisting of poems and prose), Petrarchan lyricist, and poet of the house of Aragon. There were many other openly scathing jabs at Platina, notably by Valeriano Vanetti and Pier Barozzi.

50. Agostino Nifo (ca. 1473–after 1538), a Neapolitan philosopher remembered above all for his anti-Christian interpretation of Aristotelian philosophy and his later writings as a Christian apologist.

51. Traiano Boccalini (1556–1613), political and satirical writer, most famous for his *Ragguagli di Parnaso (Advertisements from Parnassus),* in which he harshly criticized the Spanish domination of Europe. Trajano Boc[c]alini, *I ragguagli di Parnasso or Advertisements from Parnassus in two centuries with the Politick Touchstone, written originally in Italian by that famous Roman Trajano Bocalini and now put into English by the Right Honourable Henry Earl of Monmouth* (London: Dring, 1669), p. 74.

52. In his edition of Platina, *Del piacere onesto,* Emilio Faccioli has observed that these sources were listed more out of humanist convention than from actual consultation (p. 130). Pliny, on the other hand, goes mostly unmentioned despite the fact that his *Historia naturalis* was the primary source of Platina's information on plants and animals. Apicius's *De re coquinaria* served Platina merely as a structural model. The work had been rediscovered in the monastery at Fulda (Germany) by Enoch of Ascoli, after Poggio Bracciolini had listed it in a catalog he made around 1417 during his participation in the Council of Constance. Enoch acquired the manuscript and eventually lent it to humanist Giovanni Aurispa. By the time Platina began composing his tractate on cookery, there must have been several manuscript copies of Apicius circulating in Italy. Platina's friendship with Poggio went back to their days in Florence. In *De honesta,* Poggio's son, Giovanni Battista, is described as "one who frequently eats" chicken in verjuice (*pullus in acresta*), a dish reported to agree with "stomach, heart, liver, and kidneys, and [to] repress bile" (Platina, *On Right Pleasure and Good Health,* pp. 277–79).

53. Ibid., p. 103. "Writing" instead of "speaking," as previously rendered by Milham for the expression *genus dicendi.*

54. Ibid., p. 293. Imitating to "surpass" the ancients seems to be the driving force behind all aesthetic endeavors of the Renaissance. An example of a similar claim, in an area by far more pervasive than gas-

tronomy, will be made a few decades later by the celebrated Venetian courtesan and poet Veronica Franco (1546–91), who states in a letter to Tintoretto, in which she expresses her enthusiasm over her portrait:

> I can't bear to listen to people who praise ancient times so much and find such fault with our own. . . .
> [They claim] that nature was a loving mother to men of antiquity but . . . a cruel stepmother to men today . . . [and] that no one is found in the world today who matches the excellence of Apelles, Zeuxis, Phydias, Praxiteles, and other noble and famous painters and sculptors of those times. . . .
> I have heard gentlemen expert in antiquity . . . say that in our era and even today, there are painters and sculptors who must be acknowledged not only to equal but to surpass those of ancient times, as Michelangelo, Raphael, Titian, and others did, and as you do today.

Veronica Franco, letter 21 in *Poems and Selected Letters,* ed. and trans. Ann Rosalind Jones and Margaret F. Rosenthal (Chicago: University of Chicago Press, 1998), pp. 35–36.

55. Some might point out that *Le viandier (The Vivandier),* by Guillaume Tirel (more commonly known as Taillevent, 1310 [1326?]–95), circulated previous to this thunderstorm of Italian cookery. While this is true, it is also important to note that until its first printing in 1490 it could boast of a very limited and highly privileged readership, but never enjoyed the same success as *On Right Pleasure and Good Health.* Moreover, scholars of culinary history agree that his book represents a culmination of medieval cookery (in fact, it relies heavily on the spices of the Spanish and Italian traditions of the Middle Ages). Through Platina's adaptation and the many translations that would follow, Martino's book—the first modern cookery book—enjoyed an audience never before rivaled in the history of culinary-literate man. This was in part due to the novelty of the work, and in part to the new accessibility—because they were economical—of printed books.

56. Caterina de' Medici (or Catherine de Médicis; 1519–89): great-granddaughter of Lorenzo the Magnificent, Italian queen of French king Henry II, regent of France (from Henry II's death in 1559 until 1574), and mother to three kings of France. There is little doubt that she was singlehandedly responsible for changing the course of gastronomic history in France and determining the development of what we now call *grande cuisine.* Accompanying her to Paris from her native Florence were innumerable artists, musicians, dressmakers, hairstylists, dance teachers, perfume makers, etiquette masters, and, most importantly, celebrated cooks who had perfected such novelties—novel, at least, to the French palate—as aspics, sweetbreads, artichokes, truffles, macaroni, and *zabaglione.* Caterina was most probably the first to use a fork at the court of France (a new practice in Italy at the time)—a clear indication of the new sophistication in both taste and comportment that she brought with her from Italy.

57. Platina, *On Right Pleasure and Good Health,* p. 243.

58. Giacomo Albini (ca. 1320–48/49), author of a *regimen* for the prince Giacomo of Acaia, entitled *De sanitatis custodia,* a health manual for the young family of the prince and a prime example of popular medical literature (probably composed between 1341 and 1342). The *regimen sanitatis* ("health regimen") was a compilation of medical and dietetic advice often written in verse. The genre originated with the school of medicine at Salerno founded by Emperor Frederick II of Swabia, who in 1221 decreed that no one should practice medicine unless authorized to do so by the teachers at the university there. For a comprehensive edition of the corpus of medical writings from Salerno, see Salvatore de Renzi, *Collectio salernitana: Ossia documenti inediti, e trattati di medicina appartenenti alla scuola medica Salernitana* (Naples: Filiatre-Sebezio, 1852–59).

59. See Arnaldo della Torre, *Paolo Marsi da Pescina* (Rocca San Casciano: Cappelli, 1903), p. 124.

60. Lettera di Andrea Cor[s]ali allo Illu[s]tri[ss]imo Signo-/re Duca Iuliano de Medici/ Venuta Dellindia/del Me[s]e di Octobre Nel/M.D.XVI [Letter of Andrea Corsali to the Illustrious Duke Giu-

liano de' Medici, from India, in the month of October, 1516], [Florence], Giovanni Stephano di Carlo, f. a4 (recto). The Corsali document was first published in 1516 as a pamphlet and again in 1550 as the first book printed by the Venetian printer Giovanni Battista Ramusio. The original letter is in the Marciana Library in Venice (a facsimile edition is forthcoming). See Gustavo Uzielli, *Ricerche intorno a Leonardo da Vinci (Research on Leonardo da Vinci)*, 2nd series (Rome: Salviucci, 1884), p. 448.

61. Leonardo da Vinci, *The Notebooks of Leonardo da Vinci*, vol. 1, trans. Edward McCurdy (New York: Reynal, 1938), p. 90. The reference to Platina is on a folio (no. 14, recto) of anatomical studies at the Royal Library of Windsor Castle. See also A. M. Brizio, ed., *Scritti scelti di Leonardo* [Selected Writings of Leonardo] (Turin: UTET, 1952), p. 616.

62. In keeping with the subtle irony that pervades *On Right Pleasure and Good Health*, Platina advises Callimachus to avoid the last dish because it "dulls the eyes and arouses even languishing passions" (p. 285). Callimachus, otherwise known as Filippo Buonaccorsi, often called Caecus or Caeculus (Latin for "blind"), was notorious for his amorous propensities. See his biography in Milham's introduction to *On Right Pleasure and Good Health*, p. 82.

63. Robert Dal[l]intgon, *A Survey of the Great Dukes State of Tuscany* (London: Edward Blout, 1605), p. 34.

64. A true diehard of culinary lore, Castelvetro's book was reproduced in a handsome octavo edition published in 1988 under the auspices of the Ristorante I Lancellotti, in Soliera Modenese (in the province of Modena). Part and parcel of the fare are dishes prepared with fresh herbs and vegetables grown in the restaurant's garden: the varietals cultivated there are described in Castelvetro's sixteenth-century tractate. Giacomo Castelvetro, *Brieve racconto di tutte le radici di tutte l'erbe e di tutti i frutti che crudi o cotti in Italia si mangiano* (Mantua: Arcari, 1988; translation: *The Fruit, Herbs, and Vegetables of Italy*, trans. Gillian Riley [London: Viking Press, 1989]). The thrust toward eating vegetables in Italy was actually already a century old. It had begun in 1340 with Michele Savonarola's (1385?–1466?) *Libreto de tute le cosse che se manzano* (*Little Book of Everything That's Edible*).

65. Platina, *On Right Pleasure and Good Health*, p. 123.

66. Ibid., p. 377.

67. Troubled perhaps by the illustrious humanist's nonchalance in taking advantage of his humble friend's culinary wisdom, Ernesto Travi proposed that Martino's work (the date of which cannot be determined with any degree of certainty) was compiled after the publication of *On Right Pleasure and Good Health*. Maestro Martino's priority would thus disappear and his role would be reduced to that of consultant, at best. Why Martino would turn to writing down his recipes at a later date remains unexplained, and such conjecture is supported by Travi only with heuristic reasoning. Capitalizing on the apposition appearing on the title page of the Washington manuscript, "Once Cook to the most Reverend Chamberlain and Patriarch of Aquileia" (in other words, "I am no longer his cook"; see Jeremy Parzen's textual note at the end of this volume), Travi concludes that the text could not have been composed prior to 1465, the date when his eminence, Cardinal Ludovico Trevisan, passed from this world to where he had been awaited all along.

This reasoning would be plausible only if applied to an "alpha" or autograph (or idiograph) manuscript, and if we were sure that Martino remained in the employment of Trevisan until the very end of the cardinal's life. Unfortunately, neither is the case. Any well-informed copyist could have added the *once* that unleashed the Italian scholar's somewhat misguided philological passion. It is not even necessary, however, to invoke the personal initiative of a scribe. Platina himself informs us that he had completed *On Right Pleasure and Good Health* by 1464 (prior to his first "prison term"), and there is no need to move the

beginning of its composition back to 1462, as Travi does with no evidence whatsoever. But even if Platina had begun his work at that time, his debt to Martino relates only to the second half of his treatise, a section that could have been added when the end was already in sight: it was in fact a mere translation and it could have been completed in a relatively short period of time, certainly less time than any original conceptualization would have required. As has already been observed, Platina met Trevisan (and most likely Martino as well) in June 1463, at Albano (and this may not have even been the first time). Thus, all things considered, more than a year had elapsed between Platina's visit to Albano and his incarceration (which took place in October of the following year)—plenty of time for Platina's convenient appropriation of Martino's recipes.

The assertion of Maestro Martino's temporal priority, an opinion that prevails among current scholars, cannot be seriously challenged, least of all by characterizing this Renaissance cook as a consummate extemporaneous speaker, a backhanded compliment made by Platina and exploited by Travi to the hilt. Speaking and writing are not incompatible activities—not to mention the fact that Martino's style, although not uniformly represented in all manuscripts, is certainly not alien to such exquisitely oral formulations as polysyndeta, fragmentary syntax, anacolutha, and so on.

68. See Claudio Benporat, *Cucina italiana del Quattrocento (Italian Fifteenth-Century Cuisine)* (Florence: Olschki, 1996), pp. 741–45. De Rossi is keen to reassure his master that none of them came from Milan: "there was not one among them from your dominion" (Pastor, *The History of the Popes,* vol. 4, p. 484).

69. Gian Giacomo Trivulzio (1441–1518): one of the great mercenary generals of the Renaissance, who served under both Francesco Sforza and Ludovico the Moor, whose army he would later defeat while working for Ludovico's nemesis, the king of France, Louis XII, in 1500.

The two great sculptural projects to which Leonardo devoted himself wholeheartedly were not realized. Neither the huge, bronze equestrian statue for Francesco Sforza, on which he worked from about 1489 to 1494, nor the monument for Marshal Trivulzio, on which he was busy in the years 1506 to 1511, was ever completed. Many sketches of the work exist, but the most impressive were found in 1965 when two of Leonardo's notebooks—the so-called Madrid Codices—were discovered in the National Library of Madrid. These notebooks reveal the sublimity but also the practically unreal boldness of his conception. Text and drawings both show Leonardo's wide experience in the technique of bronze casting, but at the same time they reveal the almost utopian nature of the project. He wanted to cast the horse in a single piece, but the gigantic dimensions of the steed presented insurmountable technical problems. Indeed, Leonardo remained uncertain of the problem's solution to the very end.

70. Keep in mind that the townships of Blenio and Como are a stone's throw from each other, and the confusion could very well have been engendered by the greater notoriety of the latter.

71. See Aldo Bertoluzza, ed., *Libro di cucina del Maestro Martino de Rossi* (Trento: Edizioni U.C.T., 1993).

72. On July 10, 1442, Cardinal Gerardo di Landriano, bishop of Como and apostolic legate to the duke of Milan, granted Martino de Rossi use of the rectory at the monastery of San Martino Viduale. This was brought to light by E. Motta in the library of the Trivulzio family in Milan. See "Per la storia dell'Ospizio di Camperio sul Lucomagno nei secoli XIV–XV," in *Bollettino storico della Svizzera italiana* 19 (1897): 110–15. "The hospice," writes Giuseppe Chiesi,

> dates back perhaps to the 13th century.... Hidden from sight by a suffocating outgrowth of vegetation ..., only a dilapidated wall remains to bespeak its existence.... Not so in the 15th century: the woodsy path that leads from the Romanesque church of San Remigio ... to those

meager ruins was in fact a much traveled route known as the "French" or "Main Road" and was used by footmen and merchants with their beasts of burden directed toward Biasca or the Luco-magno pass.

Giuseppe Chiesi, "Martino Rossi un cuoco bleniese alla Corte Ducale," in Bertoluzza, *Libro di cucina del maestro Martino de Rossi,* p. 13.

73.   Cooks were not the only Swiss to invade the plains of Lombardy in those days. By far more notorious and feared were the mercenary soldiers whose reputation for cruelty greatly surpassed the fame of their countrymen's culinary skills, as Ariosto is wont to remind us: "Switzers, if hunger drives you to invade, / Like famished animals, the Lombard plain, / To beg among us for a crust of bread, / Or end your poverty, in battle slain" (*Orlando furioso* 17.77). *Orlando furioso (The Frenzy of Orlando),* trans. Barbara Reynolds (Harmondsworth: Penguin, 1975–77), p. 520.

74.   On April 19, 1500, Ludovico the Moor disguised himself as a Swiss foot soldier and attempted to escape his French enemies by blending in with the crowd:

> For as the Swiss were marching in military order through the French Army, he was, by the vigilance of those who were appointed to watch, or by the indication of the Swiss themselves, discovered as he was marching a-foot in the midst of a battalion, clothed and armed like a Swiss, and immediately made a prisoner; a miserable spectacle! which drew tears even from the eyes of many that were his enemies.

Francesco Guicciardini, *The History of Italy, from the year 1490 to 1532,* trans. Austin Parke Goddard, vol. 2 (London: John Towers, 1753), bk. 4, p. 374. For an accurate description of the relations—political, military, and economic—between canton Ticino and the dukedom of Milan at the time of the Visconti and the Sforza, see Giulio Vismara, Adriano Cavanna, and Paola Vismara, *Ticino medievale (Medieval Ticino)* (Locarno: Armando Dadò, 1990), chaps. 6 and 7.

75.   Besides the universally known Leonardo da Vinci, Ludovico attracted to his court and to the University of Pavia such talents as the musician Gaffurio, the Hellenist Calcondila, the historian Giorgio Merula, and the man of letters Bernardo Bellincioni, just to name a few.

76.   Grazia Rossanigo and Pier Luigi Muggiati, *Amandole e malvasia per uso di corte (Almonds and Malvasia Used at Court),* was published in Vigevano by Diakronia (1998) and reissued the same year in Milan by Editoriale Aisthesis & Magazine. From the following excerpt from a letter sent by Francesco Maletta (a diplomat) to Bianca Maria Visconti (wife of Francesco Sforza), we can gather how fastidious and pressing the ducal requests for specialties may have been:

> On this day, I was told by your Ladyship to see that you were sent some nectarines. I diligently sought them out here but only a few could be found. I was able to obtain them and am sending them to your Excellency via the present horseman. If there were any better ones to be found, I would have been happy to send them. *Lodi, August 28, 1468* (p. 74)

77.   See F. Malaguzzi Valeri, *La corte di Lodovico il Moro,* vol. 1, *La vita privata e l'arte a Milano nella seconda metà del Quattrocento (The Court of Ludovico the Moor,* vol. 1, *Private Life and Art in Milan in the Second Half of the Fifteenth Century)* (Milan: Hoepli, 1913), p. 187.

78.   *Malvasia* and *candied fried dough,* l. 4: a sweet grape varietal and the wine of the same name; "candied fried dough" is *pinocato* in the original: a candied mound of fried dough balls in the shape of a pine cone, hence the name; *son of Tereus,* l. 5: Itys, who was transformed into a goldfinch after being revived by the gods;

Ceres, l. 18: goddess of agriculture and symbol of pure "white" grain, in other words, foodstuffs made from grains.

Antonio Cammelli (1436–1502), more commonly known as "il Pistoia" after his birthplace: humanist author of comic and facetious lyrics, including 533 sonnets dedicated to Isabella d'Este. The original text may be found in *I sonetti faceti di Antonio Cammelli,* ed. E. Pèrcopo (Naples: N. Jovene, 1908), pp. 69–70.

79. This summary message was countersigned by Cichus (Cicco Simonetta), the exceptionally powerful ducal secretary who served under Francesco and Galeazzo Maria, and who was disposed of by Ludovico the Moor and replaced with Bartolomeo Calco. This, as well as all other documents mentioned below, are from the Archivio di Stato di Milano and have been transcribed by Luciano Moroni Stampa and Giuseppe Chiesi in their *Ticino ducale: Il carteggio e gli atti ufficiali (Ducal Ticino: Correspondence and Official Proceedings),* vol. 1, tome 2 (Bellinzona: Stato del Cantone Ticino, 1994), p. 128.

80. Ibid., pp. 198, 386–87, 372–73, 415, 436.

81. Ibid., tome 3, p. 103.

82. Ibid., tome 2, p. 372.

83. Claudio Benporat, "Il ricettario di Martino de Rubeis," in *Appunti di gastronomia* 13, no. 5 (1994): 5–14.

84. His large belly earned him the nickname Polyphemus: "Sum Polyphemus, ego vasto pro corpore dictus,/ Martinus proprio nomine notus eram" (Martino is my Christian name, my vast girth/ earned for me the nickname Polifemo). Antonio Beccadelli, *Hermaphroditus,* trans. Eugene Michael O'Connor (Lanham, Md.: Oxford, 2001), p. 72.

85. Antonio Beccadelli (1394–1471): poet and humanist, whose Latin poem *Hermaphroditus* openly extolled homosexual love and who later founded the Academia Pontaniana in Naples. The date of the composition of the work is discussed at length in Antonio Beccadelli, *Hermaphroditus,* ed. Donatella Coppini (Rome: Bulzoni, 1990), pp. lxxiii ff.

86. The assumption that Martino's services were first rendered to Trevisan and later to Trivulzio is also supported by the fact that the Riva del Garda manuscript (compiled for the Trivulzio) is an enlarged, though not necessarily revised, version of the Washington manuscript (the Vatican and the Pierpont Morgan Library manuscripts bear no indication of their origin). In it, a conspicuous number of "northern" recipes would seem to reflect the predilections of a new master. Recipes catering to convivial rather than gustatory experience are also more abundant and reveal a penchant for sensationalism, for which Trevisan, a bona fide gourmet, may not have had much taste. Were these recipes originally added by Martino, or are they the product of a copyist's interpolation? The question has no definitive answer, but the latter case seems more plausible.

87. The "Controversy of the Three Chapters" refers to the seminal writings of Theodore of Mopsuestia, Theodoret of Cyrus, and the letter of Ibas to Maris in which Eastern Christian philosophers asserted the monophysite (i.e., "one body") nature of Christ. These writings were condemned at the Council of Constantinople, in 382, and the ratification of this council by the pope marked the end of the schisms in the West.

88. See Emilio Montorfano, "L'opera di Maestro Martino alla luce delle ultime ricerche storiche" (The Work of Maestro Martino in Light of the Latest Historical Research), in *Maestro Martino da Como e la cultura gastronomica del Rinascimento (Maestro Martino of Como and the Gastronomic Culture of the Renaissance)* (Milan: Terziaria, 1990), p. 29.

89. See Benporat, *Cucina italiana del Quattrocento,* pp. 23–24.

90. According to Alberto Capatti and Massimo Montanari (see their *La cucina italiana [Italian Cuisine]* [Rome-Bari: Laterza, 1999], p. 13), there were twenty-two reprints of the book by Rosselli ("at times identified as a real person, at other times as a mere editorial ghost"), but none of them was printed after the first half of the seventeenth century. According to Bruno Laurioux ("I libri di cucina italiana alla fine del medioevo: Un nuovo bilancio," *Archivio storico italiano* 154 [1996]: p. 53), instead, the reprints have numbered twenty-four (the last of which dates back to 1682). We shall leave further numerological discrepancies to the investigative ingenuity of future, more resilient Maestro Martino devotees.

91. As is indeed the case with Platina, who adopts the "empty" shell of Apicius and fills it with Martino's recipes. As Mary Ella Milham writes, "for his structure, ten books, ending with one on fish, Platina turned to Apicius, which I have suggested had been edited by him or by his friend Pomponio Leto." See Mary Ella Milham, "New Aspects of *De honesta voluptate et valetudine*," in Augusto Campana and Paola Medioli Masotti, eds., *Bartolomeo Sacchi il Platina: Atti del Convegno internazionale di studi per il V centenario (Bartolomeo Sacchi, or Platina: Proceedings of the International Congress of Studies for the Fifth Centenary)* (Padua: Editrice Antenore, 1986), p. 92.

92. This bold statement comes from Apicius's famous recipe "Patina de Apua sine Apua" (Dish of anchovies without anchovies), wherein he disguises the fish by cooking it in a custard with eggs and seaweed: "ad mensam nemo agnoscet quid manducet" (no one will recognize what he is eating). Different translators have approached this recipe in different manners, in accordance with their background in Latin and their experience in the kitchen. Vehling calls it a smelt pie or sprat custard. See his translation in *Cooking and Dining in Imperial Rome* (1936; reprint, New York: Dover, 1977), pp. 100–101; but see also the later and equally problematic translation in *The Roman Cookery Book*, trans. Barbara Flower and Elisabeth Rosenbaum (New York: British Book Centre, 1958), p. 99.

93. Lacking precise instruments, Martino devises a rather peculiar way to measure time. See the recipe "How to make a good, clear, fine broth," page 63.

94. Auguste Escoffier, *Le guide culinaire* (Paris: Lagny E. Colin, 1903). For the celebrated soprano Nellie Melba, whom he had admired in *Lohengrin* at the Covent Garden in 1894, Escoffier created the dessert *pêche au cigne* (renamed "peach melba") in 1889, at the inauguration of the Carlton Hotel).

95. See Nicolas Barker's "The Aldine Italic," in *Aldus Manutius and the Development of Greek Script and Type in the Fifteenth Century* (New York: Fordham University Press, 1992), app., pp. 109–16.

96. Vehling, *Platina and the Rebirth of Man*, p. 62.

97. In many ways, Martino's book can be likened to his contemporary Luca Pacioli's *De arithmetica, geometria, proportioni, et proportionalita* and *De viribus quantitatis*, wherein the Renaissance mathematician embraces the Renaissance spirit of transmitting knowledge and technology (in regards to bookkeeping in the case of the former and magic "effects" in the latter). Pacioli even includes a few *mirabilia gulae* similar to those in Martino.

98. There are at least eleven uses of "however your master wishes" or "as suits your master's tastes" in the Library of Congress manuscript. And there is one instance when Martino refers to how his master prefers sturgeon. See "The best way to cook sturgeon," page 99.

99. See Martino's recipe for "Rice with almond milk," page 71, in which he describes a method for removing the bitter taste from a pottage if it has burned over heat.

100. Laurioux, "I libri di cucina italiana," p. 52.

101. Day 8, story 3; Giovanni Boccaccio, *The Decameron*, trans. G. H. McWilliam (Hammondsworth: Penguin, 1972), pp. 597–98.

102. See Vehling, *Platina and the Rebirth of Man,* p. 93.

103. First published in 1891, Pellegrino Artusi's book went through several revised and enlarged editions, the fourteenth of which (1910)—the last to be supervised directly by the author—became the cornerstone of modern Italian cuisine. For an English edition of this book, see *Science in the Kitchen and the Art of Eating Well,* trans. Murtha Baca and Stephen Sartarelli (Toronto: University of Toronto Press, 2003).

104. See the recipe for "Ravioli-shaped fritters," pages 94–95.

105. Odile Redon and Bruno Laurioux, "La Constitution d'une nouvelle catégorie culinaire: 'Les pâtes dans les livres de cuisine italiens de la fin du Moyen Age'" (The Making of a New Culinary Category: Pastry in Italian Cookery Books at the End of the Middle Ages), *Médievales* 16–17 (1989): 51–60. Massimo Montanari also calls attention to this referential nonchalance: "In cookery books [pasta] was described as a category of its own, combining (at least until the fifteenth century) pastas both boiled and fried, sweet and savory, simple and filled; in fact even meat or vegetable balls dredged in flour and fried were described as 'pasta.'" See Montanari, *The Culture of Food,* p. 142.

106. Anne Willan, *Great Cooks and Their Recipes* (London: Pavilion, 1995), p. 27.

107. The expression *crush* appears in the text roughly 250 times (more than once per recipe), signaling the preponderance of this action over all the others. The word *stamine* (*stamegna* in the original) comes from the Latin *stamina,* the warp in the loom of the ancients. In the vernacular of Milan, *stamegna* denotes a stingy person, because a *stamegna* holds back the more conspicuous pieces, which are of greatest value.

108. It is not just a question of deciding what constitutes a harmonious set of ingredients. Part of the process is the modality of cooking itself—whether fast or slow. In the chapter dedicated to fish, Martino explains which must be boiled and which grilled.

109. Although tomatoes were consumed in Italy not long after being introduced there (dressed with olive oil and sprinkled with salt), the fruit—it does have seeds, after all—was used to dress pasta (in meat sauces) in the early eighteenth century, and only in the late nineteenth century did it become the most popular condiment for pasta.

110. There is evidence that the ancient Greeks, Romans, and Etruscans were already cooking a rudimentary form of pasta. The Greeks cooked *laganon,* and the Romans *laganum.* The fact that Sicilians were making pasta as early as the twelfth century—long before Marco Polo went to China—is historically certain.

111. Montanari, *The Culture of Food,* p. 142.

112. And Martino invents dozens more. Besides roasts, Martino's table is graced by stews, *bondiole,* meat and vegetable tortes, puddings, and *creme cotte* (custards), dishes that can be cooked over a flame, with the flame above and below, or even far from the flame—that is to say, if we understand clearly what he is saying, over ashes.

113. Contrary to the prevailing opinion, the quest for spices, pepper in particular, did not originate with the Crusades. For centuries, Arab merchants who controlled the trade routes from Asia had assured a steady flow of these eastern products into imperial Rome. When, in the first century, spice traffic assumed gigantic proportions, Rome set up shipbuilding yards on the Egyptian Red Sea coast and launched its own vessels all the way to India. Once Roman seafarers learned how to handle the monsoon winds that carried them, the voyage was dramatically shortened: slightly less than a year. Prices, however, remained astronomical: twelve ounces of pepper could fetch as much as 200 to 250 dollars. For a long time, pepper had been used mostly for medicinal and cosmetic purposes. In Apicius's cookbook, there is hardly a recipe that does not call for pepper. After a long medieval parenthesis and the virtual cessation of all forms of commercial ex-

change between East and West, pepper resumed a role of primary importance in dietary and culinary matters. From the lands they thought they had conquered, Crusaders carried back a taste for new foods and cooking techniques. Of all souvenirs, however, the champion of the new gastronomic vogue was, once again, pepper. In the new urban realities of the twelfth and thirteenth centuries, when people had to make do with a winter's supply of salted and dried foods, spices restored a smile to the faces of many banqueters. But there is more to pepper than taste. In Reay Tannahill's *Food in History* (London: Headline Publishers, 2002), we read that, ultimately, Europe was to depend so heavily on spices that they "became a common currency, as negotiable as silver. Today, the phrase 'peppercorn rent' is sometimes used to denote a nominal sum, but in the late medieval world, there was nothing nominal about it. A pound of pepper represented the barter equivalent of two to three weeks' labour on the land" (p. 167).

114.   Terms to be appreciated etymologically: *catastrophe* = the last segment of a text where tragic events are epitomized; *incipit* = the beginning of a new mythos.

THE ART OF COOKING

COMPOSED BY THE EMINENT
MAESTRO MARTINO OF COMO,
A MOST PRUDENT EXPERT IN THIS ART,

ONCE COOK TO THE MOST REVEREND

CARDINAL TREVISAN,
PATRIARCH OF AQUILEIA

IN THE RIVA DEL GARDA MANUSCRIPT, THE TITLE READS AS FOLLOWS:

Cookery Book
Composed and Compiled
by the Eminent Master Martino di Rossi
from the Milanese Valley of Bregna, Diocese Descendant
from the Villa de Turre
Born to the Holy House of San Martino Vidualis
to the Illustrious Seigneur Gian Giacomo Trivulzio, *et cetera*
a Most Prudent Expert in This Art
As You Will Read Below.

CHAPTER ONE

MEATS FOR BOILING AND MEATS FOR ROASTING

The fatty meat of oxen and that of beef should be boiled, the loin should be roasted, and the haunch made into cutlets.

All the meat of mutton is good boiled, except for the shoulder, which is good roasted, as is the haunch.

Although pork meat is not healthful—no matter how you cook it—the chine should be roasted with onions, and when roasted, pork meat should be salted to taste.

All the meat of kid is good roasted or boiled, but the hindquarters are best roasted. The same holds for lamb.

Goat meat is good in the month of January, with garlic sauce.[1]

The forequarters of deer can be good in dainty broth;[2] the loins can be roasted and the haunch is good in pies and as cutlets; the same holds for roebuck.[3]

Wild boar is good in pepper sauce or in civet or in dainty broth.[4]

All hare meat is good roasted, but the forequarters are also good in sauce, as will be explained below.[5] Rabbit meat is better roasted than in any other way, and the loins are the best part.

Bear meat is good in pies.

---

1. See recipes for garlic sauce, pages 79 ff.

2. A dainty broth is a stew or pottage to which bits of lard are added; the result is a "dainty," or exquisitely delicious, broth. Even sauces to which lard was added were called dainty sauce. Although the modern usage of the word *dainty* makes us think of "delicately beautiful or charming," its usage in culinary terminology in the fourteenth and fifteenth centuries, and even later, was more akin to the word's Latin root, *dignus,* meaning "worthy." (In Middle English, *deinte* meant "excellent.") As will become clear below, Martino used all types of broth (fine or thin broth and dainty broth) to dress other foods.

3. Martino's pies, or *pastelli* (akin to the modern *pastele, pastelle,* or *pastille*), are savory pies made with various types of meat; unlike in a minced pie, the meat is left whole (sometimes cut into pieces the "size of your fist"); the crust is discarded and serves generally to preserve the meat. Besides the *pastello,* Martino's repertoire includes the tart *(crostata),* a short pie, and the torte *(torta),* a layered pie akin to the modern quiche.

4. *Piperata* is a pepper sauce (see page 51); the defining element of civet is that the meat be cooked in the blood of the same animal.

5. See "How to prepare a good pepper sauce for game," page 51.

HOW TO COOK CAPON, PHEASANT, AND OTHER FOWL

The meat of swan, that is, cygnet, as well as goose, duck, crane, wild goose, eagle, heron, and stork, should be stuffed with garlic, onion, and other good things and then roasted.

Peacocks, pheasants, Greek partridges, gray partridges, wild hens, partridge poults, quails, thrushes, blackbirds, and all the other good birds should be roasted.

Pullet should be roasted. Squab should be boiled but is even better when roasted. Wild squab is good when roasted but better when boiled with pepper and sage.

Good capon should be boiled, but when good and fat, it should be roasted. The same holds for pullet.

HOW TO PREPARE BOILED WHITE MEAT

When you wish to boil white meat, cut it up into pieces however you wish, and soak in cool water for an hour; and then wash in warm water and then in cool water and place over heat in a pot that is not too narrow, so that it will remain white; then you must add salt as necessary and most importantly, scum well; and in case the salt is not white, put it in a little hot water, and it will not take long for it to dissolve and become brine; and once it has settled, it can be added slowly to the pot so that the dirt will remain at the bottom; and if the meat is old and hard, especially if it is capon or hen, remove it many times from the boiling water and freshen in cool water, and thus it will remain white and it will cook more quickly.

HOW TO PREPARE A FINE ROAST

To make a fine roast with pullet, capon, kid, or any other meat worth roasting: first, if the meat is fatty, boil it, except in the case of young veal, and then lard it as roasts should be; make sure that capon, pheasant, pullet, kid, or any other meat that should be roasted is well-plucked or skinned and cleaned; then place in boiling water; remove immediately and place in cool water; this is done so that it will remain white and be easier to prepare; then lard it with chopped lard and whatever other aromatic ingredients you wish; dress as suits your master's tastes.

If you wish, stuff it with good herbs together with dried prunes or red or bitter cherries and, at the right moment, verjuice or other good things;[6] and then skewer handsomely and place over the flame and turn it slowly at the beginning so that it will be even more handsome and tasty; and when done cooking, grate a loaf of white bread and mix it with the necessary amount of salt, and sprinkle it over the roast on every side as you give it a good, quick turn over the flame; by doing so, you will have a handsome and well-browned roast; then serve, the sooner the better.

---

6. *Agrestum,* or *agresto* in Italian (from the Late Latin *acrum,* meaning "sharp" or "sour"), is an equivalent of the French *verjus* (English *verjuice*), meaning "green" or "unripe" grape juice. Martino makes a distinction between *agrestum* and verjuice; he uses the latter term to denote a particular dish, most probably of French origin (see "How to make a verjuice pottage," page 65).

HOW TO PREPARE A GOOD PEPPER SAUCE FOR GAME

Use equal amounts of water and red wine to wash the inside of the meat and then pass the wash through a stamine,[7] adding as much salt as you wish; and then cook the meat in the water and wine and when it is done cooking, remove and divide among two platters; take a libra and a half of raisins and finely crush;[8] and slice, toast, and grate the same amount of bread and soak it in good vinegar and then crush together with the raisins; and ideally, if you have the blood or pluck of the animal, crush with the other ingredients, which, once well ground, must be mixed with the broth made from the same meat, with a little *sapa,* that is, sodden wine,[9] and with the vinegar used to soak the bread; then pass this mixture through a stamine into a pot, adding spices, pepper, cloves, and *cannella,* also called cinnamon, as you deem necessary; and you can make this pepper sauce strong or sweet using vinegar and spices to taste or as suits your master's tastes.

Then boil it for half an hour over hot coals, stirring often with a spoon, so that it heats evenly; then fry the meat in good lard, divide among the platters, and cover with the pepper sauce; the darker the pepper sauce, the better.

HOW TO PREPARE DAINTY BROTH WITH GAME

To make dainty broth from all types of game: first wash the meat in good white wine mixed with an equal amount of water; pass the wash through a stamine and use it to cook the meat, adding a generous amount of lard that has been cut up into small pieces like playing dice, as well as a generous amount of sage that you have torn by hand into three or four pieces; and when it is done cooking, add some good spices, as above.

If you wish to make the dainty broth slightly thick, take two or three egg yolks, as needed, and take the same number of slices of bread and toast over a flame until dry, without overtoasting or burning, and crush; thin with some broth and add to the dainty broth; and if you have any blood or pluck from the game, crush well and cook in the broth, and it will be much better.

If you wish to serve this dainty broth on platters, remember to cut the meat into large pieces of a libra or a half libra each; if you wish to serve it in bowls, it should be chopped.

Also note that both the meat for pepper sauce and that for dainty broth are cooked in the wash so as not to lose the blood that escapes when you wash it.

HOW TO PREPARE CIVET WITH GAME

To make civet from game meat: first, cook the meat in equal amounts of water and vinegar and, when it is done cooking, remove from its broth so that it can dry. Once dried, fry in good lard,

---

7. *Stamine:* a woolen or worsted cloth used as a sieve, a fundamental tool in medieval and Renaissance cookery.

8. Martino's libra was equivalent to twelve ounces, in other words, a pound in the troy system (first used in Troyes, France), as opposed to the avoirdupois system, in which a pound is equivalent to sixteen ounces.

9. *Sodden wine:* cooked wine must.

and if you wish to make two platters of civet, take a libra of raisins and a half libra of unpeeled almonds and crush together.

Then take a libra of bread that has been sliced and dried over a flame, but not overly toasted, and soak in a little red wine and crush with the other ingredients; then add some broth from the meat, pass it through a stamine into a pot, and place it on some coals away from the flame;[10] let it simmer for a half hour; then add generous amounts of ginger and cinnamon, making it sweet or strong to taste or as suits your master's tastes.

Then take an onion and cook it in a pot with good lard that has been chopped; and when the onion is done cooking, crush it and grind it well and add it to the lard in which it was cooked; and put all of this in the pot, letting it boil for a little while; then divide the meat on platters, top with the civet, and serve.

HOW TO PREPARE A PIE WITH DEER OR ROEBUCK

To make a pie with deer or roebuck: first cut the meat into pieces the size of your fist and then cook in equal amounts of water and vinegar, just until it begins to boil, adding salt as necessary. Then remove the meat to a place where its moisture can be released and the meat dries a little. Take some whole cloves and use generously to stud each side of the meat, which then should be rolled in the spices.

Then take some good flour and make a crust, a little thicker than for lasagne.[11] Cover each piece of meat with the crust and place in the oven to cook very slowly until well done; this and similar pies will keep for fifteen days and even a month.

HOW TO PREPARE PIES WITH THE MEAT OF VEAL, CAPON, OR ANY OTHER MEAT, OR WITH OTHER TYPES OF FOWL

First, take however much lean meat you wish and finely chop using a knife; and take some good veal fat and mix well with the meat, adding some good spices as suits the common taste or as suits your master's tastes.

Then make your usual dough crust for pies and put the pie in the oven to bake. When it is done cooking, take two egg yolks and some good verjuice, a little fatty broth, and a bit of saffron; beat and add to the pie. If you do not know how to make crusts, cook it in a pan just as you would for a pie.

You can also put one or two pullets or squab in the pie, or capons, or another kind of bird, whole or in pieces.

---

10. In medieval and Renaissance cookery, temperature was controlled by moving pots and pans closer to or farther away from the flame. In this case, the pot is placed over hot coals to apply even, low heat.

11. Just as in modern-day Italy, *lasagne* were long, broad noodles.

HOW TO PREPARE A TART WITH SQUAB OR PULLET, ETC.

First, boil the meat just a little, so that it is nearly cooked; and then cut it up into small pieces and fry in some good lard. Then lay a crust of dough in a pan, topping with dried prunes or cherries, and then take some good verjuice, a little fatty broth, and eight eggs, and beat; and take some parsley,[12] marjoram, and mint, and chop up these herbs with a knife; combine in a pot and place it over heat, that is to say, place it over hot coals so that as you stir it continuously with a spoon, it will begin to stick.

Then top the crust with this fine broth; and then put it over heat as if it were a torte, and as soon as it begins to thicken, serve; and be sure that the crust is sweet or tart as suits the common taste, or however your master likes.

HOW TO PREPARE BROWNED MEAT, SQUAB, OR PULLET, OR KID

First, clean very well and quarter, or cut into small pieces, and fry in a pot with some good lard, stirring often with a spoon. When the meat is almost done cooking, discard most of the fat from the pot. Then take some good verjuice, two egg yolks, just a little good broth, and some good spices, and mix together with enough saffron to make the mixture yellow and combine with the meat in the pot; boil for a little while until cooked. Place the browned meat on a platter, top with just a bit of chopped parsley, and serve.

Browned meat can be made sweet or sour to taste or as suits your master's tastes.

HOW TO PREPARE A PIE IN A POT

First, take the meat and some good veal fat and chop and place it in the pot. If you wish, you can add some pullet or squab with the meat. Then put the pot on some hot coals away from the flame. When it begins to boil, make sure that it is well scummed; then add a small amount of raisins and take a bit of finely chopped onion fried with some good lard and add to the pot together with the lard. When it seems done cooking, add some good spices and some verjuice. If you wish, you can add one or two beaten egg yolks. As soon as the pie is done, serve.

---

12. Martino's parsley was most probably flat-leaf parsley, also known as Italian parsley or Italian plain leaf parsley (*Petroselinum crispum*).

HOW TO PREPARE CATALAN *MIRAUSE*

First, take some squab, or pullet, or capon, and dress as you would a roast, and then roast on a spit, and when half-cooked, remove from the spit and quarter; and then cut each quarter into four parts and place them in a pot. Then take some almonds that have been toasted under hot ashes and rub them with a cloth without cleaning them otherwise, and crush; and then take two or three slices of slightly toasted bread and three or four egg yolks, and crush together with the almonds; and then add a little good vinegar and some broth, and pass through a stamine; and then put this mixture in the pot over the meat, adding some good spices and a generous amount of cinnamon, ginger, and a generous amount of sugar. Then put the pot over some hot coals and boil for an hour, stirring continuously with a spoon. As soon as it is done, serve this *mirause* on platters or in bowls, whichever is more appropriate.[13]

HOW TO DRESS A PEACOCK WITH ALL ITS FEATHERS, SO THAT WHEN COOKED, IT APPEARS TO BE ALIVE AND SPEWS FIRE FROM ITS BEAK

How to dress a peacock so that it appears to be alive: first, the peacock should be killed by stabbing it in the head with a sharp knife or by slitting its throat, as you would with a baby goat. Then slice the body from the neck all the way to the tail, cutting only the skin and delicately skinning it so that you do not ruin the feathers or the skin. When you have finished skinning the body, turn the skin inside out, from the neck down. Make sure not to detach the head from the skin of the neck; and similarly, make sure that the legs remain attached to the skin of the thighs. Then dress it well for roasting, and stuff it with good things and good spices, and take some whole cloves and use them to stud the breast, and cook the bird slowly on a spit; and place a wet cloth around the neck so that the heat does not overly dry it; and wet the cloth repeatedly. When it is done cooking, remove from the spit and dress it up in its skin.

Prepare an iron device attached to a cutting board that passes through the feet and legs of the peacock so that the iron cannot be seen and so that the peacock stands up on its feet with its head erect and seems to be alive; and arrange the tail nicely so that it forms its wheel.

If you want it to spew fire from its beak, take a quarter ounce of camphor with a little cotton wool around it, and put it in the beak of the peacock, and also put a little aqua vitae or good, strong wine. When you serve it, light the cotton wool and it will spew fire for a good bit. And to make it even more magnificent, when the peacock is done, you can decorate it with leaves of hammered gold and place the peacock's skin over the gold after you have smeared the inside of the skin with good spices.

The same can be done with pheasants, cranes, geese, and other birds, as well as capons and pullets.

---

13. The term *mirause* is from the Catalan *mig-raust* (Provençal *mieg-raust*), meaning "half-cooked" or "half-roasted."

HOW TO DRESS A ROAST SUCKLING PIG

First, make sure that it has been well skinned and that it is white and clean. Then slit the suckling pig lengthwise along the chine and remove its innards and wash well. Remove the innards and finely chop with a knife together with some good herbs, and take some finely chopped garlic, and a bit of good lard, and a little grated cheese, and a few eggs, and crushed pepper, and a bit of saffron, and mix all these things together and put the mixture in the suckling pig, inverting it and turning it inside out as you would with a tench.[14] Then sew it together and tie it up well and cook on a spit or on a grill. But cook it slowly so that the filling is as well cooked as the suckling pig. Make some brine with vinegar, pepper, and saffron, and add two or three sprigs of laurel, or sage, or rosemary, and baste the suckling pig repeatedly with this brine.

The same can be done with geese, duck, crane, capon, pullet, and similar fowl.

[HOW TO PREPARE BOILED PULLET WITH VERJUICE][15]

To make boiled pullet with verjuice, the pullet needs to be cooked with a bit of salt-cured meat. When half-cooked, take some whole verjuice grapes, and cut in half, removing their seeds, and cook together with the pullet. When done cooking, take a bit of finely chopped parsley, mint, ground pepper, and saffron, and add all these things together with the pullet and the broth on a platter and serve.

[HOW TO PREPARE ROAST PULLET]

To prepare roast pullet: when it is done roasting, take some orange juice, or good verjuice mixed with rose water, sugar, and cinnamon; put the pullet on a platter, and then dress with this mixture and serve.

HOW TO PREPARE ROULADES WITH VEAL AND OTHER GOOD MEAT

First, take some lean meat from the haunch and cut it into long slices and beat it on a cutting board or table using the knife handle, and take some salt and ground fennel seeds and spread over the cutlets. Then take some parsley, marjoram, and good lard, and chop together with some good spices and spread this mixture over the cutlets. Roll them and cook them on a spit, but do not let them get too dry over the flame.

---

14. See "Tench," page 104.

15. Where the Library of Congress manuscript gives no title for a particular recipe, the Vatican manuscript title has been used, and brackets have been introduced by the translator. This editorial convention was first suggested by Benporat (see the bibliography), who noted that the Library of Congress and Vatican manuscripts were virtually the same, save for the fact that the Library of Congress manuscript lacked titles for a good number of recipes.

HOW TO PREPARE ROMAN-STYLE *COPPIETTE*

Cut the meat into pieces the size of an egg, but do not detach completely, because the pieces of meat have to remain attached to one another; and take some *pitartima* seeds,[16] also called coriander seeds, or some ground fennel seeds, and dredge the pieces of meat in this mixture, put in a press for a little while, and roast on a spit, inserting a thinly sliced piece of lard between each piece to make sure that the *coppiette* remain tender.[17]

HOW TO PREPARE VEAL MORTADELLA

Take some lean meat from the haunch and chop it up with a little lard and some good veal fat, just as for the meat used in pies. Then take some finely chopped parsley and marjoram and an egg yolk, together with the necessary amount of grated cheese and spices and saffron; and mix all these things together with the meat; and then take some caul fat from a pig or mutton or from another type of meat, as long as it is good; and tie the mixture together in the caul fat, shaping it into pieces about the size of an egg; roast slowly on a spit so that they do not overcook.[18]

HOW TO PREPARE *TOMACELLI*

Take some pork livers and some other livers and boil, but do not overcook; then grate as you would cheese; take the necessary amount of salt-cured pork belly and chop. Take a bit of aged cheese and fatty cheese and a little marjoram and parsley, raisins, spices, and two or three eggs, as needed, and grind all these things together with the livers. Then shape the *tomacelli* into pieces the size of walnuts or eggs, and wrap each one separately with pork caul fat. Then cook in a pan with good lard, slowly, so that they will not overcook.[19]

HOW TO PREPARE KING OF MEATS WITH PORK OR YOUNG VEAL

Take some lean meat trimmed of all its sinew, in other words, from the haunch, and some good pork fat or veal fat. Then take some good aged cheese and a bit of fatty cheese and some good spices and two or three eggs and take the necessary amount of salt; and carefully mix all these things together and make them yellow with some saffron; and take some large pork intestines and clean well, making sure that they are thin and that no fat has remained; and fill with the

---

16. *Pitartima:* a fifteenth-century name for coriander seeds, borrowed from the Greek.

17. The name *coppiette* literally means "little couples": as prepared by Martino, the result is paired pieces of meat cooked on a spit, separated by a piece of lard. The modern-day version of this dish calls for the meat to be ground: "nothing more than classic meatballs" fried in lard, according to Alessandro Molinari Pradelli, author of the recently published *Grande libro della cucina italiana* (*Great Book of Italian Cuisine*) (Rome: Newton and Compton, 2000).

18. Modern mortadella is a type of cured pork (the original Bolognese sausage, hence "baloney"); its name means "seasoned with myrtle," from the Latin *mirtus.*

19. The word *tomacelli,* from the Latin *tomaculum,* meaning "liver sausage," survives today in the Ligurian dish *tomaxelle*—braised veal roulades filled with ground meat, sweetbreads, spinal cord, and mushrooms.

mixture and press it into the intestines, making the sausages as long or as short as you like; and they should be boiled within two days because after that they will no longer be as good. Nonetheless, they can be conserved for fifteen or twenty days, or longer, if properly handled.[20]

WHEN YOU WISH TO MAKE GOOD SAUSAGE WITH PORK OR OTHER MEAT

Take some lean meat and some fatty meat trimmed of all its sinew and finely chop. If you have ten librae of meat, add one libra of salt, two ounces of well-washed fennel seeds, and two ounces of coarsely ground pepper. Mix well and let set for one day. Then take some well-washed and trimmed intestines and fill with the meat and then smoke to dry.

HOW TO PREPARE TWO PLATTERS OF ASPIC

Take forty mutton feet, skin, remove the bones, and soak in cool water for three to four hours. Then wash well and cook in a jug of white vinegar mixed with a jug of white wine and two jugs of water, adding salt as necessary.[21] Simmer very slowly, scumming with great care. When half-cooked, take a quarter ounce of whole peppercorns and a quarter ounce of long pepper,[22] a quarter ounce of cardamom, a quarter ounce of whole cinnamon, and an eighth of an ounce of spikenard. Grind all these things together and add them to the water where the mutton feet are cooking. Simmer until reduced by one-third. When the feet are well cooked, remove and return the broth to the heat and when it begins to simmer again, add ten egg whites that have been beaten until frothy. Stir with a spoon and then immediately pass the broth through a wool sack two or three times so that the mixture is repeatedly strained of the spice mixture, which will remain in the sack; the more times you strain, the clearer and more pure it will be.

Then take the meat of an already cooked pullet or kid, or capon; remove the skin from the meat, which should be very white and clean; place the meat between two pieces of white cloth to dry, and then arrange on the platters and top with the broth; place the platters in a cool place and let them congeal.

[HOW TO COOK A QUARTER OF KID WITH GARLIC]

Take a quarter of kid and dress well for roasting, lard and fill with a generous amount of peeled cloves of garlic, the same way you would as if you wished to baste or lard it. Then take some good verjuice, two egg yolks, two crushed garlic cloves, a little saffron and pepper, and a bit of fatty broth, and mix all these things together and put this mixture in a pot beneath the kid while it is roasting, and baste it every so often with this sauce. When it is done cooking, put the kid

---

20. This recipe used *cervellata* in the original, a type of blood sausage still made in southern Italy. By the end of the seventeenth century, this dish had become known as the "King of Meats" (*Re delle Carni*).

21. A jug, or *boccale,* was roughly equivalent to a liter in volume.

22. *Piper longum,* or long pepper, is a type of pepper still cultivated in South Asia and imported to Europe, as it was in Martino's day.

on a platter, top with the sauce, and a bit of finely chopped parsley. The kid should be well done and served very hot.

HOW TO PREPARE A VEAL CUTLET

Take some lean meat from the haunch and thinly slice, but not too thinly, and then beat with a knife handle. Coat the cutlets with salt and fennel seeds, and keep them pressed for half an hour, if you have the time. Then roast them over a grill, turning as necessary; keep moist by topping with a slice of lard. These cutlets should not be overcooked, and they should be served very hot. They will give great pleasure and whet the appetite for drink.

HOW TO PREPARE THE LIVERS OF FOWL, PULLET, PORK, OR OTHER ANIMALS

If using veal livers, cut into pieces the size of a walnut and roll in salt, fennel seeds, and sweet spices; and wrap them in pork caul fat or that of veal, or better yet, that of kid, and cook them on a spit but be careful not to overcook.

HOW TO PREPARE RASHERS

Take some salt-cured meat that is marbled with fat, and together with some lean meat cut into slices and cook in a pan without overcooking.[23] Then put on a platter and top with vinegar, a bit of sugar, cinnamon, and finely chopped parsley. The same can be done with *sommata* or prosciutto by adding orange juice, lemon juice, or whatever you wish instead of vinegar, and this will make drinking all the better.[24]

HOW TO COOK THRUSHES WITH SAUCE

Dress and roast the thrushes as you usually would. Then take some well-peeled, crushed almonds and mix with a generous amount of sandalwood extract so that the sauce will be red, and then mix with a little verjuice and broth, adding generous amounts of ginger and cinnamon.[25] Then pass this sauce through a stamine into a pot; and then boil for about a quarter of an hour; and when the thrushes are done cooking, put them in a small pot and top with the sauce; and you

23. Martino's rashers (essentially fatty pork meat either fried or grilled), or carbonade, are a distant relative of the modern carbonade, or *carbonata* in Italian; its name is possibly derived from the fact that it was cooked over hot coals, *carboni* in Italian.

24. In other words, it will enhance one's thirst; *sommata* was salt-cured pork loin; prosciutto (*presutto* in Martino's terminology) is today's ubiquitous salt-cured pork thigh.

25. See Martino's method for blanching almonds in "Marzipan," page 87.

can also make them differently by topping the thrushes with orange or lemon juice together with salt and sweet spices.

HOW TO COOK A VEAL'S HEAD OR THAT OF AN OX

Once the veal or ox has been butchered, remove the head and scrape it with warm water as you would with suckling pig; clean well and then boil. Serve with garlic sauce.[26] If you wish to roast it, do so in the oven after stuffing with garlic and good herbs and other good spices. It is very good when prepared in this way.

HOW TO DRESS VEAL'S BRAINS

Once the head has been boiled, remove the brains, and crush well. Then take two egg yolks, a bit of crushed pepper, verjuice, and salt, and mix all these things together with the brains; and fry in a pan with a little rendered lard; and when it begins to thicken, remove and put it in a bowl, and top with sweet spices. Serve immediately.[27]

ROASTED FIGPECKERS

Take some figpeckers and pluck them well without cutting or gutting the giblets. Then take some grape leaves and fill them with salt, fennel seeds, and a little lard, and wrap the figpeckers in the leaves and cook them for a half hour or less, because they will cook quickly over hot ashes. If you wish to roast them, bind them around a skewer with their heads and feet together; this is done so that they are not torn by the spit.[28]

HOW TO DRESS PARTRIDGES IN THE CATALAN STYLE

Take a partridge and roast, and when it is done cooking, remove from heat and spread open the wings and detach the meat from the breast of the body. Then insert a bit of salt, a small amount of sweet spices, and a bit of crushed cloves that have been mixed together with a little orange or lemon juice, or verjuice; and this should be done when the partridge is still hot, and not over-cooked, but rather green and almost bloody; that is, not well done but very hot; turn it quickly, not slowly.

HOW TO PREPARE RENDERED PORK LARD

Take some fresh pork fat or fresh lard and cut into pieces the size of a chestnut, and add a generous amount of salt. Then crush well and let set for a day; and then place in a pot over heat; and for a hundred librae, add ten or twelve jugs of water and let boil slowly until thoroughly melted. Then strain the rendered lard through a stamine; and very slowly scum the top so that

---

26. See "White garlic sauce" and "Violet garlic sauce," page 79.
27. The Vatican manuscript calls this recipe "How to dress veal or ox brain, or whatever type" of brain.
28. The Vatican manuscript calls this recipe "How to cook figpeckers when they are very fatty."

you do not remove the water below, and place the rendered lard in a clean jar and keep in a cool place. With this method, it will keep for a year.

HOW TO MAKE A STUFFED VEAL BELLY

Take a veal's stomach and make a hole in the side big enough so that you can fill it with the stuffing, which should be made with the following things: some good aged cheese, four eggs, a little slightly crushed pepper, saffron, some raisins, and a bit of chopped parsley and marjoram; and mix all these things together; and then place in the stomach and boil until well done.

[HOW TO DETERMINE WHETHER A PROSCIUTTO IS GOOD]

Stick a knife into the prosciutto, and then hold it to your nose; if the knife smells good, the prosciutto is good, and the same holds for the contrary. If you wish to cook it and you wish it to keep even longer, take some good white wine or vinegar and an equal amount of water—although it would be better without water—and boil the prosciutto in the wine until half-cooked; then remove from heat and let it set in its cooking water until cooled; then remove it from the pot, and by doing this, it will taste very good and it will last quite some time.

[HOW TO DETERMINE WHETHER A COW'S UDDER IS GOOD]

First of all, the udder should not be too fatty, and it should be reddish in color; and it should be cooked the same way as a prosciutto, above; and the same holds for tongue; and the fatter the tongue is, the better; and it should be cooked a little longer than prosciutto. And all salt-cured meat can be cooked in this way.

HOW TO PREPARE A PIE WITH COCKSCOMBS, LIVERS, AND TESTICLES

Cut each one of the cockscombs into three parts and the cock's livers into four, and leave the testicles whole; and take a little lard and finely chop, but do not beat; and take two or three ounces of good veal fat and beat well; and even better if you have ox marrow or that of veal; and take thirty or forty dried sour cherries, cinnamon and ginger, a generous amount of sugar, and a few turnip greens;[29] and mix all these things together, and make a pie and cook in the oven or in a

---

29. It is not clear whether Martino intended for turnip greens to be included in this recipe. In the Library of Congress and Vatican manuscripts, *raffiuoli* or *rafiuoli* (which elsewhere denote modern ravioli) are listed among the ingredients for this recipe (the Riva del Garda manuscript omits *raffiuoli,* as does Platina in his adaptation of the recipe). While Benporat and Faccioli are unable to explain the term (Faccioli wrote that "the presence of ravioli in this dish does not seem justifiable"), it is probable that, owing to an error of the scribe, the term *raffiuoli* was intended to denote turnips, turnip greens, or even beet stalks. In fact, John Florio's posthumously revised Italian-English dictionary (London: R. H. and W. H. for R. C., T. S., G. W., and R. R., 1690) lists *ravelli* as "young turneps" *[sic]* and *ravizze* as "turnep leaves or stalks." Even in more recent times, the term *ravazzuolo* denotes turnip greens; the morphological affinity of the terms is evident.

pan. When it is half-cooked, take an egg yolk, some saffron and verjuice, and beat all these things together and put them in the pie, and cook through.

HOW TO COOK A BONELESS SQUAB

Clean and dress the squab well and soak in vinegar for twenty-four hours; and then wash it well, and stuff it with good things and good spices; and boil it or roast it, as you wish; and by doing so you will find it to be boneless.

HOW TO PREPARE TWO SQUAB OUT OF ONE

Take a squab and skin well without using water, and be careful not to break the skin. Then remove the innards and turn the skin inside out, keeping it whole, and then straighten it out and fill it with a stuffing of good things, and it will seem to be a whole squab. Then dress the squab's skinned body and boil or roast both of them, as you wish. If you roast, take a bit of grated bread and some salt, and when the squab is half-cooked, coat it with the grated bread; and take an egg yolk and brush it over the squab so that it will make a little crust, and hold over a flame for a little while to brown. By doing so, it will appear to have not been skinned; and thus it will appear to be two squab.

CHAPTER TWO

HOW TO MAKE EVERY TYPE OF VICTUAL

FIRST: HOW TO MAKE A BLANCMANGE OVER CAPON

To make twelve servings: take two librae of almonds and crush well. In order that they may be as white as possible, soak in cool water for a day and a night. Then crush them, and when they have been crushed, add a little cool water so that they do not purge their oil. Then take a capon breast and crush together with the almonds; and take some bread white and soak it in lean capon broth; and crush with the other ingredients; and take a little verjuice, a half ounce of ginger, well peeled so that it is all white, and a half libra or more of sugar; and thin with some lean capon broth; and pass through a stamine into a well-cleaned pot; and place the pot over hot coals away from the flame, stirring often with a spoon; and let it cook for a half hour; and when it is done cooking, add three ounces of good rose water. Then serve in bowls or cover the entire capon, or whatever fowl it may be, with the blancmange, and serve. If you cover the capon with the blancmange, to make it even more beautiful, top generously with pieces of apple. If you wish to give this dish two colors, take an egg yolk and some saffron, and mix together with a part of the dish, and make sure that it is more sour with verjuice than the white version. When prepared in this way, the dish is said to be "broomish."[1] If you have two capons, dress one white and the other yellow.

HOW TO MAKE TWELVE SERVINGS OF BLANCMANGE IN THE CATALAN STYLE

Take two jugs of goat's milk and eight ounces of extra fine rice flour and boil the rice flour in the milk. Then take the half-cooked breast of a capon that was butchered the same day and rip into strings as thin as hair and place in a mortar and give them no more than two turns of the pestle. Then, when the milk has simmered for a half hour, add the breast to the milk together with a libra of sugar; and let it boil for about a quarter of an hour more; and you must stir continuously, from the beginning to the end. You can tell that it is done when you remove the spoon and you see that the blancmange is syrupy. Then add some rose water, as above; and serve in bowls, topped with a bit of sugar.[2]

---

1. So called for its yellowish color, reminiscent of the broom's flowers.
2. See also "Blancmange in the Catalan style," page 75.

HOW TO MAKE CONSOMMÉ WITH CAPON, PHEASANT, PARTRIDGE, ROEBUCK, SQUAB, OR WILD SQUAB

Take some of the above-mentioned things and clean very well. If you wish to prepare consommé from capon and make two servings, take a pot filled with four jugs of water and place the capon in the pot after breaking all of its bones; and place over heat; then add an ounce of lean salt-cured meat and thirty or forty crushed peppercorns and a bit of crushed cinnamon, and three or four cloves, and five or six sage leaves torn into three pieces each, and two sprigs of laurel, and let it simmer in the pot for seven hours, until reduced to only two servings of broth, or less, if you want it to be good; and be sure not to add any salt. If you are making this broth for someone who is sick, do not use salt-cured meat, and add just a small amount of spices; and by doing so, you will make it good for both the healthy and the sick.

[HOW TO MAKE A GOOD, CLEAR, FINE BROTH]

To prepare ten servings of fine broth, take thirty egg yolks and some good verjuice, and some good meat broth, or better yet, capon broth, and a bit of saffron, and a small amount of sweet spices, and mix all these things together before passing through a stamine into a pot; place the pot over hot coals away from the flame, stirring continuously with a spoon; and when you see that spoon begins to stick, remove from heat; but do not stop stirring with the spoon until you have said ten Lord's Prayers.[3] Serve the pottage in bowls, topped with a small amount of sweet spice, as above; and make the pottage sweet or sour to taste.

HOW TO MAKE TEN SERVINGS OF WHITE FINE BROTH

Take a half libra of almonds, peel, and crush well; and then add some cool water so that they do not purge their oil. Then take ten egg whites, a bit of bread white, verjuice, and meat or capon broth, and a little white ginger, and crush all these things together; and pass through a stamine together with the almonds; and cook in the same way as the pottage mentioned above.

HOW TO PREPARE A GREEN FINE BROTH

Take all the things in the first pottage, except for the saffron, and take some chard,[4] and a bit of parsley, and green sprigs of wheat if available; and crush all these things together, pass through a stamine, and cook as above.

---

3. That is, stir thoroughly. Even when recited quickly, it takes about thirty seconds to say a Lord's Prayer in Latin.

4. For Martino, the words *biete* and *beta* meant "chard" or the "green leaves of beetroot," both of which belong to the genus *beta* and were called *beta*. As we moderns know them, red beets did not appear in Europe until the fifteenth century, according to the *Oxford Companion to Food,* with the earliest known mention of a "swollen root," that is, the globular root of the plant itself, in 1587. In modern-day Italy, the word *bietole,* a diminutive of Martino's *biete,* is commonly used to denote Swiss chard, while the term *barbabietole* is used to denote the globular root of the plant. Known as *erbette* in Emilia, chard is commonly used as a coloring agent for green pastas (in Martino, the term *erbette* or *herbette* denotes a mixture of herbs, chard, and borage; see "Pottage of greens," pages 70–71).

HOW TO MAKE *ZANZARELLI*

To make ten servings: take eight eggs and a half libra of grated cheese, and a grated loaf of bread, and mix together. Then take a pot of meat broth made yellow with saffron and place over heat; and when it begins to boil, pour the mixture into the pot and stir with a spoon. When the dish has begun to thicken, remove from heat and serve in bowls, topped with spices.[5]

GREEN *ZANZARELLI*

Do as above, but do not add the saffron, using instead the herbs used in the above-mentioned green broth.

[HOW TO MAKE *ZANZARELLI* DUMPLINGS]

To make white, green, or yellow *zanzarelli* dumplings, prepare the mixture as described above for the desired color, but make it thicker; and when the broth begins to boil, shape the mixture into dumplings as big as fava beans using a small spoon; and drop them into the broth one by one.

[HOW TO MAKE WHITE *ZANZARELLI*]

To prepare white *zanzarelli*, take a little almond milk and grated white bread, and some egg whites, and mix them together with some good meat broth, or better yet, fatty pullet broth in a pot with a little almond milk. Then cook as above.

FARRO WITH CAPON BROTH OR OTHER MEAT BROTH

To make ten servings: first of all, clean and wash the farro well, and cook in good capon broth or fatty pullet broth, and let it simmer for a long while.[6] When done cooking, add some good

---

5. That Martino's *zanzarelli* are a precursor of the modern-day *stracciatella* seems evident (see page 151). The name of the dish is most probably a northern Italian pronunciation of the word *ciancerelle*, from the onomatopoeic *ciance* (CHEE'AHN-cheh), meaning idle chatter, and by extension, when in verb form, from *cianciare*, "to chew with difficulty" or "to fiddle around." The entry for *ciancerelle* in John Florio's posthumously revised Italian-English dictionary (1690) gives the following definition: "also a kind of pottage made of herbs, eggs, cheese and spices." The name of the modern version of this dish, *stracciatella*, is a diminutive of the Italian *straccio*, meaning "rag," from *stracciare*, "to rip," which in turn comes from the spoken Latin *extractiare*, literally "to pull off." In Artusi's great nineteenth-century cookbook, this dish is called *minestra del paradiso*, or "paradise soup," because of its "heavenly" streaks.

6. Experts continue to clash over whether farro is properly denoted as *Triticum dicoccum* (emmer) or *Triticum spelta* (spelt), but most, including the *Oxford Companion to Food*, concur that Italian farro is emmer, while spelt is more commonly found in eastern Europe. Once a preferred grain of the ancient Romans, farro has become so popular in North America that many package it marked simply as "farro." That Martino includes it as one of the primary grains—indeed the first—indicates that farro was widely popular many centuries before the farro mania of the late 1990s.

spices; and take three egg yolks and a bit of cooled farro, and mix together. Then drop into the farro; and make yellow with some saffron.

RICE WITH MEAT BROTH

Prepare as for farro broth. But many do not like eggs with their rice, so you should leave it up to your master's tastes.

MILLET WITH MEAT BROTH

Cook the millet in meat broth, simmering slowly, stirring well, and making sure that it does not burn; and it should be made yellow with some saffron. But it should be first well cleaned and washed with warm water, as with rice.

HOW TO MAKE A FINE BROTH OF BREAD, EGG, AND CHEESE

Boil grated bread for a quarter of an hour in meat broth; and take a bit of grated cheese and beat it with some eggs, and let the boiled bread cool thoroughly; and then add the beaten egg and cheese to the boiled bread and mix. This pottage should be made yellow with some saffron and it should be very thick.

HOW TO MAKE A VERJUICE POTTAGE

Take four fresh egg yolks, a half ounce of cinnamon, four ounces of sugar, two ounces of rose water, and four ounces of orange juice, and beat together; and cook as you would a sauce; and this pottage should be made yellow with some saffron. This pottage is best during summer.[7]

CRUSHED FAVA BEANS

Take some crushed fava beans that you have picked over; clean and wash well before placing over heat. When they begin to boil, pour off their water, add enough water to cover by one finger, and season with salt to taste. Simmer, covered, over hot coals away from the flame; cook thoroughly until the water has been absorbed and then crush in a mortar. Then return to heat in a pot.

Take a finely chopped onion and fry in a pot with some good oil, being careful not to burn. Take a bit of sage and some figs or some finely chopped apples, and add to the oil with the onions, and heat well. Then serve the crushed fava beans in bowls topped with some good spices.

---

7. While verjuice (called *agresto* still in Italy) is not an ingredient in this recipe, Martino calls it *verzuso* or *vergiuso*, a calque of the French *vertjus* (i.e., "verjuice"), probably because of the sourness added to the dish by the orange juice.

FRIED PEAS WITH SALT-CURED MEAT

Take some unshelled peas and boil. Take some marbled salt-cured meat and thinly slice into pieces half the size of your finger and lightly fry; add the peas to the salt-cured meat. Add a little verjuice, some sodden wine, or some sugar, and a bit of cinnamon. Beans can also be fried in a similar fashion.

FRYING FAVA BEANS

Take some fava beans, and sage, and onions, and figs, and some apples, as above, and some good herbs as well, and mix together; and fry in a pan with oil; and after you have finished preparing this fry, remove and top with some good spices.

MEAT POTTAGE

Take some lean veal that has been boiled, and finely chop; boil again in some fatty broth, adding some grated bread white, a bit of pepper, and some saffron, and simmer for a half hour. Then let cool; and take some eggs, grated cheese, well-chopped parsley, marjoram, and mint with a little verjuice, and beat together, and add to the meat, stirring slowly with a spoon. This pottage should be as thick as a sauce. And the same can be done with pluck.[8]

TRIPE POTTAGE

First of all, tripe should be well cleaned and well washed; make sure that it is white. To make it tastier, cook well with a bone taken from salt-cured meat, but to preserve its whiteness do not add salt; and when done cooking, cut into small pieces and add some mint, sage, and salt, and bring to a boil. Then serve in bowls, topped with spices, and with cheese, if desired.

TROUT TRIPE POTTAGE

First of all, clean the trout's tripe well and be sure to cook for a long time.[9] When it is half-cooked, add some finely chopped parsley and mint, and a bit of pepper. As soon as it is done, serve in bowls, topped with sweet spices.

TROUT ROE POTTAGE, PREPARED SO THAT IT APPEARS TO BE PEAS

Boil the roe until only slightly cooked. Remove from the broth and separate the eggs from one another; and add some white bread to the broth so that it is not too light, and then pass through a stamine; or take some broth from real peas, which would be much better to use if you can get

---

8. The Neapolitan manuscript calls this recipe "Cardinal soup," probably referring to the red meat of the veal or—even more likely—the pluck (*pluck*: heart, liver, and lungs).

9. *Tripe*: trout's intestines.

some; and whatever type of broth you use, cook the eggs in the broth together with a small amount of spices, and some parsley, and some finely chopped mint.

ROSE-APPLE POTTAGE

Cook the apples in meat broth.[10] When they are nearly done cooking, add a bit of parsley, and finely chopped mint. If the broth is too light, add some bread white and then strain as above. When the apples are done cooking, serve in bowls, topped with spices.

LETTUCE POTTAGE, PREPARED SO THAT IT APPEARS TO BE SQUASH

Take the internal leaves, the whitest of them all, in the center, and cook them as you would squash with eggs and verjuice.

[KNOWING HOW TO COOK DURUM WHEAT FLOUR]

Durum wheat flour is cooked with fatty meat broth, or fatty pullet broth, and it must be added slowly to the broth, stirring continuously with a spoon. Let it simmer for a half hour on hot coals away from the flame, because it can burn easily. Serve in bowls, topped with cheese and spices. During Lent, cook it in almond milk with sugar and rose water.

[HOW TO MAKE TURNIP POTTAGE]

Clean the turnips and cut them into large pieces, and cook well in meat broth. Then pass them through a large slotted spoon, or crush them, and then return to the pot with fatty broth and a little salt-cured meat, some pepper, and some saffron.

[HOW TO MAKE FENNEL POTTAGE]

Fennel is cooked the same way as cauliflower, except that it should be more finely chopped; it takes longer to cook and should be prepared with a bit of pepper and salt-cured meat, or oil.

ROMAN-STYLE MACARONI

Take some white flour, and add water and make a sheet of pasta slightly thicker than that for lasagne, and wrap it around a stick; and then remove the stick and cut the pasta into pieces the size of your little finger, and they end up with the shape of thin strips or strings. Cook in fatty broth or in water, depending on the season.[11] But they need to be boiled when you cook them.

---

10. In the *Grande dizionario della lingua italiana,* the Italian equivalent of the *OED,* Martino is cited as perhaps the first to mention the rose apple in Italy: *Syzygium jambos* (also known as *Eugenia jambos* and *Caryophyllus jambos*), a member of the Myrtaceae family.

11. That is, whether a Lenten (lean) or non-Lenten (fat) period.

If you cook them in water, add some fresh butter and a bit of salt. When they are done, place on a platter with some good cheese, and butter, and sweet spices.

ANOTHER WAY TO PREPARE MACARONI

Prepare the pasta as above. And cook it in the same way, and dress it using the same things, but make the sheets of pasta a bit thicker and cut more thinly and into smaller pieces. This pasta is called *triti* or *formentine*.[12]

PARSLEY ROOT POTTAGE

Take some parsley roots,[13] remove the middle stalks, clean well, and cook in meat broth. Then finely chop and add again to good fatty meat broth with a little pepper and saffron.

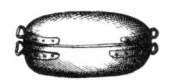

[HOW TO COOK MUSHROOMS]

Clean the mushrooms well and boil in water with two or three cloves of garlic and bread white. This is done because they are poisonous by nature. Remove and strain well all their water, until dry, and then fry in good oil or lard. When they are done, top with spices.

You can dress mushrooms in another way by first cleaning well and then placing them over hot coals and dressing them with lard and garlic chopped together and pepper. You can dress them similarly with oil. You can also cook them in the same manner in a pan as if in a torte.

FRIED SQUASH

Take some squash and clean well;[14] and then cut crosswise into slices as thin as the blade of a knife; and then bring them to a boil in water and immediately remove; and then let set until dry. Sprinkle with just a bit of salt, dredge in flour, and fry in oil. Then remove, and take a few fennel fronds, a little garlic, and some bread white, and crush well, and thin with enough verjuice to make watery, and pass through a stamine, and use this sauce to top the squash. They are also good topped with just verjuice and fennel fronds. If you want the sauce to be yellow, add a bit of saffron.

---

12. *Formentine*, or "frumentines": evoking the size of a grain of cereal; *triti*: from the Arabic *itrya*, meaning "dried dough" (in Sicilian dialect, the word *tria* is still used to denote dried pasta). Others maintain, however, that Martino's *triti* comes from the Latin *tritum*, "chopped" (or possibly from the Latin *triticum*, meaning "wheat").

13. Martino refers here to what today is called Neapolitan parsley, generally larger than other parsley plants; the stems of these plants are consumed like celery in southern Italy.

14. Martino's *zucca*, or squash, denoted many different varietals of *Cucurbitae*, a term that most probably encompassed both the famous *zucca marina di Chioggia* (similar to the American pumpkin; used today for pumpkin ravioli in Lombardy and Emilia) and the ubiquitous winter squash of Italy.

QUINCE POTTAGE

Cook the quince in lean meat broth. Then crush and thin with some almond milk made with meat broth or good fatty pullet broth, if the season permits; and pass through a stamine and put into a pot with sugar, ginger, and cinnamon, and a bit of saffron; and set it to boil away from the flame on hot coals so that it will not burn, and stir often with a spoon. And it would be best to add a little butter or fresh rendered lard. Then, when it appears to be done, serve in bowls, topped with sweet spices and sugar.

STUFFED FAVA BEANS

Soak the fava beans with skins on and gently crack open the lighter side; carefully remove the beans without breaking the shell; and then take some peeled, blanched almonds and grind well with a little rose water so that they do not purge their oil; and add a generous amount of sugar; and use this mixture to fill the shells, and then press back together so that they appear to be half-cooked fava beans; heat them in a pot or pan or another container without water or anything else, being careful that they do not burn. Then distribute the fava beans in bowls and top with some hot meat broth, a bit of finely chopped parsley with a little finely chopped and fried onion, and then a small amount of sweet spice. You can omit the onions if not desired.

HEMP SEED POTTAGE

To make twelve servings, take a libra of hemp seeds. Clean well and boil in a pot until they begin to open; and then take a libra of white, well-ground almonds, and add to the seeds; grind well and add some bread white. Thin with some meat broth or lean pullet broth and pass through a stamine. Boil in a pot over hot coals away from the flame, stirring often with a spoon. Then add a half libra of sugar and a half ounce of ginger and a bit of saffron with rose water; and serve in bowls, topped with sweet spices.

RAVIOLI FOR NON-LENTEN TIMES

To make ten servings: take a half libra of aged cheese, and a little fatty cheese and a libra of fatty pork belly or veal teat, and boil until it comes apart easily; then chop well and take some good, well-chopped herbs, and pepper, cloves, and ginger; and it would be even better if you added some ground capon breast; incorporate all these things together.

Then make a thin sheet of pasta and encase the mixture in the pasta, as for other ravioli. These ravioli should not be larger than half a chestnut; cook them in capon broth, or good meat broth that you have made yellow with saffron when it boils. Let the ravioli simmer for the time it takes to say two Lord's Prayers.[15]

---

15. Just one or two minutes.

Then serve in bowls, topped with grated cheese and sweet spices mixed together. You can make similar ravioli from pheasant breast and partridges and other fowl.

SICILIAN MACARONI

Take some very white flour and make a dough using egg whites and rose water, or common water. If you wish to make two platters, do not add more than one or two egg whites, and make sure that the pasta is very firm; then shape it into long, thin sticks, the size of your palm and as thin as hay. Then take an iron rod as long as your palm or longer, and as thin as string, and place it on top of each stick, and then roll with both hands over a table; then remove the iron rod and the macaroni will be perforated in the middle.

These macaroni must be dried in the sun and they will last for two or three years; they will last particularly well if you make them under an August moon; cook them in water or meat broth; and place them on platters with generous quantities of grated cheese, fresh butter, and sweet spices. These macaroni should be simmered for two hours.[16]

VERMICELLI

Thin the pasta as above,[17] cut it into thin strings, and break into small pieces with your fingers just like little worms;[18] and set it to dry in the sun, and it will keep for two or three years. When you wish to cook it, do so in meat broth or good, fatty pullet broth, for one hour. Then serve in bowls, topped with grated cheese and spices.

In case it is not a meat day, cook it in almond milk with sugar or in goat's milk. But because this milk cannot achieve the sufficient boil required by vermicelli, boil first in a little water, as is done for rice. And the same holds for lasagne and *triti,* also called *formentine.*[19] All of these pasta dishes should be made yellow with some saffron, except when they are cooked in milk.

POTTAGE OF GREENS

Take some chard leaves and a little borage and boil in clear water that is already boiling when you add them; then remove and finely chop with a knife. Take a bit of parsley and raw mint, and

---

16. Clearly, Martino's advice about making the pasta during an August moon is in earnest: anyone who has ever made dried pasta (today's *pastasciutta,* literally, "dried dough") knows that the quick drying of the pasta is the key to its lasting. It is not clear, however, why he says to cook it for two hours: it is possible that the quality of flour in his time made the pasta harder than the pasta we are accustomed to eating today. It is more likely that the modern concept of *al dente* (meaning "pleasing to the bite"), that is, the notion that pasta should not be made too soft by overcooking, was entirely foreign to Martino. (In fact, pasta was probably not served *al dente* until the birth of its national popularity in Italy thanks to the advanced techniques of nineteenth-century Neapolitan *mugnai,* or pasta makers.)

17. As for "Sicilian macaroni," the previous recipe.

18. *Vermicelli* means literally "little worms."

19. See "Another way to prepare macaroni," page 68.

similarly chop with the other herbs. Then grind well in a mortar and add to some fatty broth in a pot and simmer for a short while. If desired, you can add pepper.

RICE WITH ALMOND MILK

To make ten servings, take a libra of almonds and peel until white. Take a half libra of rice and wash two or three times in lukewarm water and place over heat with clear water and cook well. Then remove and set to dry. Then crush the almonds well, wetting and spraying them with a little cool water, so that they do not purge their oil; and thin with cool water; and pass through a stamine and simmer this milk in a pot, adding a half libra of fine sugar. When it begins to boil, add the rice and place the pot over hot coals away from the flame, stirring very often with a spoon so that it does not burn; and simmer for a half hour. Rice can similarly be cooked in goat's milk or other types of milk.

Because such a pottage can easily burn, in case it does, remove the burned taste as follows: pour out the pottage from the pot, being careful not to touch the bottom, and place it in a clean pot. Then take some white cloth and fold it over itself three or four times and wet it with cool water. Then squeeze the water out and place the folded cloth over the pot with the pottage; and let it set there for a quarter of an hour; and if necessary, wet it again and put it back over the pot; and by doing so you will remove the burned taste. Nor do I know a better remedy. And the same can be done with farro.[20]

ALMOND POTTAGE

To make eight servings: take a libra of peeled, blanched almonds, and crush well, adding cool water often, as above, so that they do not purge their oil; and add some bread white. Thin with cool water, pass through a stamine, and put in a pot to boil over hot coals. Simmer for an eighth of an hour. Also add a half libra of fine sugar to boil with the almonds. This almond pottage should be slightly watery. And it can be made even more tasty by adding a little rose water.

CAPON SKIN LASAGNE

Take boiled capon skin, cut into pieces and put in fatty capon broth; and simmer for a half hour with a bit of saffron. Then serve in bowls, topped with a bit of cheese and spices.

RED CHICKPEA BROTH

To make eight servings: take a libra and a half of chickpeas, wash with warm water, and put in the pot you want to cook them; and they should be dry; and add a half ounce of flour, that is, sifted flour, a little good oil and salt, and about twenty crushed peppercorns, and a bit of crushed cinnamon, and mix well with your hands. Then add three jugs of water and a pinch

---

20. See "Farro with capon broth or other meat broth," pages 64–65.

of sage, rosemary, and parsley root, and simmer until reduced to the quantity of eight servings. When it is almost done, add some oil. But if you are making this broth for someone who is sick, add neither oil nor spices.

FREGOLA POTTAGE

To make ten servings: take three loaves of bread, remove the crust with a knife, grate well, place on a table, and place a libra and a half of white flour around it; add four or five eggs to the bread and beat well with a knife, continuously sprinkling the bread with the flour. When it seems that it is as small as candied anise seeds, pass it all through a stamine, remove the flour, and set the remaining bread to dry. When you want to cook it, do so in meat broth or good pullet broth. And make it yellow with saffron, and simmer slowly for a half hour; top each serving with a bit of cheese and spices.[21]

COOKING SQUASH

Give the squash a good washing, and then cook in meat broth, or in water, and add the necessary amount of onion. When it seems to be done, remove and pass through a slotted spoon or crush well, and cook in a pot with fatty broth and a little verjuice. Make yellow with saffron; and when it is done, remove from heat and let cool for a little while. Then take the necessary amount of egg yolks and beat them with a little aged cheese and mix with the squash, stirring continuously with a spoon so that it does not stick. Then serve in bowls, topped with sweet spices.

SQUASH WITH ALMOND MILK

Cook the squash in water and then remove as much of the water as you can; pass through a stamine or slotted spoon and simmer in the milk with sugar and a little verjuice, as suits your master's tastes.

SQUASH IN THE CATALAN STYLE

Take some *carbassa*,[22] that is, some squash, clean well, and put in a dry pot with some good chopped lard; and put the pot over hot coals away from the flame and simmer, stirring continuously with a spoon. The squash should simmer in this manner for four hours. Then take some good fatty broth that has been made yellow with a bit of saffron, and add it to the pot together with some sugar and sweet spices with a little verjuice, as suits your master's tastes or the tastes of others. As we said above in the first recipe for squash, you can add a few beaten egg yolks with a bit of good aged cheese.

---

21.   Similar to couscous, fregola has enjoyed a renaissance of its own in recent years—mainly in the Sardinian style.

22.   *Carbassa*, Catalan for squash or gourd.

FRESH FAVA BEANS WITH MEAT BROTH

Take some fava beans and clean with warm water as you would almonds; and then boil in good broth. When they appear to be done, add a bit of parsley and chopped mint, allowing the beans to simmer with some good salt-cured meat as well. Make this pottage slightly green because it looks better that way. You can prepare peas in a similar way, and every other fresh legume; but note that they should not be cleaned with warm water like fava beans; instead leave them as they are, with their thin shell.

LENTEN VERJUICE

To make ten servings: take a libra and a half of almonds that have been peeled in lukewarm water, and crush well, as above, adding a little cool water so that they do not purge their oil. Take some bread white and soak it in good verjuice. Then take some of the almonds, the bread white, some orange juice, and rose water, and incorporate, adding an ounce of cinnamon and a libra of fine sugar. Pass through a stamine and make yellow with some saffron. Then put in a pot to simmer away from the flame. To make sure that it does not burn, stir often with a spoon. It should simmer for about an eighth of an hour.[23]

LENTEN BLANCMANGE

To make ten servings: take a libra and a half of peeled almonds and crush well, as above, and take some bread white that has been soaked in white pea broth. If you do not have any peas, substitute with another broth by boiling very white bread in water for half an hour and then soak the above-mentioned bread white in this broth. Then take some good saltwater fish or some good freshwater pike that has been boiled. Take a half libra of its most firm and white meat and crush well with the almonds and bread white, a little broth, a half libra of peeled ginger, eight ounces of sugar, and some orange juice, which, if unavailable, can be substituted by a little verjuice to which rose water has been added. Incorporate and pass through a stamine; cook in a pot for an eighth of an hour, away from the flame so that it does not burn; and stir continuously with a spoon.

LENTEN PEAS

You can prepare peas similarly with almond milk during the time of Lent, as in the recipe above for blancmange.

---

23. The defining factor, making the dish acceptable for Lent, is the omission of eggs. As above, the fact that Martino calls it *verzuso* instead of *agresto* would seem to indicate its French origins. See "How to make a verjuice pottage," page 65.

HERBS WITH ALMOND MILK

Take some herbs and boil them in a little water, which must be boiling when you add the herbs. Remove to a table or a cutting board, and finely chop with a knife; and grind well in a mortar; and then boil in almond milk, adding a sufficient amount of sugar.

HERBS WITHOUT MILK

Take some herbs and first boil them as above. Then use them to make meat or lean broth, depending on the period,[24] and serve however you wish.

[HOW TO MAKE HEMP SEED POTTAGE]

Take some hemp seeds and soak for a day and a night, discarding those kernels that come to the surface because they are no good.[25] Then take some well-peeled almonds and crush with the hemp seeds. Once they are well crushed, add some cool water and good pea broth, adding fine sugar as well, and a little rose water. Then cook for about an eighth of an hour, stirring continuously with a spoon.

ROMAN BROCCOLI

Take the twisted broccoli and break apart with your hands as common practice requires; place in water when it begins to boil.[26] When it is almost half-cooked, discard the water and take a generous or at least sufficient quantity of good chopped lard and add to the drained stalks, stirring well with a spoon. Then take some good fatty broth and let them simmer in the broth over heat for a short time.

YELLOW POTTAGE DISH

To make twelve servings, take a libra of unpeeled almonds and crush well, and take some capon breast, or that of another type of fowl that you like, boiled or roasted, as you wish, with four egg yolks; crush well with the almonds, adding a half libra of sugar, cinnamon, ginger, and a bit of saffron.[27] Then thin with fatty pullet broth, or other good broth, and a little bit of verjuice and pass through a stamine. Then place over hot coals very far from the flame so that it does not burn; stir continuously with a spoon and let simmer for an hour. Remember that when it is half-cooked you need to add two ounces of good rendered lard or fresh butter; then serve in bowls, topped with sweet spices.

---

24. That is, whether a Lenten or non-Lenten period.
25. That is, because they are hollow.
26. Martino's broccoli were most probably the famous green cauliflower of Rome, *broccoli romaneschi*.
27. The quantity half libra pertains probably only to the sugar.

ELDERFLOWER POTTAGE

To make twelve servings during Lent, take a libra and a half of peeled, well-crushed almonds, as above. Take three ounces of dried elderflowers. First soak them in cool water for an hour, squeezing and pressing out the water afterward. Crush half of the flowers with the almonds, adding bread white and a half libra of sugar with a bit of ginger.

If you wish for it to be yellow, add a bit of saffron; and pass the whole thing through a stamine; and cook as in the preceding entry. When you place over a flame, top with the elderflowers that have been left whole. When it is sufficiently cooked, serve in bowls, topped with good sweet spices.

If you wish to make this pottage during nonfast days, add three egg yolks and thin with fatty pullet broth, or other good broth; pass through a stamine and add sugar and the other spices with the whole flowers, as above. But note that when it is half-cooked, you must add two ounces of good rendered lard or fresh butter.

WHITE *ZANZARELLI*

To make ten servings: first of all, take a libra of peeled, crushed almonds, as above, crushing them together with a bit of elderflower; thin with cool water and pass through a stamine. When you see that you have more than enough for eight servings, cook this liquid mixture in a pot, first reserving one common cup from the raw mixture; and take the white of two loaves of bread that has been well grated and ten *albumena,* also called egg whites. Beat them together with the reserved cup of almond milk above, together with the grated bread and a half libra of sugar. As soon as the milk starts to boil, add this other mixture, but do not stir it or anything else. Then, once you see that it has thickened, serve in bowls, topped with sweet spices.

BLANCMANGE IN THE CATALAN STYLE

To make ten servings, take a libra of well-peeled and well-crushed almonds which you have thinned with fatty pullet broth, or another type of broth, and pass through a stamine; boil in a well-cleaned cooking pot, adding two ounces of rice flour that has been thinned with almond milk and strained; and simmer for an hour, blending and stirring with a spoon all the while, adding a half libra [of sugar and] capon breast that has been cooked in the almond milk in the beginning and then finely chopped and well crushed.[28] When the whole mixture is done, add a little rose water; serve in bowls, topped with sweet spices.

---

28. The absence of sugar in this part of the recipe was most probably due to the scribe's oversight (compare with "How to make twelve servings of blancmange in the Catalan style," page 62). See Bruno Laurioux ("I libri di cucina italiana alla fine del medioevo: Un nuovo bilancio," *Archivio storico italiano* 154 [1996]: 33–58), who notes that in the corresponding recipe of the Vatican manuscript there is a blank space where the word *sugar* would appear; he observes, rightly, that this would seem to indicate that the Washington and Vatican manuscripts derive from the same model (p. 49).

CHAPTER THREE

HOW TO MAKE EVERY TYPE OF SAUCE

WHITE SAUCE

Take the necessary amount of well-peeled and well-crushed almonds. As I have said many times before, add a little cool water as you crush them, so that they do not purge their oil. Take a bit of bread white that has been soaked in verjuice and crush with the almonds, adding some white ginger; that is, well-peeled ginger. Thin this mixture with good verjuice, or orange juice or lemon juice, and pass through a stamine, making it more or less sweet with sugar and tart with verjuice or orange juice, as suits your master's tastes or whoever's. This sauce should be served with all boiled meats in time of nonfast days or during Lent.

GOLD OF PLEASURE SAUCE

Take some raisins and crush well. Take two or three slices of toasted bread that have been soaked in red wine, adding more or adding less, as needed. Crush all the above things together. Then take a little red wine, some sodden wine, and verjuice, and for those who do not like verjuice, use vinegar, making it sweet or tart as you wish. Pass all of this mixture through a stamine, adding a generous amount of good cinnamon, a few cloves, and some crushed nutmeg.[1]

PEACOCK SAUCE

Take two hard-boiled egg yolks and pullet livers that have been boiled, and the necessary amount of toasted almonds. Crush all these things together well with good vinegar or verjuice; thin and pass through a stamine, adding some cinnamon and a bit of ginger and some sugar. Make sure that you briefly cook this sauce and that it is made yellow with saffron.[2]

DRIED PRUNE SAUCE

Take some prunes and soak them in red wine and remove their bones;[3] and crush them well with a few unpeeled almonds, and a little roasted or toasted bread that has been soaked in the

---

1. The recipe is entitled "Gold of pleasure sauce" not because gold of pleasure (a green herb with a golden flower, also known as myagrum or cameline) is an ingredient, but because the sauce resembles the color of the flower. The early-fifteenth-century English cookery book *Liber cure cocorum* lists this "dainty" sauce: "this sawce fyne, that men calles camelyne."
2. This recipe is called "peacock" for its bright colors.
3. That is, their stems and seeds.

wine where the prunes were soaked. Crush all these things together with a little verjuice and a bit of the wine mentioned above, and a bit of sodden wine, or sugar, which would be much better; thin and pass through a stamine adding some good spices, especially cinnamon.

To make pepper sauce, see the recipe above where it is described, and follow it to the letter.[4]

GREEN SAUCE

Take some parsley and wild thyme and a little chard, with some other good herbs, with a bit of pepper, and ginger, and salt. Crush all these things together well, thinning with some good strong vinegar, and pass through a stamine. If you want it to taste of garlic, add some baby garlic fronds to crush together with the other ingredients. But do only for those who like garlic.

PEACH BLOSSOM SAUCE

Take some peeled, blanched almonds that have been well crushed with the bread white of some bread, a little ginger and cinnamon, verjuice, and red wine, and some pomegranate juice, adding to all of these things some sandalwood extract. Then thin and pass this mixture through a stamine, and make it sweet with red wine or tart for those who like it like that.

BROOM FLOWER SAUCE

Take some almonds, and saffron, and egg yolks, and the almonds must be peeled and crushed as they ought to be; thin and pass through a stamine with some good verjuice, adding some crushed ginger.[5]

GRAPE SAUCE

Take some good red grapes and crush them in a pot together with a loaf or a half loaf of bread, as needed; and add a little good verjuice or vinegar so that the grapes are not too sweet. Simmer these things over a flame for a half hour, adding some cinnamon, ginger, and other good spices.

MULBERRY SAUCE

Take some well-peeled and well-crushed almonds together with a little bread white; and take the mulberries and carefully grind them together with the other ingredients. But do not beat or crush them, so as not to break those tiny seeds that they have inside; then add some cinnamon, ginger, and a bit of nutmeg. Pass it all through a stamine.

---

4. See "How to prepare a good pepper sauce for game," page 51.
5. This sauce's name is due to its yellow color, which is like broom flowers.

BLACK CHERRY OR SOUR CHERRY SAUCE

To make a similar sauce, follow the order given and described above in the recipe for making grape sauce. But you can make it with a different color, darker or lighter, depending on the ingredients that you add.

CORNEL CHERRY SAUCE

Follow the same method above for cherry and grape sauce.

MUSTARD

Take some charlock and soak for two days,[6] changing the water often so that it becomes whiter; and take some almonds that have been properly peeled and crushed. Once they have been well crushed, add them to the mustard and then crush together well. Then take some good verjuice or vinegar and crush some bread white in it; then thin and pass through a stamine. Make it as sweet or as strong as you wish.

RED OR VIOLET MUSTARD

Take the charlock and crush well; and take some raisins and crush them also, as well as you can. Take a bit of toasted bread and a little sandalwood extract and some cinnamon, and a little verjuice or vinegar, and sodden wine, and thin this mixture; and pass through a stamine.

MUSTARD THAT CAN BE CARRIED IN PIECES ON HORSEBACK

Take the charlock and crush as above, and take some raisins that have been well crushed; add some cinnamon and a few cloves to these things. Then you can make little round balls the size of those that you shoot with a crossbow, or square pieces of whatever size you like; let them dry for a little while on a table, and once dried, you can take them from place to place, as you wish. When you want to use them, you can thin them with a little verjuice, or vinegar, or cooked must, that is, sodden wine.

HEAVENLY SUMMERTIME SAUCE

Take some wild mulberries that grow in thickets and a small amount of well-crushed almonds with a bit of ginger. Thin these things with some verjuice and pass through a stamine.

YELLOW PEPPER SAUCE FOR FISH

Take a loaf of bread and slice it; toast the slices, and then take some red wine, mixed with a little vinegar, and some cooked wine must, and use it to boil the bread slices; then pass through a stamine, adding some good sweet and strong spices; and make it yellow by adding a bit of saffron.

---

6. *Charlock: Sinapis arvensis,* or wild mustard, also known as *lapsanā,* as in the Latin saying *lapsanā vivere,* "to live on a meager diet."

WHITE GARLIC SAUCE

Take some almonds that have been carefully peeled and crush; when they are half-crushed, add however much garlic you like, and crush together adding some cool water so that they do not purge their oil. Then take some bread white and soak it in lean meat broth, or fish broth if on a fast day; and you can serve this garlic sauce to suit all seasons, fat and lean, as you wish.

VIOLET GARLIC SAUCE

Follow the order in the recipe above, except it is not necessary to add broth, but take some red grapes and crush well by hand in a pot or other container; simmer for a half hour; then strain this must, which you will use to thin the garlic sauce; and the same can be done with cherries. This garlic sauce can be used in times of meat or fish, as you wish.

GREEN VERJUICE

Take some bitter herbs, the ones called sorrel or garden cresses, crush well and add a bit of salt; and add to some old verjuice that you have thinned by passing through a stamine.

SAUCE

Take some vine leaves and crush well, and if you like, you can add some garlic fronds with a little bread white and some salt. Thin these things with vinegar or verjuice, and pass through a stamine.

VERJUICE WITH FENNEL

Take some garlic, if you like, and the best and sweetest fennel fronds you can get; crush well together adding some new verjuice, and use the verjuice to thin this mixture, and pass through a stamine; and make sure that you add just enough salt.

ROSE-APPLE SAUCE

The rose apples should be a little green, that is, not too old or overly ripened; and once obtained, crush well and add a garlic clove to crush with them, for those who like garlic, and for those who do not, leave as is. Then thin with a little verjuice, and pass through a stamine.

CONSERVING CORNEL CHERRY JUICE FOR THE WINTER

Take some ripe cornel cherries and crush by hand in a pot or other container—as much as possible; add a generous amount of new verjuice, and some pepper, and a lot of salt; simmer for two hours or more and pass through a loose stamine, putting the juice in some jar or other container that you have for preserves. Remember that it is important it be well salted; this juice will be good for making any other sauce as dark or as light as you wish.

CHAPTER FOUR

HOW TO MAKE EVERY TYPE OF TORTE

WHITE TORTE

Take a libra and a half of good fresh cheese, finely chop, and crush well; and take twelve or fifteen *albumena,* or egg whites, and mix well with the cheese, adding a half libra of sugar and a half ounce of the whitest ginger you can get; similarly add a half pound of rendered lard from good, lean pork; or, instead of lard, the same amount of good, fresh butter; and likewise add the necessary amount of milk, probably a good third of a jug. Then make the dough or rather crust in a pan, suitably thin, and cook very slowly, applying heat from below and above; and be sure that it is browned on top by the heat; and when it seems to be done, remove from the pan and top with some fine sugar and some good rose water.

BOLOGNESE TORTE

Take the same amount of cheese, as in the recipe above for white torte, and grate. Note that the fatter the cheese, the better; then take some chard, parsley, and marjoram; once cleaned and washed, chop well with a knife and add to the cheese, crushing and mixing it with your hands until well incorporated, adding four eggs and as much pepper as necessary, and a bit of saffron, and likewise, some good rendered lard or fresh butter, mixing and incorporating all these things together as I have said. Place this filling in a pan with a crust below and above, applying medium heat. When it appears to you that it is half-cooked, to give it an even more handsome appearance, make it yellow by brushing it with an egg yolk that has been beaten with a bit of saffron. You can tell that it is done when the crust on top rises and puffs up; it is best to remove it from the flame at this point.

HERB TORTE FOR THE MONTH OF MAY

Take the same amount of cheese as above, and crush well; and mix fifteen or sixteen egg whites with a cup or about a cup of good milk;[1] and take a good amount of chard, that is, as the main ingredient, and a little marjoram, a lot of sage, a bit of mint, and a lot of parsley. Crush all these

---

1. Every Martino manuscript, save for the so-called Neapolitan Recipe Collection, reports "un quarto o [vel] circa di latte." As in modern Italian, a *quarto* was a quarter of a liter, roughly a cup. The Neapolitan manuscript reports a *foglietta,* roughly a half liter or a pint in Renaissance Italy. A pint of milk would seem excessive here.

herbs together well, squeezing out their water, and pass through a stamine. Add their water together with the things above and add to them a half libra of good rendered lard or fresh butter; and take a few leaves of parsley and just a few leaves of marjoram, and cut and chop as finely as possible; and grind well in a mortar, incorporating them with the above things, adding a half ounce of white ginger and eight ounces of sugar. Make sure that this mixture is well incorporated in a pot that you put over hot coals, away from the flame, stirring continuously with a spoon or other appropriate tool for this purpose, until it seems to begin to thicken like a fine broth. When this has been done, prepare a thin dough in a pan, and fill it with the above things, that is, this filling, gently applying medium heat on the top and on the bottom. When it appears to you to have thickened, remove and top with fine sugar and some rose water. As for such tortes or herb tortes, whatever you may wish to call them, the greener they are, the better, as they will have a more handsome appearance that way.

[HOW TO MAKE SQUASH TORTE]

Take some squash and clean well and grate as you would cheese; and boil for a little while in good broth or good milk. Take a large amount of fresh cheese, as in the above recipes, adding and mixing with it a little good, aged cheese. Take a libra of good pork belly or veal's udder that has been well boiled and finely chopped with a knife. If desired, in place of these two things, you can use butter or rendered lard, adding a half libra of sugar, a little ginger, and cinnamon, with a cup of milk and six eggs. When it appears to you that the squash is done, remove from the water and pass through a stamine; and make this mixture yellow with some sesame oil; then put it in a pan with a thin layer of dough on the bottom, but not on the top, and apply moderate heat from below and above; and when it appears to you to be done, layer on top, in place of the crust, with some small lasagne. When it is sufficiently cooked, top with some good sugar and rose water.

[HOW TO MAKE TORTES WITH TURNIPS, PEARS, AND QUINCES]

Similarly, depending on the period and the season, you can make tortes using turnips and also cooked pears that have been well ripened under coals, and you can also make tortes with quinces by first cutting them into quarters or smaller or larger pieces, peeling and cleaning them well; and you cook their insides by boiling them in good broth. If you prefer, you can also cook them under hot coals, which is perhaps better, and then pass them through a stamine, adding the other things mentioned earlier, just as for the squash recipe, above.

[HOW TO MAKE *MIGLIACCIO*]

To make a *migliaccio* for four or five persons, crush a libra of the freshest cheese that you can get until it resembles milk; and take three or four ounces of sifted flour and eight or ten egg whites, and a half libra of sugar, and mix all these things together, incorporating well. If you do not have sifted flour, take some bread white and grate finely, adding it in place of the flour. Add some good rendered lard to a pan, without any dough or crust, and place the pan over hot coals until the lard is well heated; and then toss the mixture in, applying moderate heat below and above, as for the other tortes. As soon as it is done, remove, and top with some good sugar and rose water.[2]

[HOW TO MAKE AN ELDERFLOWER TORTE]

Take some elderflowers, crumble, and neatly remove any stalks; incorporate well with the mixture described in the recipe for making a white torte.[3] But note that when made with flowers, this mixture should be more compact and thicker. This is done so that the flowers will be more evenly distributed, so that there is just as much in the bottom as in the middle, and above and equally throughout.

[HOW TO MAKE A VINE-SHOOT TORTE]

Take the shoots produced by a vine and simmer them after first chopping and crushing with a knife; the same can be done with red roses; and take some good, fresh cheese, and a well-boiled veal udder, and chop together well. If you prefer, in place of the udder, you can use rendered lard or butter, adding ginger and cinnamon and sugar as necessary. Place this mixture in a pan, with a crust below and on top. When it is almost done, pierce or make holes in the top crust, almost throughout. When it has finished cooking, top with some sugar and rose water, in generous amounts, as needed.

[HOW TO MAKE A NON-LENTEN RICE TORTE]

Wash and clean the rice well, and cook in milk or good fatty broth until it is well cooked; and then remove to a cutting board and let dry, and take a little well-crushed good, fresh cheese and

---

2. Martino's *migliaccio* seems to have nothing in common (save for the linguistic affinity) with the modern Neapolitan *migliaccio* (a pudding of alternated layers of polenta, blood sausage, and mozzarella; polenta, as it is made today and is used in modern *migliaccio*, did not exist in Martino's time—corn is a New World ingredient). Perhaps more closely related is Artusi's *migliaccio di Romagna*, a flat cake made with chocolate, or Tuscan *castagnaccio* (often referred to as *migliaccio*), a flat cake made with chestnut flour. The Neapolitan Recipe Collection calls this dish *migliaccio* "in the Florentine style." The word *migliaccio* comes from the Late Latin *miliacium* (from *milium*), meaning "millet" or simply "meal." Indeed, Martino's torte is made of meal (flour). Platina points out that this dish was more rightly called *polenta* (in Martino and Platina's time, the word *polenta*, from the Latin *puls*, meaning "powder" or "dust," referred to ground meal).

3. See "White torte," above, page 80.

add to the rice, adding ten egg whites as well, some sugar, and some rose water. If desired, you can also add a little milk, as much as a small glass will hold. Once you have mixed all these things together well, cook in a pan, following the directions and method described above for a white torte. Note that this requires, without doubt, a lesser amount of cheese than for the other tortes described above.

[HOW TO MAKE A FARRO TORTE]

Clean the farro well and cook in good fatty broth, and remove and let dry, just as above for rice. Take a libra of fresh cheese, and a half libra of good aged cheese, crushing the one and grating the other, as one customarily does. Take a pork belly or a veal udder that has been cooked almost to the point that it breaks apart and finely chopped with a knife, adding some good spices and sugar if desired, and fifteen eggs with a bit of saffron. Mix all these things together well; place in a pan to cook with a crust only on the bottom. When it appears to you to be almost done, take some well-dried lasagne and add them on top, in a thick layer; and let it continue to cook; and when it has finished cooking, top with some sugar and rose water.

VEAL, KID, OR YOUNG CAPON TORTE

Take whichever of the meats listed above that you wish, boiling them first, and making sure that the meat is lean and fatty; and once you have removed every nerve, finely chop with a knife; then crush slightly in a mortar; and take some fresh cheese, and little bit of good aged cheese; likewise a little parsley and marjoram, finely chopping the one and the other, and ten or fifteen eggs with a pork belly or veal udder that has been well boiled and very finely chopped, adding a bit of pepper, some ginger, some cinnamon, some saffron, and cook the same way you would a white torte.

[HOW TO MAKE A CHESTNUT TORTE]

Boil the chestnuts, and once you have crushed them slightly, pass through a stamine with a little good milk, adding all the other spices and things that go into the filling and mixture for the farro torte, described above, and make it yellow with saffron.

COMMON TORTE

Take some good cheese with eight eggs and good pork fat or that of veal, or butter, some whole raisins, some ginger, some cinnamon, and a little grated bread, with a little fatty broth that has been made yellow with saffron; and dress it as we have said above for a white torte.

[HOW TO MAKE A MILLET TORTE]

Take some well-crushed and well-washed millet that is white and clean, and cook it in some good goat's or cow's milk, and make sure that it thickens as it cooks and that it is well cooked. Take a bit of sifted flour and two egg whites, and mix together, thinning the flour; and for those

who do not like eggs, milk can be used to thin the flour, and once it has been thinned, add it to the millet, stirring well with a spoon; and let it simmer for a little while as well, adding some good sugar, stirring again and mixing well. Then remove this mixture to a large cutting board, spreading it out and extending it the same way you would make a filling for a torte, and let cool. When you wish to make the torte, cut it on the table making larger or smaller slices as you like, and fry them in a pan with some good rendered lard, turning a few times; and cook until they color a little bit on both the bottom and the top. As you remove them one by one, place them on a platter, sprinkling with some sugar and some rose water. Similarly, you can make this dish during Lent, by using almond milk in place of other milk, as above, and by frying in good oil. Likewise, you can dress rice in these two ways described above.

[HOW TO MAKE A RED CHERRY AND ROSE TORTE]

Take the blackest cherries you can find, and after you have removed the pits, grind well in a mortar, and take some red roses that have been finely chopped with a knife, with a little fresh cheese and a bit of good aged cheese, adding some spices, that is, cinnamon, ginger, and a little pepper, and some sugar; and mix all these things together very well, adding also three or four eggs as needed; and cook slowly in a pan with a crust on the bottom. As soon as it is done, top with some sugar and some rose water.

[LENTEN CRAYFISH TORTE]

Take some crayfish and boil;[4] remove the good part and crush well in a mortar; and make some good, thick almond milk, by passing the almonds or milk through a stamine with a little rose water, and if you do not have any, in its place it is good to use pea broth or that of crushed white chickpeas;[5] and together with these things, crush a small amount of raisins and four or five figs, adding another small amount of whole raisins as well, a bit of parsley, and marjoram, and chard that has been fried first in good oil and finely chopped with a knife, adding some ginger and cinnamon, and some sugar. This filling or mixture should be crushed well in a mortar. In order

---

4. The original title in the Vatican manuscript for this recipe is "Torta di gambari nella quaresima." In modern Italian, the term *gambero* (plural *gamberi*) is a generic one, denoting everything from tiny shrimp to crayfish and crawfish. It is highly unlikely that Martino intends "shrimp" here. By *gamberi* (or *gamari*, as they are called in the Library of Congress manuscript), he means crayfish, with claws. For Martino, the diminutive of *gambero*, *gambarelli* (or *gamarelli*, as the case may be), denotes what anglophones call shrimp. See also recipes for "Crayfish," "Stuffed crayfish," "Spiny lobster," and "Lobster" (pages 106–107), as well as "Mantis shrimp," "Bay shrimp" (page 102), and "Crab" (page 108).

5. That is, the peas' or beans' cooking water.

to make it thicken like for the other tortes, add a little powdered starch, incorporating well with the other ingredients, or a small amount of pike roe that has been crushed and passed through a stamine because it will solidify and help it to thicken better. Make a crust for the bottom and the top as for other tortes. As soon as it is done, top with some sugar and rose water.

[HOW TO MAKE AN EEL TORTE]

Skin and cut the eel into pieces as large as two fingers and boil for a little while, but do not let it overcook. Make some fine, blanched almond milk by passing the almonds with some good verjuice and some rose water through a stamine, and make sure that the milk is very dense, that is, with a thick even consistency. Crush a small amount of raisins with three or four dried figs. Then take some spinach and tear it crosswise with your hands into small pieces and fry it a bit in oil, adding a little finely chopped parsley, an ounce of whole raisins, and an ounce of pine nuts that have been peeled and cleaned, and some ginger and cinnamon, and some pepper, and the necessary amount of saffron. Mix these things together with your hands, incorporating together well, and place a crust in the bottom of a pan and dress it with this filling or mixture, using it to make a first layer on the crust, and then another layer of eel; and thus, step by step, as you wish, you can continue until the mixture is finished; top with another crust and cook slowly, applying moderate heat from below and above. When it is half-cooked, take a little verjuice and some rose water with sugar; and make many holes in the top crust so that this liquid can penetrate; sprinkle the top with this liquid without removing the torte from the heat until well cooked.[6]

DATE TORTE WITH ALMONDS AND OTHER THINGS

Take a libra of peeled almonds and crush well, and together with some good fatty fish broth and a little rose water, pass it through a thick stamine; and take a half libra of good, clean dates, with a small amount of raisins and four or five dried figs, and crush together well; likewise crush together with two ounces of well-cooked rice; and crush all these things together well in a mortar; and take a small amount of spinach, parsley, and marjoram, and fry in good oil and chop with a knife; and add, together with the herbs, a few fish livers or else the fat of a nice fish would be good, chopping it together with the herbs. Then take an ounce and half of whole pine nuts that have been peeled and cleaned, and use them to stick into the filling once it has been spread out; also take an ounce of whole raisins and a half libra of sugar, cinnamon, ginger, and a bit of saffron, and mix all these things together, incorporating well. To make it thicken, take a half ounce of powdered starch or fine starch; or a bit of pike, as above, incorporating well with the filling; and put a crust on the bottom and top with lasagne in the same way shown in other recipes above.[7]

---

6. See also "How to make an eel torte," pages 88–89, and accompanying note 14.
7. See "How to make a farro torte," above, page 83.

Let it cook slowly and when it appears to you to be done, top with sugar and a bit of rose water. Note that this torte should be short.

WHITE RICE TORTE

Take a libra of peeled almonds that have been well crushed, and a little rose water, and a little rice broth that you took from the pot when the rice was almost done cooking, and incorporate with the almonds; and pass through a stamine; and take eight ounces of rice, and once it is cooked, grind together with the almonds, adding two ounces of white yeast and a quarter of an ounce of fine starch, or a small amount of pike roe that has been crushed and passed through a stamine, as above,[8] and a half ounce of sugar; likewise a half ounce of peeled pine nuts that have been crushed slightly in a mortar, but not ground. Mix all these things together and cook them with a crust on the bottom. When it is half-cooked, top with some thin, dried lasagne. When it has finished cooking, top with some sugar and rose water. Be careful to not overcook this torte.

[HOW TO MAKE A RED CHICKPEA TORTE]

Cook a libra of red chickpeas, crush well, and together with their broth pass through a very thick stamine; and take a libra of well-peeled, blanched almonds that have been very well crushed, because they should not be passed through a stamine; and together with the almonds, crush two ounces of raisins and three or four dried figs; likewise an ounce and a half of slightly crushed pine nuts, not ground, adding some sugar, rose water, cinnamon, and ginger, mixing all these things together well. To make it thicken, incorporate some fine starch or some pike roe, as above, and cook it with a crust on the bottom; and when it appears to you to be nearly done cooking, top with some sugar and some rose water, and apply heat again from above from a high flame. Note that this torte should be short.

FISH ENTRAILS AND MILT TORTE

Boil a fish with its entrails and take a libra of peas that have been boiled and well crushed; and pass them through a stamine; and similarly, crush the fish, the entrails, the milk, carefully removing all the bones, and if you have any trout roe or tench roe, it would be good to crush and add to the other ingredients. Then take some parsley and some marjoram and finely chop before crushing and adding together with the other ingredients in a mortar, adding some sugar, ginger, and cinnamon as necessary, and once you have mixed in a little rose water, incorporate all of these things together well; and cook this torte slowly until well cooked, following the method that has been repeatedly described in previous recipes.

Note that all the tortes described above can be made with varied and diverse colors at the same time in the same pan, depending on the period, and also with different fillings and with

---

8. See "Lenten crayfish torte," above, pages 84–85.

different ingredients, by fashioning thin dividers that you can use to separate the tortes into halves, or thirds, or quarters, whichever you prefer.

TORTE IN BROTH

Make a thick dough as you would for a pie, of whatever size you like; and take some pullet or squab that has been slightly boiled and quartered, and cut each quarter into two or three parts; and take some well-crushed almonds and a few egg yolks, some saffron, and some good fatty broth with a little verjuice; and first let the dough dry as you would for a pie, and in order to make the edges stand up straight, fill it with flour, topping it with a cover of dough; and let it cook until it appears to you to stand up straight. Then cut away the cover, and pull out the flour, and put the pieces of meat inside, arranging them the same way you would for a pie; and top this mixture with broth and the other things mentioned above; and make sure to add enough ginger and a bit of pepper. Cook this torte in the oven, or in a pan, the way other tortes are cooked.

MARZIPAN

Peel the almonds well and crush as much as possible, because they will not pass through a stamine otherwise. Note that in order to make the almonds whiter, more tasty, and sweeter in the mouth, they should be soaked in cool water for a day and a night or even more, so that they will peel themselves when you squeeze them with your fingers. When you crush them, wet them with a bit of rose water so that they do not purge their oil. If you really want to make it good, take an equal weight of sugar as of almonds, that is, a libra of the one and a libra of the other, or more or less, as you wish, and add also an ounce or two of good rose water; and incorporate all these things together well. Then take some wafers, also called *nevole*,[9] made with sugar, and wet them with rose water; dissolve them in the bottom of a pan and add this mixture or filling on top. Once you have sprinkled and spread the filling over the wafers, wet it again with a little rose water, and top with some good powdered sugar. When you have spread the entire surface with the sugar, cook it in the oven or over a flame, just as with the other tortes, slowly, being very careful to apply moderate heat and checking it often so that it does not burn. Remember that, similarly, marzipan tortes should be short and thin rather than tall and thick.[10]

---

9. *Nevole* (NEH-voh-leh) was a name for wafers made of sugar and flour.

10. Martino's *marzapane* is essentially modern marzipan, but the term itself meant something different to him. As this and the following recipe reveal, the name *marzipan* refers not to the filling—a mixture of ground almonds and sugar—but rather to the casing for the filling. The term *marzapane* comes from the Arabic *mauthaban*, which initially denoted a coin and, by extension, the box in which the coins were contained. For Martino, *marzapane* most probably meant a "casing that contains something sweet." It is not a coincidence that the following recipe is for calzones (Martino's term *caliscione* is merely a variant of the term we use today): from the Latin *calceus*, meaning "shoe," the term refers explicitly to the casing for the sweet contents. It is not surprising that Platina would—albeit erroneously—Latinize the term into *canisiones*, a term that seems more akin to the Latin *canistrum*, meaning "basket," than to *calceus*.

HOW TO MAKE CALZONES

Take a similar filling or mixture like that described above for marzipan, and prepare the dough, which you make with sugar and rose water; and lay out the dough as for ravioli; add this filling and make the calzones large, medium-sized, or small, as you wish. You can use a wooden mold, working it with the right skill, to shape and press them on top so they will be more handsome to look at. Then cook them in a pan, like marzipan, watching over them diligently so that they do not burn.

HOW TO MAKE *OFELLA*

Take some good Parmesan cheese[11] that has not been overly aged, and a bit of another type of fresh cheese, and grate, adding some egg whites, whole raisins, some cinnamon, ginger, and a bit of saffron. Mix all these things, incorporating well, and make sure that this filling is slightly thick. Then take a thin dough, like that used for making lasagne, and wrap the *ofelle* in this dough, making them large, medium-sized, or small, as you wish, giving them some yellow coloring on top with saffron, or whatever other color you wish; and cook them in the oven, and be careful that the oven is not too hot, because they should not be overcooked.[12]

[HOW TO MAKE AN EEL TORTE]

Take an eel that has been skinned and cleaned, and in case you wish to use another type of fish, take one that has been similarly deboned and cleaned, and cut it into pieces as large as two fingers; also take some good fish fat and milt, finely chop, and place on top of the pieces. Likewise, take a bit of finely chopped mint and parsley and an ounce of raisins, cinnamon, ginger, pepper, and crushed cloves. Mix all these things together, incorporating well. Then take its dough, which should be well made and aged,[13] and fill it with this mixture; top with some good oil and cook; and when it is almost done, take two ounces of almonds that have been cleaned and well crushed;

---

11. Even in Martino's time (and indeed long before Martino's time), the unique microclimate of the modern provinces of Parma and Reggio Emilia (in the region of Emilia-Romagna) was recognized as the only place where the inimitable cheese could be produced. Today, it is more properly referred to as Parmigiano Reggiano: regretfully, the Italians' battle to protect the name *Parmesan* has not stopped poor imitations (for example, Argentine and American "Parmesan"), which bear no resemblance to the unmistakable grainy texture of the famed cheese.

12. An ancient dish of Rome, *ofella* (from the Latin *offa,* meaning "morsel" or "small bite") was a sweet flatbread (what would come to be called *focaccia* in modern Italian, a term derived from the Latin *focum,* "fire" or "hearth"). In the *Aeneid* (6.420–22), the Sibyl subdues Cerberus with a drugged *ofella.*

13. That is, dried.

thin with some verjuice and pass through a stamine, and use them to top the pie, adding a bit of saffron; and simmer all these things together until properly cooked. Note that in times when you can eat eggs, you can thin two egg yolks with verjuice and add together with the other ingredients, making the pie much better and certainly not making it any worse.[14]

DRIED PIES MADE WITH WHOLE FISH

Take a fish that has been cleaned and deboned and make a shallow incision on either side near its spine; and season well, inside and out, with salt and good spices that have been mixed together. Then take a slightly thick dough, arrange and wrap the fish in it, and cook in the oven slowly until cooked through.

QUINCE PIES

Prepare the dough as described for other pies, and take some quinces that have been peeled and neatly cleaned; and remove the seeds and all of the hard core that the fruit has in its middle, making a suitably large and wide hole in each one; and fill each hole with good ox or veal marrow together with a generous amount of sugar and cinnamon; and arrange the quinces neatly in the pie, topping with some more marrow, inside and outside of them; sprinkle with sugar and cinnamon, and generously season this pie on every side; and once you have placed the dough or cover on top, cook the pie following the directions and method for the others described above.

LENTEN ALMOND JUNKET

Take some cleaned, blanched almonds and crush well along with a little rose water so that they do not purge their oil. Then add two ounces of sugar and two ounces of rose water, and a quarter jug of good fish broth which must be made from pike or tench, because no other fish will be as good, whether from the sea or from freshwater. Be careful that you do not make the broth too salty, but make sure that it is strong and that the fish is very fresh. Thin all of the above things together and put them in a stamine, passing them through and vigorously squeezing this mixture, so that none of the substance of the almonds is left in the stamine. Let this junket[15] set overnight on a platter or other pot, and in the morning you will find that it has curdled and thickened in the same way a junket made of real milk does; and if you like, you can thicken with leaves or herbs the same way that other junkets are dressed, or you can leave on platters and top it with sugar or candied anise.

LENTEN IMITATION RICOTTA

Take a libra of cleaned almonds that have been well crushed, just as above in the previous recipe, and take four ounces of sugar, an ounce of rose water, and a half cup of fish broth of equal qual-

---

14. Although different in technique and ingredients, this and the previous eel torte recipe (page 85) have the same title in the Vatican manuscript.

15. Junket is curds.

ity as that mentioned in the previous recipe. Once you have thinned all these things together, pass through a tight stamine. Place this mixture in a mold in a cool place, during the evening, until morning. Then turn the molds onto platters or cutting boards and serve this ricotta, but do not forget the sugar or anise, which will not hurt this dish.

LENTEN IMITATION BUTTER

Similarly, take a libra of cleaned, well-crushed almonds, as above, and pass through a stamine together with a half cup of rose water, until thick; and to make it properly thicken, add a bit of powdered starch, or, even better, a half cup of pike broth with four ounces of sugar and a bit of saffron to make it yellow, passing it all through a stamine, as I said, to make it as thick as you can. Then shape the butter like a loaf of bread; let it thicken from evening to morning in a cool place.

HEMP-SEED-MILK SOUP

Boil a small amount of hemp seeds until their shells begin to open, and crush well in a mortar, adding a small amount of peeled almonds; and after thinning with some cool water, pass through a stamine. Then simmer for a little while, adding a bit of salt and sugar as necessary; likewise, a little pepper to the taste if you wish; and let it simmer again for the time it takes you to say a Miserere;[16] and take some sliced bread that has been slightly toasted, and arrange the bread slices one at a time in a bowl, topping with the milk of the seeds in layers one by one, as you arrange the slices; when this has been done, empty out all the milk from each bowl, holding the bread in place so that it remains as is. And, again, add the hemp-seed milk, and repeat two or three times. Then top everything with some good sweet spices and serve.

CUSTARD

Prepare a dough as for a pie and fill well with flour so that it is flat, and cook it in a pan until it is a little bit dry.[17] Once you have done this, remove the flour and take some egg yolks, some milk, some sugar, and some cinnamon. Once you have mixed these things together, place on the dough and cook the same way you would a torte, turning it all around, and stirring often with a spoon. When you see that it begins to thicken, add a little rose water and stir well with a spoon. When it has finished thickening, it is done. Note that it should not be overcooked and it should tremble like a junket.[18]

---

16. Even when recited quickly, it takes about two minutes to say a Miserere (see also the reference in chapter 2 to the Lord's Prayer, also used as a timing device). The Miserere is the Vulgate version of Psalm 51.

17. This is Martino's method for "blind" baking.

18. Martino's name for this recipe, *diriola,* seems to be a diminutive of *tardiola,* probably from *torta* (perhaps from *torta di latte,* "milk torte," or *tortello di latte*). It is defined in John Florio's dictionary (1690) as "a plain custard." Fourteenth-century Italian cook Cristoforo Messisbugo cites it as a French dish. As in French, there is no term in modern Italian for custard: it is generically referred to as *crema* (as in *crema pasticciera,* or "pastry cream," or, after the French, *crème,* as in *crème caramel*). In fact, the term *custard* is derived not from the cream itself, but from the crust (Middle English *crustade,* "a pie with a crust," probably from the Provençal *croustado*).

HOW TO MAKE A LENTEN CUSTARD

Take some almond milk and sugar, and some rose water and some cinnamon. In order to make it thicken, add a little powdered starch; follow the same directions as in the recipe above.

PAN-FRIED CHEESE

Take some fatty cheese that is not overly aged or salted and cut it into thin slices or square mouthfuls, or however you wish; and take some pans made especially for this purpose; put a little butter in the bottom of the pan, or some freshly rendered lard, and heat over hot coals; and add the pieces of cheese; and when they obtain the tenderness that you desire, turn them, topping with some sugar and cinnamon; and serve immediately, because they should be eaten very hot at the end of a meal. You can also prepare the cheese in another manner by toasting it; that is, by first browning some bread slices until they begin to color on both sides, and then arranging the slices in a row in a torte pan; then top with the same number of cheese slices, thinner than the slices of bread; heat the pan cover and put it over the pan so that the cheese begins to melt or uncurdle. Once you have done this, top with some sugar and a bit of cinnamon and ginger.

GARNISHED TURNIPS

Cook the turnips under hot coals, or boil them whole and uncut, and cut them into large slices as thick as the spine of a knife; and take some good fatty cheese that has been cut into slices the same size as the turnips, but thinner; and take some sugar, some pepper, and sweet spices that have been mixed together; and in the bottom of a torte pan, arrange the slices of cheese the same way you would make a bottom crust, and add a layer of turnips, topping with the spices described above and a generous amount of good, fresh butter; and continue to layer the turnips and cheese in the same manner until the pan is full, and cook for a quarter of an hour or more, in the same way you would a torte. This dish should be served after the others.[19]

GOLDEN SOPS

Take some bread slices that have been trimmed of their crusts; and make them into squares, toast slightly, just enough so that they brown on all sides. Then take some eggs that have been beaten together with a generous amount of sugar and soak the bread slices in the beaten eggs; and carefully remove them and fry them quickly in a pan with a little butter or rendered lard, turning often so that they do not burn. Then arrange them on a platter and top with a little rose water that you have made yellow with a bit of saffron and a generous amount of sugar.

---

19. Professor Terence Scully, translator of Martino and many other medieval and Renaissance cookery texts, must be credited with the artful rendering of the original title of this recipe, *rape armate,* "armored turnips."

CHAPTER FIVE

HOW TO MAKE EVERY TYPE OF FRITTER

ELDERFLOWER FRITTERS

Take some good fresh cheese and a little aged cheese, and crush well, adding a bit of sifted flour to them and the necessary amount of egg whites; likewise, a little milk and some sugar; and grind all these things well together, remove from the mortar, and add a sufficient amount of elderflowers at your own discretion; they should not be crushed or crumbled, so as not to make the mixture too clear, that is, too liquid, so that you can form the round fritters using your hands, or in whatever shape you like, and then fry them in good rendered lard or butter, or in good oil; and serve very hot.

FRITTERS MADE WITH EGG WHITES, SIFTED FLOUR, AND FRESH CHEESE

Follow the directions and method described in the preceding recipe, but add neither milk nor elderflowers to these fritters.

FRITTERS MADE WITH JUNKET OR CURDLED MILK

Take the junket and pass it through a stamine together with some garlic sauce,[1] until you have eliminated its whey or excess water. Once this has been done, take the whey that has remained in the stamine, and mix it together with the necessary amount of egg whites, sugar, and some rose water. This mixture should not be too thick; carefully shape the fritters using a spoon, a little bit at a time, as large or small as you like; and fry them in good rendered lard or butter so that they will be well seasoned.

RICE FRITTERS

Cook the rice well in milk, and when you remove it, follow the directions and method described above, except you do not have to add either cheese or any more milk.

SAGE FRITTERS

Take a little sifted flour, and mix it with eggs, sugar, and a bit of cinnamon and saffron to make it yellow; and take some whole sage leaves and dredge them one by one in this mixture and fry in rendered lard or good oil.

---

1. See "White garlic sauce" and "Violet garlic sauce," page 79.

APPLE FRITTERS

Peel the apples and thinly slice, removing the seeds and core that they have in their middle, and fry a few of the slices in rendered lard or oil; then remove and dry on a cutting board. Dredge or batter them in a mixture similar to that in the previous recipe, and again, these should be fried in good fat; and in times of Lent, you can fry them in oil, but add neither fat nor eggs.

BAY-LEAF FRITTERS

Fry some bay leaves in some good fat or lard. Then remove and let dry; and these fritters are made with a mixture similar to that for sage.

ALMOND FRITTERS

Take some blanched and well-crushed almonds and pass them through a stamine with some rose water and a little milk, and take a boiled pullet breast and crush separately from the almonds; likewise, a bit of sifted flour, two or three egg whites, as needed, and mix all these things with a little sugar; give these fritters any shape you wish and fry them slowly in good rendered lard or butter and make sure that you do not overcook them.

ON LENTEN FRITTERS

ELDERFLOWER FRITTERS

Take some almonds and crush well, or some pine nuts, if you prefer, and pass the almonds or pine nuts through a stamine with a little rose water and some pea broth; and take a little good, white yeast and some elderflowers, as seems enough to you, and mix all these things together with a bit of sifted flower. Note that this mixture should be prepared the night before, so that the fritters will be spongy; and in the morning, add a little sugar, give them any shape you like, round or otherwise, and fry in good oil.

BITTER HERB FRITTERS

Take some sifted flour and a bit of yeast, and mix with some finely chopped herbs; prepare the mixture the night before so that they come out spongy; in the morning add minced dried figs and some raisins. This mixture should not be too thin. Then shape the fritters and once you have fried them in some good oil, top with sugar and honey.

[RICE FRITTERS]

Cook the rice well and once cooked, remove and dry on a cutting board, and if you wish to crush it, you can do so; if not, leave it whole. Take the necessary amount of almonds; crush well and pass through a stamine with a little rose water or a bit of the cooking water from the rice. Make

this almond milk very thick. Then take some sifted flour and some sugar. Once you have mixed all these things together, give the fritter any shape you like and fry in good oil.

[APPLE FRITTERS]

Peel and clean the apples well and boil or cook under coals; remove the hard part from their middles and crush well; and add a little yeast together with a bit of sifted flour and some sugar; and prepare the fritters, frying them in good oil.

STUFFED FIG FRITTERS

Take a small amount of almonds and the necessary amount of pine nuts, and crush well; make sure that they have been blanched and cleaned, adding two dried figs and a small amount of raisins before crushing. Then take a bit of finely chopped parsley, a few whole raisins, and some good spices. If this mixture is too thick, add a little rose water; take some dried figs that have been opened and cored from the bottom, that is, from where the blossom is; fill well with this mixture and fry slowly in good oil, sprinkling them with a little flour.

[FISH FRITTERS]

Boil the fish and crush its whitest flesh; and take a little thick almond milk and a bit of sifted flour with some sugar; and thin all of these things with a little rose water or plain water; then give the fritters any shape you wish and fry them in good oil.

FISH-SHAPED FRITTERS

Peel and blanch some almonds, and take the flesh of some good fish and crush it well together with the almonds, adding some raisins as well to be crushed with a little sugar; likewise, a bit of parsley and marjoram finely chopped with some good spices and a little saffron; prepare beforehand a thin dough in the same manner that lasagne are made, encasing and binding this mixture in the dough, in bigger or smaller pieces, as you wish. Then take some wooden molds that have been carved in the shape of fish of different qualities and in different manners, as you like, and use them to shape the dough with its filling. These fritters should be fried in good oil and they can also be cooked dry in a pan the same way as a torte; and once cooked, they will resemble fish.

MORE FISH-SHAPED FRITTERS

Crush some almonds and thin with rose water and sugar; and take some flour that has been thinned with plain water and sugar; and make the fritters by mixing all these things together, shaping them like fish as described above. Note that these fritters should be cooked dry in a pan like a torte.

RAVIOLI-SHAPED FRITTERS

Prepare a mixture similar to that described above in the previous recipe, with almonds, flour, and sugar, and use this mixture to make the fritters. To make another, similar fritter, take some

almonds that have been cleaned or some pine nuts or some walnuts, and crush well with a small amount of raisins and dried figs; and by adding some fish milt or fish livers, they will be excellent, and likewise some parsley and marjoram that have been finely chopped with some good spices. Make this mixture yellow with saffron. Then shape the fritters and fry them in good oil.

FRITTERS IN THE SHAPE OF SMALL PIES

Cook some rice in water until well done and crush a small amount of almonds; and pass through a tight stamine with a little rose water, thus incorporating the rice with the almond milk; add some sugar and a little powdered starch; be careful not to add too much. Give these fritters the shape of little pies and fry in oil.

WIND-FILLED FRITTERS

Take some sifted flour and some water, salt, and sugar; thin the flour, thus making a dough that is not overly hard, and roll it out as for lasagne on a table; using a round wooden mold or a glass, cut the dough and fry in good oil. Be careful that your dough has no holes; in this way, the fritters will puff up and will appear to be filled but will be empty.

ANOTHER WAY TO PREPARE FRITTERS

Prepare a mixture in the same way and shape as above in the recipe for making junket fritters;[2] and take some fennel that has blossomed, and if desired, you can leave the fennel fronds attached; otherwise, if you like, you can separate the fronds and stalks one by one, or in pairs of two, if you wish, and then dredge and turn them well in the mixture and fry in good rendered lard or in equal amounts of oil and butter.

SKIRRET

Clean well and once you have removed the hard core in the middle, boil; once cooked, dredge well in flour and then fry in oil.[3]

---

2. See "Fritters made with junket or curdled milk," page 92.

3. Martino's *pastinache grosse* are most probably *Sium sisarum*, commonly known as skirret, similar to the parsnip (what Italians still call the "white carrot") and perhaps more common in ancient Italy than *Pastinaca sativa*, the common cultivated parsnip. The fact that this recipe for skirret is added at the end of the fritter section should not be considered exceptional: a fifteenth-century scribal amanuensis commonly would insert an overlooked or forgotten text wherever he might find an empty spot to accommodate it (he did not have the luxury of the modern word processor, and erasure or reordering of the text would have been time-consuming and extravagant). He also includes fried fennel (the previous recipe) among those for "fritters." Moreover, the one common element of Martino's "fritters" is that they are fried (as the word's etymon, *frigere*, "to fry," reveals): while no dough or batter is involved here, the vegetable is dredged in flour before it is fried. (Compare this recipe with "How to prepare large skirret," page 125, in the Riva del Garda section.)

CHAPTER SIX

HOW TO COOK EGGS IN EVERY WAY

FRITTATA

Beat the eggs well together with a little water and milk to make the frittata[1] softer; likewise, add some good cheese that has been grated and cook the frittata in good butter to make it more fatty. Note that, for it to be good, it should not be stirred or overly cooked. If you wish to make it green, take the things mentioned above and add the water from the following herbs: chard, a generous amount of parsley, borage, mint, marjoram, and a lesser amount of sage, passing through a stamine to obtain their water; then remove the herbs that will have been crushed in the stamine.

Another way to make a frittata with herbs is to take the above herbs, finely chop, and fry in good butter or oil, and then by mixing them together with the eggs and the other ingredients mentioned above, you make the frittata which should be carefully cooked when well seasoned, but not overcooked.

DEEP-FRIED EGGS

Put some oil in a pan and make sure that it is somewhat hot; and break fresh eggs in the pan and cook through slowly; and as they fry, continue to top the eggs with the frying oil, using a ladle; and when they have taken and become white on top, they are done, but they should not be overcooked.

EGGS POACHED IN WATER

Bring some water to a boil and break the freshest eggs and drop them into the water; and when they have taken, remove from the water, and they should be very tender; top with some sugar, rose water, some sweet spices, and a little orange juice or verjuice; and if you prefer, instead of the things mentioned above, you can top with good grated cheese and some sweet spices.

---

1. The term *frittata* has become so prevalent in anglophone cookery that the most recent and revised *Joy of Cooking*, published in 1997, gives three different "frittata" recipes. The word comes from the Latin *frigere*, "to fry." And while purists claim that the Italian frittata is distinguished from the French omelet (a term derived from the Latin *lamella*, meaning "small, thin plate"), inasmuch as it is turned over to finish cooking it, Martino's recipe for frittata, perhaps the earliest on record, resembles modern scrambled eggs rather than the modern frittata or omelet. There are, however, two key elements that link it to the contemporary frittata: the addition of cheese to the beaten egg, and the use of green herbs or vegetables (today, zucchini and parsley are generally used).

EGGS POACHED IN MILK OR SWEET WINE

Prepare as specified in the previous recipe, but do not top with cheese.

STUFFED EGGS

Boil fresh eggs whole in water until hard; and once cooked, cleanly peel and slice in half; remove the yolks, being careful to leave the whites intact, and crush part of the yolks with a small amount of raisins, a little good aged cheese, and a bit of fresh cheese; likewise, some finely chopped parsley, marjoram, and mint, adding one or two egg whites, or more, as needed, with sweet or strong spices, as you prefer. Once you have mixed all these things together, make the mixture yellow with some saffron, use the mixture to fill the reserved egg whites, and then fry slowly in oil; and to make a good sauce to top them, take some of the remaining egg yolks with a small amount of raisins, and once you have crushed them together, thin with a bit of verjuice or *sapa,* that is, sodden wine; pass through a stamine, adding a bit of ginger, a few cloves, and a generous amount of cinnamon, and simmer this sauce for a little while. When desired, serve the eggs topped with this sauce.

EGGS ON THE GRILL

Beat two fresh eggs together and heat an empty pan until very hot; and drop the beaten eggs into the pan, allowing them to spread all over the pan, in the same manner as for a frittata as thin as paper. When they appear to be done, fold into four quarters so that it is square just like a little box. Place it on the grill, breaking over it as many fresh eggs as you think it is able to hold on top, and apply moderate heat from below and above like a torte, topping with sugar and cinnamon; and when it appears to you that the eggs have taken, remove from the grill and serve together with their square beneath them.

EGGS ON A SPIT

Heat the spit well and then insert into the eggs lengthwise or crosswise, however you prefer;[2] and turn it over the flame in the same way as for a roast. When they appear to be done, remove and serve.

EGGS IN A PAN

Put some good butter into small pans or copper pans and heat slightly; and take some previously prepared fresh egg yolks, separated from the whites, if you prefer, and cook them in the pan, topping with some sugar and cinnamon; apply moderate heat from below and above, making sure that they do not overcook. Then top with a little orange juice or rose water.

---

2. Presumably, Martino intended that the cook use a very lean spit to thread the egg.

EGGS IN HOT ASHES

Place fresh eggs in hot ashes, carefully turning often, so that they feel the heat on every side equally. When they begin to sweat a lot, remove them because they are done.

EGGS CODDLED IN THEIR SHELLS

Place fresh eggs in cold water and boil for the time it takes you to say a Lord's Prayer, or a little bit longer, and remove.[3]

DEEP-FRIED EGGS IN THE FLORENTINE STYLE

Take fresh eggs and break them one by one into a pan when the oil is very hot; and as soon as you put them in the oil, use a spatula or spoon to push the outside of the eggs into the center, making them as round as possible, and turn often as you are cooking them so that they are well browned on the outside and not too hard or overcooked on the inside, but rather soft and tender.

EGGS POACHED ON HOT COALS

Take a whole egg and toss it onto hot, burning coals, and tap it with a stick on top until it breaks, and let it cook; and when it appears to you to be done, remove and top with a little vinegar and parsley.

STUFFED DEEP-FRIED EGGS

Prepare deep-fried eggs in the Florentine style, as above, making sure that they are not overcooked; and on one side, make a hole in each one and cleanly remove all of the yolk inside. Then take a bit of good, fatty, aged cheese that has been grated, with a little finely chopped mint and parsley; likewise, just a small amount of raisins and a bit of pepper with one or two or more raw egg yolks, as needed; mix and incorporate all of these things together and fill the eggs through their holes; fry again until the filling is cooked, turning often, and when they have finished cooking, top with a little orange juice or verjuice, and a bit of ginger.

EGGS IN THE SHAPE OF RAVIOLI

Make a dough like that for lasagne, which is not too thin or tender, and break some fresh eggs over the dough, and after topping with sugar and sweet spices with a little salt, wrap these eggs in the dough in the same way you would ravioli; and boil or fry, however you prefer. But they are better fried; similarly, you can arrange the eggs in the shape of pies, topping with the same things as above and adding a little verjuice, if you like, and then cooking the pies like a torte, or frying them, but make sure that the eggs are not overcooked, because the more an egg is cooked, the harder and worse it becomes; this is its nature.

---

3. "The time it takes you to say a Lord's Prayer" would be about one minute.

CHAPTER SEVEN

HOW TO COOK EVERY TYPE OF FISH

In this final section, it should be noted in general that every fish to be boiled or fried should be scaled and scraped on the outside, and then opened; and the entrails should be removed before the fish is washed; and conversely, a fish that is to be roasted should not be scaled or scraped or opened, except for saupe, which should be opened and its entrails removed, and similarly shad, from which a certain forked bone, to which its intestines are attached, must be removed through the gills before cooking or roasting.

THE BEST WAY TO COOK STURGEON

First of all, do not cook the sturgeon until it has softened, bruised, or become tender, but not fresh; and if you wish it to be perfect, take some good white wine or vinegar mixed with pure water in equal parts and a sufficient amount of salt and boil it well, simmering as long as you would veal or beef, cutting into pieces at your discretion, depending on its size. But for those who prefer to cook it whole, to make it all the more pleasing to the eye, it should be prepared in large, capacious pots, the way my master does, because every type of fish is better when cooked whole, rather than in pieces or in any other way.

STURGEON SAUCE

Sturgeon should be served with white sauce and a generous amount of ginger, or good white garlic sauce, or mustard, depending on the season and appetite; for these sauces, see the individual recipes above.

[HOW TO PREPARE UMBRINE]

Umbrine should be prepared and cooked in the same way as sturgeon, except that it should be boiled for a shorter amount of time, because it cooks more quickly; and prepare a sauce as I said above for sturgeon.

[HOW TO PREPARE DENTEX]

Dentex should be boiled while still very fresh; not as much wine or vinegar is required as in the recipe above for sturgeon. But remember that wine or vinegar causes it to seize up and become firm; it conserves the fish longer and it also makes it taste better than does water, salted or unsalted.

A GIANT SEA BASS

Boil as stated above; when it is less than four or five librae, fry it in good oil or roast it on a grill; remember, as mentioned above, it should not be scraped or opened; a brine should be prepared with vinegar and oil and a generous amount of salt, and using a laurel or rosemary branch, baste the fish with the brine repeatedly, turning it often on the grill and allowing it to cook slowly so that it cooks through. Note that every type of fish should be well cooked, because they are damp by nature, and when not well cooked are unhealthy.

GIANT CORB

Boil it similarly to sea bass; but if it is small, roast or fry. When fried, it should be accompanied by slightly garlic-scented green sauce and a generous amount of ginger. Likewise, it can be served with mustard, if you prefer.[1]

GILTHEAD

If it is a large gilthead, boil and season well. If it is small, fry or roast in the ordinary way.[2]

TURBOT

This fish should be boiled, but, because it is very delicate and breaks easily, it should be cooked in a basket, or tied to a cutting board so that it can be removed whole when it is done; and it should be simmered very slowly. Note that in general every type of fish should be simmered slowly, but it is necessary to be able to discern and know the quality of all fish because there are those that are more firm and hard than others; likewise, there are those that are more tender and soft; thus, they should be cooked for longer or shorter periods of time, as necessary, but they all should be simmered softly, gently, and slowly, until cooked through.

SOLE

Sole should be fried and topped with a bit of fine salt and orange juice or verjuice, and a generous amount of chopped parsley.

---

1. The corb, as it is commonly known in English, belongs to the drum and croaker family. Like its Italian names (*corvo, corvalo,* or *corvolo*), the English name comes from the Latin *corvus,* meaning "crow," because of the fish's dark coloring.

2. Mediterranean gilthead bream has become so popular in North American restaurants that by now it is usually referred to by its Italian name, *orata.*

BONITO

Bonito and tunny[3] should be boiled like sturgeon, and the same spices should be used. If small, both of them should be fried, since they cannot be roasted because they do not have scales. But if you decide to fry, cut large ones into slices crosswise, the size of one or two fingers, and fry well slowly. Top with a generous amount of orange juice and some good strong spices and a little chopped parsley if you like.

RED BREAM

When large, it is good boiled, roasted, and fried; when small, it does not matter how you cook it; it should be served with green sauce.

RED MULLET

They should be roasted very carefully and they should not be opened but only washed and basted often with the brine mentioned above;[4] and if you wish to conserve them for eight to ten days, arrange them one on top of the other in an orderly fashion on a plate or in a pot; and top with enough of the brine to cover; and in this manner, you can conserve them.

SAUPE

Because of its quality, it should be fried after having first removed all of the intestines, for it has a lot of tripe; and when you wish to roast it, remove the intestines through the smallest hole that you can possibly make.

GOBY

Because of its nature and quality, it is better boiled than in any other way.

SCORPION FISH

When large, it should be boiled. When small, it should be fried.

RED SEA BREAM

Red sea bream is better fried or roasted than boiled.

WHITE SEA BREAM

White sea bream is good fried or roasted, as you prefer.

---

3. In Faccioli's transcription of the Library of Congress manuscript, he reports, "la palamita o 'l fondo," with the following note: "This term [*fondo*] seems to be used alternately with *palamita*, although it is not registered in any dictionary." In the transcription of the Vatican manuscript, Benporat reports instead: "la palamita ol tondo." Faccioli appears confident in his transcription, *fondo*, and it is possible that this was an oversight of the amanuensis. Morphologically, *tondo* has an affinity with the Latin *thunnus*, or tunny; hence, the translation, *tunny*. In fact, bonito (or *palamita* in Italian) is often called a "type of tuna," and the two fishes are often prepared in the same fashion.

4. See "A giant sea bass," page 100.

MORAY EEL

First skin or peel with warm water and discard the head and a piece of the tail; fry well and serve with garlic-scented green sauce.

MACKEREL

They should be fried, but they are also good boiled with pepper and parsley.

GRAY MULLET

By its nature and quality, this fish should be roasted, but when it is very big, it must be boiled; and its sauce, when roasted, is brine, and when boiled it is white sauce.

FLOUNDER

It is good boiled with a bit of parsley. It is also good fried, topped with orange juice.

CATFISH

Boil in equal parts wine or vinegar and water, and a very strong garlic sauce should be used as its sauce, considering that every catfish is vile and more suited for farmers than for gentlemen.

DOGFISH

Boil as in the previous recipe. Then mix some strong garlic sauce with a little strong mustard, and fry with these sauces; but no matter how well you dress it, it will never be good because it is not good to begin with.

EEL

Large eels should be roasted on a spit after being skinned and well cleaned; cook very slowly because this more than any other fish needs to be well cooked. To better season, it is cut into pieces as large as your hand or a little bit bigger. Small eels should be fried in oil; you can also boil a large eel and the small by adding some aromatic herbs to them as they simmer, like parsley, sage, and some bay leaves, with some pepper and a little verjuice.

MANTIS SHRIMP

They should be boiled just like freshwater crayfish, and they should be dressed with vinegar.

BAY SHRIMP

They also should be boiled with some fennel seed and dressed with vinegar.

[HOW TO COOK OYSTERS]

Oysters are cooked over hot flaming coals, and when they open they are done, and they can be eaten. They should be removed from their shell, fried in a little oil, and topped with some verjuice and strong spices.

[HOW TO COOK DOLPHIN FISH]

Dolphin fish should be fried and topped with orange juice.

SHAD

It is good roasted, when the forked bone and intestines are removed through the gills, as stated above; its sauce is green sauce, and it is also very good boiled; when prepared in this manner, it should be accompanied by white sauce.

MUSSELS

Take a dry pan and place the mussels in it over heat; and when they open, they are cooked; as soon as you see them open, add a little verjuice to the pan and some pepper and finely chopped parsley, and flip them once or twice in the pan. Likewise, they can be cooked on a hot iron rod or on hot coals, and when they open they are cooked. But note that they will be better if soaked in well-salted water for a day or a night, because it will make them purge the sand that they have inside.

CODFISH

Boil and serve with white mustard as its sauce.

FRESHWATER PIKE

Boil when it is large, first removing its entrails, but do not scrape outside, because it should be descaled only after it has been cooked; and serve with white sauce, garlic sauce, or mustard. Fry if the pike is small.

GIANT TROUT

Clean well and slice crosswise in pieces as large as your hand; arrange the pieces in layers in a cauldron or whatever pot you wish to cook them in, making sure that the cut side is facing up; and as you layer them on top of one another, sprinkle each one with a generous amount of salt. Once you have completed this for the desired quantity, cover completely with water but be very careful not to wash away the salt with which you have topped the fish, and also add a little vinegar, just enough so that the cooking water comes to about two fingers above the fish; bring to a boil and scum well. When it stops producing scum, remove almost entirely from the flame so that it will simmer as slowly as possible until done cooking. Then remove and place on a clean

table to dry, and top with some sweet spices. Serve this trout with white sauce made with a generous amount of ginger.

If the trout is on the smaller side, clean well and cut lengthwise along its back from one end to the other. Add salt into the incision and similarly to the rest of the body. Then put it in a press between two cutting boards with a weight on top for two or three hours. Once this is done, dredge in flour and fry well, slowly, in good oil. In this way, you can conserve it for three or four days if you like.

TENCH

There are three good methods.

The first: boil if it is large and top with a fine broth made of verjuice, spices, finely chopped parsley, and a little of its cooking water.

The second method: you can turn it inside out; if it is large, scrape and clean well, slicing it from head to tail along its back, removing all the entrails, and breaking the ribs on both sides; then take its roe, fat, and liver; if the tench does not have any, those taken from another fish are just as good; take some parsley and some other aromatic herbs, chop well together with the liver, roe, and fat from the fish, adding a bit of finely chopped garlic, that is, in small pieces, a bit of pepper, some saffron, some salt, and a little oil; likewise some dried damson plums or some black cherries, red cherries, or raisins, also known as *zibibbo*,[5] with a generous amount of peeled pine nuts; likewise, one or two fresh egg yolks, depending on the period; incorporate all these things well together and use this mixture to cover the inside of the tench, that is, its skin, which is now on the inside; and then sew it up with a needle and thread, or tie it well round and round with a string so that it holds this filling; and place it on a grill over low heat, because it will take a long time to cook; if roasting, make a brine with vinegar, oil, salt, saffron, pepper, and a little sodden wine; when you turn it (it should be turned a number of times), baste well with this brine.

The third and last method: if the tench is small, after you have cleaned it well, cut and open it similarly along the back, top with a bit of salt, and dredge it in flour inside and out before frying in good oil. For a sauce, top with orange juice or verjuice.

PERCH

When it is large, it should be boiled after removing the entrails, but do not scrape it at all on the outside; if it is very fresh, cook it in pure water if you have no vinegar to add to the water. When it is cooked, skin and clean outside as above for pike. If it is small it should be scraped and fried in oil. It is also good roasted and basted with brine.

---

5. *Zibibbo*, from the Arabic *zabib*, meaning "raisin" or "dried fruit." In modern Italian, the term *zibibbo* denotes a grape varietal cultivated in Sicily, *moscato di Pantelleria*, or *moscatellone*, which is dried and made into preserves or pressed to make a sweet (and sometimes fortified) wine.

LAMPREY

Soak it in a little water and scrape away its sticky outer layer, but do not break or tear the skin; remove the tongue and the teeth, and in the bottom of its belly, where its sex is, make a small hole as big as the tip of your finger with a knife or sharp wooden stick, and through this hole, lift out enough of the intestines so that the rest can be removed by pulling them out with your hand wrapped in a piece of cloth; pull it out completely so that it comes out whole without being torn, because the lamprey has nothing foul in its body except for the intestines. Collect all of its blood and use it to make its sauce; put a half of a nutmeg seed into its mouth and whole cloves into all of the small holes around its head; at this point, curl the lamprey into a spiral and place it an earthenware pan big enough to accommodate it; add a half ounce of good oil with a little verjuice and the best white wine that you can get, adding liquid until it covers the lamprey more than halfway. Top with a bit of salt and cook slowly over hot coals like a torte. When it begins to cook, use a knife to open those little holes below its head and press down on it with a cutting board or something else until all of its blood comes out and mixes with the other ingredients; to make things easier, if you wish, you can also remove the blood before placing it over the flame.

To make its sauce, take some almonds or hazelnuts; without peeling them, toast them in hot ashes, and after you have peeled them, crush with a small amount of raisins and with a slice of toasted bread; thin with verjuice and sodden wine and with some of the wine and the other liquids above in which the lamprey has been cooking; once you have passed all of these things through a stamine, add a little ginger and just a few cloves and a generous amount of cinnamon; likewise, some of the blood that you reserved earlier before cooking it; and mix it with the things mentioned above, which you will add to boil with the lamprey when it has cooked through; transfer to a platter with its sauce, and serve.

It can also be cooked in another way, that is, it can be roasted on a spit, holding a container made for this purpose underneath when you turn it to collect the blood and the fat that comes out and drips down as the lamprey is cooking, because this is what makes it taste so good. Using this, you can make a sauce following the directions above, which you serve with the lamprey; if the lampreys are small, in which case they are called *lampredoze,*[6] they should be roasted slowly on a grill, and their sauce should be made with orange juice and sodden wine. If you do not have any oranges, add some verjuice with a little oil and some salt and sweet spices in their place. While they are roasting, baste often with this sauce. Once cooked, top with the remaining sauce and serve.

BARBEL

Prepare it as you wish: it is not reputed to be a good fish and its eggs are dangerous to eat, especially during the month of May.

---

6. A diminutive variant of Italian *lampreda*.

GRAYLING

Grayling is an excellent fish; prepare it however you like, for it is good in all manners, but its natural method for cooking is frying.

SEA CONGER

Roast as you would eel, that is, put a sage or bay leaf between each piece.

CRAYFISH

Boil in a small amount of water and vinegar, that is, equal amounts of water and vinegar, and a generous amount of salt, and because they will purge their own water, do not add too much cooking water; boil until they expel their juices themselves. In order to know when they are cooked, pay attention to when the cooking water has increased two or three times in the cauldron, as has been explained; then they should be fine, but to know for sure, taste them and you will not be fooled.

STUFFED CRAYFISH

Cook them as stated in the previous recipe and using the tip of a small knife, skillfully open their belly between their legs and remove all that is contained in their belly, tail, and claws; crush the inside of the tail and the claws with almonds and a small amount of raisins; and when eggs are allowed, add one or more egg yolks to these things, as needed; you can also add a bit of cheese, finely chopped parsley, and marjoram. Fill the crayfish with this mixture and fry gently and slowly in good oil as long as possible; in time of Lent, add neither the eggs nor the cheese. If you wish, for some variety in their filling, take some almonds crushed with sugar and rose water to fill the claws, or fill half of the crayfish with one filling and the other half with the other.

SPINY LOBSTER

Stuff its mouth and the hole that it has under its tail with cotton wool so that its good meat is not lost when you cook it; and place it as is, dry, to cook slowly in an oven, or over a hot and well-cleaned and well-swept hearth, making a ring of hot coals around it, just wide enough so that they do not touch it. This is done so that it will cook better and more quickly. Turn it often so that it does not burn.

Likewise, if you prefer, you can boil it with water and vinegar as for crayfish, allowing to boil a little bit longer at your discretion, because it is larger and harder than other crayfish and the like. Dress it with vinegar.[7]

---

7. A spiny lobster is one without claws.

LOBSTER

Stuff its holes as above and cook in the same way as for spiny lobster.[8]

RUDD

Cook it however you like, because it is nothing special nor is it a commendable fish.

COMMON CARP

Boil when large; you can also roast and fry them when they are small.

[HOW TO COOK SALMON]

The salmon is a very fine fish and the natural method for cooking it is boiling; it is also good in every other way that you may wish to prepare it.

BEAKED CARP

They should be fried slowly so that they do not burn; serve with green sauce or green verjuice as its sauce.

SMELT

They should be fried; serve with green sauce or green verjuice as its sauce.

MULLET

Fry similarly; and serve with a sauce as in the previous recipe.

GARFISH

Its natural method for cooking is frying but it is also good boiled or roasted.

CORKWING

Boil if large; if it is small, fry, and serve with mustard as its sauce.

FRESHWATER SHAD

They are good boiled, topped with parsley, some butter and spices; similarly, they are good fried and topped with orange juice or verjuice.

SARDINES

The natural method for cooking them is frying, but you can also roast them, if you wish.

---

8. Here the recipe is for a lobster with claws.

[HOW TO COOK OCTOPUS]

Octopus is a vile fish of little worth; cook it however you wish.

CRAB

Prepare in the same way as stated above in the recipe for shrimp, and serve with vinegar as its sauce.

[HOW TO COOK EEL IN ANOTHER WAY]

Enough has been said on eel in another recipe,[9] but do not forget that when you place the pieces of eel, one by one, on a spit, you should always place a sage or bay leaf between them, and you should turn the spit as slowly as possible; baste often with a brine made as described above. When the pieces seem to be done, take some flour or grated bread, with cinnamon and salt mixed together, and skillfully sprinkle over the eel to make a crust around it in this manner, which will make it taste good. If the eel is small, boil with water and wine, herbs, and spices, as above in the other recipe.

LAKE GARDA CARP

Take some brine prepared in the same manner as that for saltwater fish, and as soon as you get the freshest carp,[10] toss it into the brine and let it soak for two days; then fry it in a generous amount of good oil until cooked through. By using this method, that is, by frying them and re-frying them, and even two or three times if necessary, you can conserve the carp for twenty days, and even for a month or longer. But note that every time they are fried, they lose some of their substance and become less good, because this method was invented only to make them last longer. If they are large, boil them, if they are small, fry, being careful not to be pricked by that poisonous spine on their head.

SQUID

The smaller they are, the better they will taste. Wash well and prepare a filling, as is described for stuffed tench,[11] even a better one if you know how; fry in good oil, topping with some orange juice and some good spices. You can boil large squid by cutting them into pieces in the same way as veal or ox tripe, with a little broth; make sure that it is cooked through, and you can add finely chopped parsley with some spices. Likewise, large squid can be prepared in this other manner, by washing it first with a little white wine and verjuice and some sodden wine, thus squeezing out the squid's ink with these things, which is used to make its sauce; take an ounce

---

9. See "How to make an eel torte," page 85; "How to make an eel torte," pages 88–89; and "Eel," page 102.

10. Martino's *carpione* is most probably the famed *carpione del Garda,* a type of large carp (currently in danger of extinction) found only in Lake Garda; it should be distinguished from other types of carp.

11. See "Tench," page 104, second method.

of toasted almonds that have been toasted in hot ashes, crush a bit of toasted bread—or omit, if you prefer—and crush these things together. Thin all these things with the squid's wash, pass through a stamine, and simmer for a little while, adding some cinnamon, ginger, and a few cloves; fry the squid in good oil and top with this sauce.

FISH ASPIC

Take some water, wine, and vinegar, and so that it can be preserved and will last longer, add just a little water and a lot of seasoning. And in order that you may know which is the best and richest fish for making the broth for aspic, I say that tench and pike are the most fatty, and the larger they are, the better. Note that such a fish should not be scraped, but only opened, and it should be very fresh; cook through slowly in just enough broth to cover, and this is done so that the broth will become richer. When the fish appears to be done, remove and skin entirely, and reserve the skin, but return its skin for a short while to simmer in the broth. When it appears to have simmered long enough, strain the broth well, following exactly the directions and method described in the recipe for meat aspic,[12] and by doing so you will clarify and fine this aspic, as you would for any other broth. Remember you should season it well and it should taste well seasoned. In this broth, you can make aspic with different sea fish that you have cooked separately and individually, and likewise whatever type of fish you please.

HOW TO MAKE MEAT OR FISH ASPIC WITH TWO OR THREE COLORS IN A CARAFE

To make it clear, take some very pure, aged white vinegar or white verjuice, and mix with two parts water. Take some mutton or kid feet, well skinned and cleaned principally and especially between the hooves; slice crosswise, remove the bones, that is, the tendons of the legs, and wash well in cool water, and boil in the vinegar and water mixture as above, as slowly as possible, adding some well-peeled ginger that has been cut up into pieces, and likewise some melegueta peppercorns that have only been slightly crushed;[13] when the feet appear to be done, remove and let the broth simmer without them for a good while; then prepare ten fresh egg whites, or more or less, as needed, following all the directions for straining, clarifying and everything else as stated above in the recipe for meat aspic; and get your platters prepared with capon or pullet or whatever else you wish to put in the aspic, and top with just such a neatly prepared decoction, returning the platters to their cool place so that it will thicken and congeal better; once it has fully congealed, to make the various colors, cut out a quarter of the gelatin on the dish and place in a pot over heat until it dissolves and melts, that is, becomes broth again; you can make it yellow with saffron, and when it chills again, return the broth to the same place in the carafe, but be

---

12. See "How to prepare two platters of aspic," page 57.
13. Melegueta pepper, also known as Guinea pepper or grain of paradise (*Aframomum melegueta*).

careful that it is not too hot when you return it; and once this has been neatly arranged, when it has thickened and congealed, remove another quarter and make it red with cornel cherries using a method similar to that for yellow; and one by one, take the other white quarter, and to make it green, take some green wheat or barley shoots budding and grind together with some well-crushed parsley, and use it for coloring in the same way as for the other two colors. Similarly, you can make the other white quarter violet by getting some carrots that have been cooked under hot coals and peeled;[14] using a knife, carefully remove the violet part on top and put it in the bottom of the sack in which you strain the decoction for the aspic, and, repeatedly, over and over again, pour the reheated white broth until it has taken on this color; once you have done the same, following this method, for all the other colors above, again arrange this last one in its place like the others. If you desire more colors, use your own judgment, because using this method, you can make as many as you wish.

ASPIC IN A BASKET

Take a fine, well-prepared decoction and a basket or a small, new reed chest; neatly arrange pullets inside the basket, or other meat that you desire to place in the aspic, just as you would do on a platter; and take another, well-cleaned, and large pot, large enough to accommodate the basket, and place it inside, fill with the previously prepared decoction, and return to a cool place to thicken and congeal. When it has fully congealed, take a knife and heat slightly; run it around the basket in order to remove it more easily from the pot, and clean the basket all around with white cloth or by some other means; you will be able to take the aspic in the basket wherever you wish, and similarly you can make the aspic in a cage if you like. And during Lent, you can make this using the same method, placing a whole cooked fish inside; it will appear to be alive and it will be a fine thing to see.

HOW TO KNOW WHETHER SPINAL CORD IS GOOD

Cut it crosswise into slices about half the size of your finger, clean well all around, and cook over a grill, turning often and basting continuously with oil and vinegar mixed together in equal parts. Be aware that it should not dry out too much, and when it appears to you that the heat of the flame has penetrated on either side, it will be done; then top with the oil and vinegar and serve. To know whether the spinal cord is good, cut it and if you find it to be well colored and red, that is a good sign. But be careful that it is not too old and that it is not rancid.

---

14. It is well known that carrots were generally purple or purplish-red in color until the mid-sixteenth century, when white carrots first began to appear (the earliest references to truly orange carrots date back to the seventeenth century). When Martino refers to the "part on top," he means the layer just under the skin.

HOW TO PREPARE STURGEON ROE CAVIAR AND COOK IT AS WELL

Take some bread slices and toast until slightly browned, and slice the caviar the same size as the bread slices, but a little thinner, and lay them on top of the bread; place the bread slices on the tip of a knife or fork suited to this purpose and expose to the air around the flame until the caviar hardens like a slightly browned crust. Likewise, you can prepare it in any other way by first washing well in lukewarm water so that it is not so salty; take some good, small herbs that have been finely chopped, grated bread white with a bit of finely chopped and gently cooked onion, and a bit of pepper, to which you add a cup of water; mix all these things together with the caviar, shape into one or more fritters, and fry as you would with eggs.

To make the caviar, take some sturgeon roe, during the season and period when sturgeon are best, remove from the roe all the nerves inside, and wash with some good white vinegar or with good white wine. Place on a table and allow it to dry; then put it in a pot, adding salt to taste; stir well with your hands, but carefully so as to crush as little as possible. And once this has been done, take a white sack made of rather loose canvas, and toss in the caviar for a day and a night so that the water it purges will be strained out. Once this has been done, put the caviar back in a pot, well pressed and thick, in other words by pressing it down with your hands. Three or four small holes at the bottom of the pot will allow moisture to escape in case the caviar was not properly strained. Keep the pot well covered and you can eat the caviar as you wish.

A GOOD TUNA BELLY

Take some water with a little vinegar and a generous amount of bran to remove the salt; boil the tuna belly in it, simmer moderately, but not too long. Once cooked, remove, clean, and soak in vinegar. You can tell whether it is good or not by the fat: the more, the better. It should be from the belly of the tuna and it should be solid and hard, not soft.

LITTLE TUNNY

Soak in lukewarm water for six hours, changing the water two or three times; simmer for a little while, that is to say, bring it to a boil two or three times; then remove and put it in vinegar.

SALTED EEL

Skin the eel and cut into pieces as large as your hand, and boil in water for a half hour; then discard the cooking water and put it in cool water, and boil until cooked; then remove and top with vinegar and parsley.

SALTED TROUT OR OTHER SALTED FRESHWATER FISH

Soak in lukewarm water for four or five hours and change the water and boil for an hour, or more or less, as necessary, depending on whether they are large or small; and you can prepare every other salted fish in the same manner. Note that for all qualities and types of fish, you should always favor the largest, just as the proverb goes: old fish and young meat.[15]

BOTTARGA

Take the roe of fresh gray mullet, also called *muzano,* and make sure that it is very fresh, that is, for it to be good it must be in season; and be careful not to break that thin membrane that is around the roe; sprinkle with chopped salt to taste—neither too much nor too little; let it set like this with salt on top and beneath for a day; then put it in a press for a day and night. Once this has been done, remove and thicken by smoking just far enough from the flame that it is not affected by the heat. Once it has dried, preserve it by arranging it in a wooden box or barrel, adding a generous amount of bran. *Bottarga* is generally eaten raw, but those who wish to cook it can do so by heating it under ashes or on a clean, hot hearth, turning it over until it is hot all the way through.

FRYING TROUT LIKE CARP

Clean the trout well and remove the entrails; prick them in many places with the tip of a knife on both sides and make a brine of water and vinegar in equal parts, adding a generous amount of salt, which will make it dissolve; put the trout in the brine for a half day or longer. Once this has been done, put them in a press on a table for three or four hours, and fry well in a generous amount of good oil, making sure that they cook through but do not burn. You can conserve these trout for a month, refrying them again if you wish and preparing them like carp.[16]

HOW TO MAKE PIKE OR OTHER LARGE FISH, COOKED WHOLE IN THREE DIFFERENT WAYS

Take a large fish, remove the entrails, wash well, and tie a cloth or sheet of damp canvas around its head so that it covers a third of the fish; this is done to cover the part to be boiled; then turning yourself to the tail, scrape the other third of the fish and split open the part from the tail just as you would for a fish to be fried. Begin first cooking the part of the tail, frying it very carefully so that it does not ruin the rest. Once this has been done, take a small thin board the length and width of the fish, on which you carefully tie the fish so that it does not break. Boil the part of the head tied with cloth, leaving it tied, simmering very slowly, and making sure that the cooking water does not touch the fish save for where it is tied with the cloth. Once boiled and

---

15. That is, the older and therefore bigger the fish, the better; the younger the meat, the better.
16. Compare "Lake Garda carp," page 108.

sufficiently cooked on this side, remove and untie it slowly from the board so that it does not break. Put it over a grill whole, as is, and make a small bed of coals underneath it so that the heat of the flame cannot touch it save for that part in the middle that is not cooked. And in order to keep the flame from ruining the boiled and fried parts, take two square stones, high enough for this purpose, and put them under the grill and arrange the coals for roasting between them; as you roast it, baste with the brine described in the recipe for roast fish.[17] When it appears to have cooked through, remove and slowly untie the cloth, using your hands to clean the boiled part as I have shown for other fish. Place it on a dish and serve, and if you like, you can serve it with the three sauces suitable for boiled, fried, and roasted fish.

LENTEN IMITATION EGGS

Take some cleaned almonds that have been blanched as much as possible and crush well, moistening them with a little rose water so that they do not purge their oil. Thin with cooled, good, fatty, and rich pike broth; pass through a stamine, turning it into milk; take a half libra of rice that has been cleaned and washed, or more or less, as needed; cook it well in half of the above almond milk, and also take three ounces of the best and whitest starch you can get, and add it to the remaining milk until you see that the starch is fully dissolved; then boil this milk and starch together for a half-quarter of an hour, stirring continuously with a spoon, and make sure that it does not burn. Once this has been done, take the rice with all the milk and pass together through a stamine by the force of your hand; the thicker the mixture, the better it will be, and do not forget to add a generous amount of sugar. At your discretion, take the quantity or part of this mixture that you think is sufficient, make it yellow with saffron, and shape it into small round balls like egg yolks; then take two wooden molds shaped like eggs; and if you do not have the molds, you can use two egg shells in their place; put the white mixture beneath and above and all around the egg yolks, thus making it look like eggs. And one by one, arrange them on a dish, and they will appear to be hard-boiled eggs that have been peeled. Thin and make liquid a bit of the white composition with rose water and sugar, hot or cold as you wish, and you can use it to top the eggs and it will appear to be milk. If you like them dry, leave them as they are without topping with this liquid, but in its place top with fine, powdered sugar.

RICE PREPARED IN A BETTER WAY THAN ABOVE

Wash the rice with hot water until very white and set it to dry on a cutting board; once dried, boil with goat or almond milk, depending on the period, and this is done because it makes the rice richer than when cooked in water. Also add a moderate amount of salt, being careful not to make it too salty. If you want it to taste really good, do not hesitate to add a generous amount of sugar.

---

17. See "A giant sea bass," page 100.

FLYING PIE

[Note that this remarkable pie is for amusement.][18]

Make a mold for a large pie, and in the bottom make a hole large enough that your fist can pass through, or even bigger if you wish, and the sides around it should be slightly higher than the common usage; fill it with flour and cook in an oven. Once it is cooked, open the hole on the bottom and remove the flour; beforehand, prepare another small pie filled with good stuff that has been well cooked and seasoned and that has been made as big as that hole in the large mold; place this pie through the hole into the mold; and in the empty space that remains around the small pie, put some live birds, as many as it will hold; and the birds should be placed in it just before it is to be served; and when it is served before those seated at the banquet, you remove the cover above, and the little birds will fly away. This is done to entertain and amuse your company. And in order that they do not remain disappointed by this, cut the small pie up and serve. I say one pie, but you can make more—as many as you wish. You can make tortes in a similar fashion, mixing the ingredients and adapting them so that they will go well together.

18. The Riva del Garda scribe added this note.

THE RIVA DEL GARDA RECIPES

These recipes either are not included in the Library of Congress and Vatican manuscripts or appear there in significantly different versions.—Translator

HOW TO MAKE A PEPPER SAUCE IN THE GENOESE STYLE

To make a pepper sauce in the Genoese style, from meat or fish, take the necessary amount of very tender lean meat, and a handful of salt, or more or less, as needed, and the same amount of bread, which has been soaked in lean broth; and once you have ground the meat, thin it with broth together with the other ingredients, and add a generous amount of pepper and saffron; then pass all these things through a stamine and simmer in a pot, stirring often; and this pepper sauce should be served hot; and similarly you can make it using fish; and note that pepper sauce made with roebuck or hare or pork or other game should be made black; take some dried squash and char on a pale;[1] and once it has been charred, drop into cool water; then crush together with the pepper sauce on top. Similarly, if you do not have any squash, take some mutton spleen—cooked or raw—and crush together with the pepper sauce.

HOW TO MAKE MACARONI IN THE GENOESE STYLE, ACTUALLY CALLED *TAGLIARINI*

Make a thin macaroni with good flour; this pasta should also contain half an egg white, or more, as needed. Once it has been thinned with lightly salted water, let it harden somewhat and roll it out thinly, adding a generous amount of flour. Wrap it around a stick, remove it, and then cut it into strips as thin as a piece of string. Then let it dry for a little while or prepare it fresh, if you wish. Take some good, aged Parmesan cheese,[2] and a *provatura,*[3] neither too hard nor too fresh, and grate them together; then take some arugula and make sure that its leaves are free of worms, and crush as fine as possible; then add it together, as I have said, with the cheese, with a bit of saffron; then place on a platter or in bowls, and incorporate all these things together; add a layer of macaroni, that is, of *tagliarini;* every dish made with macaroni should have fresh butter.

---

1. That is, on a spit.
2. See note 11, page 88, on Parmesan cheese.
3. A buffalo-milk cheese similar to mozzarella (i.e., a plastic cheese), but harder.

HOW TO MAKE DRIED SQUASH IN THE GENOESE STYLE

Take squash that has been well washed in hot water and then set a cauldron full of water to boil; toss in the squash and let it cook, but do not soak in the evening for the following morning because it will take forever to cook it; finely chop after it has cooked and dressed as fat as you wish; then boil with a little salt-cured meat because it would not be worth anything without it; every vegetable should have salt-cured meat if it is to be good; boil in a pot with good broth. You can also make it with eggs and cheese as for other squash.

HOW TO MAKE TWO PLATTERS OF RAVIOLI

Take a libra of good Parmesan cheese and another of good fatty cheese; then take some good herbs, that is to say, chard, different types of mint, and saffron; crush well together and once they have been crushed, boil or fry in good butter. Then mix together with the cheese and incorporate well and make them fat with butter, or with some veal teats or even some good veal or pork belly, depending on the period. Make a thin pasta and encase the filling in it, making the ravioli as long as a good-sized finger and a little wider. Note that these ravioli should be boiled in good broth or in water with salt; and after they have cooked slowly the length of four Lord's Prayers, remove to a platter and top with good aged and fresh cheese mixed together with cinnamon and saffron. Other ravioli can be prepared in the same manner.

HOW TO MAKE YELLOW RAVIOLI

Take some good aged Parmesan or other fresh cheese, a bit of good pork belly—fatty and lean—that has been well boiled and cooked, and crush together with two or three eggs, as needed, with some pepper, cinnamon, cloves, and yellow saffron.

HOW TO MAKE WHITE RAVIOLI

Take some good, fresh, fatty *provatura* that has been well crushed in a mortar with a little butter and the necessary amount of white ginger, and for each *provatura,* add three or four egg whites that have been well beaten together with sugar to taste; and incorporate all these things together. Then make the ravioli as long as a large finger and bind with sifted flour. Note that these ravioli should be made without pasta. Cook slowly so that they do not break apart, and when they have come to a boil, remove and top with sugar and cinnamon. Serve these ravioli on a platter or in bowls, as you wish.[4]

---

4. White ravioli are akin to what the Tuscans call *gnudi,* meaning "nude" dumplings, in other words, the filling of ravioli cooked without the pasta.

HOW ONE MUST COOK ON PAPER OR PARCHMENT

Mold the paper in a shape that resembles a pan, in such a way that the oil cannot escape; add enough oil so that it is half a finger above the paper; then heat this oil over hot coals or over a candle until very hot; then slowly break the egg and let it cook; allow for some salt to be added and make sure that the paper in which you have cooked the egg is not near the candle, that is to say, that it is not above it. This is done to cook it and to entertain.

HOW TO MAKE SALTED MUSHROOMS IN THE GENOESE STYLE

Take the mushrooms and soak in lukewarm water for two or three days. Change the water every day. Then boil until well cooked and let them dry for a little while. Cut them into morsels half the size of a chestnut. Then fry in good oil. Then take a clove of garlic and a half of one of the mushrooms; crush together in a mortar with an amount of bread crust equivalent to a chestnut, and a little verjuice. If it is too strong, add some water and let [. . .]⁵ some of the oil in a pan. Then add this sauce and fry together and serve. These [. . .] how people like them, and they should be seasoned with pepper.

HOW TO MAKE LENTEN CAVIAR POTTAGE

Take some good caviar, making sure it is not rancid, and remove the outside part; then crush well in a mortar, and when it has been well crushed, to make eight servings, take half of the caviar and then crush in a mortar twenty-five almonds that have been well blanched and an ounce of bread white; thin with a little cool water and pass through a stamine, adding more water with the almond milk so that there will be enough for eight servings. Then place over a flame and add a bit of good oil and some herbs, that is to say, marjoram, mint, and parsley that have been finely chopped. Then bring to a boil with the milk. Then add the caviar to the milk after first thinning it with a bit of the milk in the mortar. Then put all these things in the pot and give it a stir with a spoon. Add a bit of saffron and pepper; and once you have stirred it, remove. Then take some and serve in bowls, topped with sweet spices. Similarly, you can make this with pike roe, but it must be well crushed and passed through a stamine. You can also make it with sturgeon roe.

HOW TO MAKE BUTTER POTTAGE TO BE SERVED AT THE END OF A MEAL

To make eight servings, take thirteen hard-boiled eggs; then take all the yolks without the whites and crush thoroughly; then take two librae of fresh butter that has been washed with cool water. Pour off the water and pass through a stamine, pressing it through. Then add to the egg yolks and churn for an hour, adding a half cup of fined rose water and up to eight ounces of sugar and a drop of saffron; pass through a stamine without letting them go through, that is, the saffron

---

5. The text is illegible here. Hereafter, ellipses in brackets denote illegible text in the original.

threads. Then take a copper-plated strainer that has holes like an armored sieve,[6] and pass this butter through the holes; put a little bit in each bowl and this pottage will look like it has vermicelli in it.

HOW TO COOK EGGPLANT SO THAT IT IS
NEITHER TOO STRONG NOR ILL PREPARED

Cut them into quarters and peel carefully, like a pear. Then bring them to a boil in a little water with salt; and when the water begins to boil, add the eggplant and boil for two Lord's Prayers; then remove and dry. Dredge in flour and fry like fish and when they have been fried, drain off the oil, leaving a little bit in the pan with the eggplant. Then take a clove of garlic and crush with a quarter of the eggplant. Then take a little of the oregano that is used to top anchovies, crushed with garlic with a bit of bread, saffron, pepper, and salt, and thin these things with verjuice; or, if the verjuice is too strong, with some water. Then add all these things together in the pan and cook with the eggplant for a little while. Then put on a platter and serve.

HOW TO MAKE A GOOD ZABAGLIONE

To make a cup, take four eggs, that is, the yolks, and some sugar and a sufficient amount of cinnamon, and some good sweet wine; if the wine is too strong, add a little water or lean broth. Then cook the same way that fine broth is cooked, stirring all the while with a spoon. When it thickens, remove the zabaglione from the heat. Then put it in a cup. It is to be served in the evening at bedtime. Note that it soothes the brain.

HOW TO MAKE TEN SERVINGS OF FINE MEAL

Take a capon breast that has been boiled and that was butchered two days before. Then take a half libra of Parmesan cheese and half of a hard *provatura,* which is not too hard but fatty; then take as many wattles as it would take to fill half an egg; clean and crush well in a mortar with the capon meat; then add a veal teat and a half libra of fatty pork belly together with spices, that is, pepper, cinnamon, ginger, and a bit of saffron; break in two eggs; make a thin pasta as you would for lasagne, but a little thicker; take the mixture and shape it into morsels the size of half of a chestnut; cut this pasta in the shape of ravioli, and if you do not have the mold, cut it with a glass; then cook in good capon broth or other fatty broth, with saffron in it; when the broth comes to a boil, drop them in, letting them simmer slowly for the time it takes to say four Lord's Prayers. Serve in bowls, topped with a little Parmesan cheese mixed with cinnamon. Note that the saffron must be boiled from the moment the salt clouds; be careful because saffron becomes

---

6. That is, a ricer.

black, especially if it boils too long.[7] Let it suffice that a lot has been said of this dish and pottage, both what is missing and what is below. Note that every vegetable should be prepared with salt-cured meat.[8]

HOW TO MAKE TEN SERVINGS OF MARZIPAN

Take a libra of marzipan that has been well crushed, and add together with a two-day-old, tender capon wing; then crush together since there is no need to pass through a stamine; then take an amount of bread white equivalent to a hen's egg and wet it with lean capon broth, adding a little verjuice, rose water, and a little capon broth, crushing all these things together; place in a pot over hot coals away from the flame and add a bit of white ginger and let it come to a boil. When you wish to serve, top with some sugar and cinnamon.

HOW TO MAKE MELON POTTAGE

Take the melons and cook as will be described below for the melon torte; and put them in a stamine and let them become very tender; then crush well, adding some fatty capon broth or suckling calf broth and let it simmer for a short while; remove and place a well-beaten egg yolk in each bowl, together with some good cheese, a little verjuice, ginger, and pepper, and enough saffron to make it yellow, and when you wish to serve, top with sugar and cinnamon; this pottage should be very thick.

HOW TO MAKE VEAL AND KID SWEETBREADS POTTAGE

Take a libra of sweetbreads and boil well; when cooked through, crush thoroughly on a cutting board as you would with the best of them; and take five hard egg yolks that have been well crushed and add together with the sweetbreads in a mortar and grind; then take a little good fatty capon broth or suckling calf broth and thin; put in a pot on hot coals away from the flame, and when it boils, add a little verjuice, if it pleases your master; and when it is done, remove from heat and add a bit of saffron and ginger; then take three or four well-beaten egg yolks and add, stirring vigorously so that the pottage does not go bad; and before dividing in bowls, add a half ounce of rose water, and when you serve, top with sugar and cinnamon. Veal and kid sweetbreads can be prepared similarly. Note that they should be only lightly seasoned.

---

7. The advice on when to add saffron ("Note that the saffron must be boiled from the moment the salt clouds") probably refers to the boiling temperature of salted water. The medieval and Renaissance cook probably did not know that salted water boils at a higher temperature than unsalted water does. This would seem to explain why the scribe recommends adding the saffron only after the salt has clouded: if it is added when the cooking water has reached its boiling point, it needs to be boiled for a shorter period of time.

8. The last line of this recipe would seem to indicate that some type of vegetable is to be used; and, indeed, even today vegetables are cooked with salt-cured meat. Nonetheless, it is unclear why the scribe added this note at the end of the recipe.

HOW TO MAKE TURNIP POTTAGE

Take some peeled turnips, cut them into small slices, and crush well as you would salt; then put them in white vinegar for a half hour; squeeze the vinegar out well and cook in good fatty broth with salt-cured meat; serve in bowls, topped with pepper.

HOW TO PREPARE ROTTEN PEARS OR BRUISED PEARS OR APPLE-PEARS

Clean the pears well and then toast over hot coals; and when they have been toasted, put them in wine or water; then clean with your hands and cook them in boiled must with a generous amount of cinnamon.

HOW TO MAKE A CATALAN GINGER POTTAGE

Take a half libra of rice flour and two jugs [roughly two liters] of goat milk, a half libra of sugar, up to a half ounce of white ginger, and twenty dates without their pits and without the white skin inside; then cut into pieces the size of playing dice; and then take two ounces of well-peeled and cleaned pine nuts, making sure that they are not rancid, and crush only slightly in a mortar; then two ounces of very large raisins without seeds and cut into pieces as you did for the dates; then, when you have boiled the milk and flour for a half hour, stirring all the time, add these things together with a tender capon wing that has been cut into pieces and slightly crushed; and allow them to boil for another half hour; and make it yellow with saffron—which can also be done with broom flowers—thinning the saffron with some rose water and passing it through a stamine. During Lent, similarly, in place of goat milk, add almond milk, and in place of capon, add a little pike or lobster tail that has been crushed together with the same things above; and this soup should be thick and you must be careful not to burn it.

HOW TO MAKE FOUR OR FIVE SERVINGS OF MARZIPAN

Take a libra of marzipan that has been crushed in a mortar as thoroughly as possible; then take a tender capon breast and crush it in this marzipan; then take a glass of rose water and a little verjuice, as suits your patron's tastes, and some fatty capon broth; and set it to boil for a little while; and this pottage should be thick and should not be passed through a stamine; each serving should be topped with sugar and cinnamon.

HOW TO MAKE A GALLIMAUFREY IN THE FRENCH STYLE

Take a mutton breast, or veal breast, cooked, or even half-cooked; then take some finely chopped onions that have been fried slowly in rendered lard; then take the meat, and cut it into small pieces the size of walnuts; then add all these things together in a pan and fry with a bit of strong mustard or a good quantity of pepper and verjuice.

HOW TO MAKE TWELVE SERVINGS OF LEMON POTTAGE

Take a libra of peeled and well-crushed almonds; then take a tender capon breast that has been crushed; then take a lemon in a salted mixture, with the seeds removed, finely chopped, and crush together with the things above, and with bread white soaked in a quarter of a liter of capon broth; thin all these things again with the broth and verjuice mixed with a generous amount of white ginger and a half libra of fine sugar; pass through a stamine; then place in a pot over hot coals, stirring often so that it does not burn; it should be as thick as blancmange and should be served with boiled meats, topped with sugar and cinnamon.

HOW TO MAKE AN IN-BETWEEN COURSE CALLED BULLETS

First take a good tender capon and cook a little more than halfway; then finely chop and put it in a mortar; crush until it resembles butter; then add together with a quarter of a fresh *provatura*; crush all these things together well; then take four ounces of veal teat that has been well beaten with a knife; then add a [. . .] of chicken egg with one or two beaten;[9] and this mixture should be slightly hard; incorporate all these things together with a generous amount of fine sugar and a bit of white ginger; shape this mixture into balls the size of missiles that are launched with a bow; boil them in lean capon broth, but before you add these bullets, take two well-beaten egg whites and batter these bullets in the egg whites. Note that the broth must first boil before you add these bullets. Let simmer in a large pan very slowly for the time it takes to say three Lord's Prayers.

HOW TO MAKE A SAUCE FOR THESE BULLETS

Take a half libra of almonds that have been well peeled and well crushed; then take two ounces of starch flour and soak in lean capon broth, adding a generous amount of fine sugar and rose water; then put all these things in a mortar and thin it all together before passing through a stamine with just enough orange juice to flavor the mixture slightly; and put in a small pot on hot coals away from the flame, stirring all the while to avoid burning. Note that this sauce should be thick but not as thick as blancmange, nor should it be too dark or too clear; then there should be a pomegranate seed on each bullet to make it more handsome to see; and first place the little bullets on a plate, over the sauce, and then add the sauce on top, to be served as a dish before the meal or after, however you wish.

---

9. Here, not only is a portion of text illegible, but an evident scribal error has been made, resulting in a nonsensical phrase.

HOW TO COOK SNAILS

Snails should be gathered and taken from rosemary or fennel, or from vines and from grapes and other fruits, for they are not good when taken from other fruits. Let them set in a pot for two days and a night until they have purged themselves in some durum wheat; then wash well and rewash; and then put them in a pot with the water from which you wish to make the broth; and add rosemary, fennel, and other good mints, and boil together.

HOW TO PREPARE TWELVE SERVINGS OF WHITE *ZANZARELLI*

First take a libra of sweet almonds that have been peeled and crushed together with some elderflower and thin with some water before passing through a stamine; when you see that you have passed enough through for eight servings, cook in a pot, reserving a cup of the uncooked liquid; if desired, take ten egg whites together with the reserved liquid, together with milk and grated bread; crush all these things together with a half libra of sugar and when the milk first begins to boil, add this other mixture, stirring once with a spoon, and remove; then, when you see it has thickened, serve in bowls, topped with sweet spices.

HOW TO MAKE TEN SERVINGS OF A POTTAGE THAT RESEMBLES BLANCMANGE

Take a libra of peeled and well-crushed almonds; thin with fatty pullet broth or other good broth, and pass though a stamine into a pot to boil with an ounce of rice flour thinned with almond milk; allow it to boil for an hour, stirring all the while and adding a half libra of sugar and a bit of finely chopped and crushed capon that was cooked first in milk; when all this mixture is cooked, add a little rose water; serve in bowls, topped with sweet spices.

HOW TO MAKE AN APPLE TART IN THE FRENCH STYLE

Cook the apples as above;[10] take some well-crushed pine nuts and add the apples to them with a generous amount of sugar, cinnamon, ginger, saffron, and a little well-crushed pike roe, and thin everything together with rose water or other water before squeezing through a stamine to make it thicker, but not too much so; then make a dough thinned with a little oil, sugar, water, and salt, making it hard but allowing it to be elastic; make this dough, which is made with the ingredients mentioned above, the thickness of a finger, and it should be cooked in the oven or in a pan over low heat; then have some wafers made with sugar and turn them into powder with a little sugar and pulverize; sprinkle with rose water.

HOW TO MAKE A WHITE TART

Take some belly or milt of a good fish that has been cooked in well-crushed almond milk; add everything together in a mortar, adding a bit of pike roe and some sugar and a generous amount

---

10. See "How to make tortes with turnips, pears, and quinces," page 81.

of white ginger with rose water and more water; squeeze through a stamine; then cook with the other ingredients and a generous amount of that wafer powder; and when served, top with rose water and pine nuts.

HOW TO MAKE A WHITE OR GREEN TORTE THAT HAS GLASSES INSIDE OR WHATEVER COLOR YOU PLEASE

Take a veal's head that has been properly skinned and dressed for boiling; once cooked, remove and clean the brain, and crush in a mortar with cinnamon, sugar, and rose water, and if you wish to make six or seven glasses, add two or three egg yolks and a bit of saffron, using glasses that are slightly large and two fingers high; then make a thin dough in a pan and arrange the glasses in the torte. Note that the ingredients should be passed through a stamine and the filling should also be added to the glasses. Cook slowly and once cooked, add pepper, sugar, and cinnamon, and serve hot, giving each person a glass.

Note that you cut the torte on the table and you place one glass per man on the cutting board.

HOW TO MAKE A CAULIFLOWER TORTE, USING THE FLORETS OF TWISTED CAULIFLOWER, WHICH RESEMBLE TURNIPS

Peel well and cut into thin slices; then boil in broth until well cooked; once cooked, squeeze out their water; crush in a mortar, and once crushed, add four or five eggs, as needed; pass through a very loose stamine, and take a libra of fresh cheese and a half libra of Parmesan cheese, pepper, and saffron, and make sure to season generously with the pepper, and this torte should be short and very fatty with butter or with good pork belly. This torte is good during the winter and it should be prepared like the Bolognese torte.[11]

HOW TO MAKE AN ONION TORTE IN THE GENOESE STYLE

Take some peeled onions, slice into thin rounds, and place into a pot to fry with oil; and once they are cooked, make two sheets of dough, one below and the other on top; thin with oil and crushed salt; then roll out the dough in a thin pan; put in the onions, making sure that they have been thinly sliced, and cook with a generous amount of pepper and salt in an oven or over moderate heat.

HOW TO MAKE A SPINACH TORTE IN THE GENOESE STYLE

Take well-washed and cleaned leaves; first boil some water for a little while and toss them in; remove quickly, and finely chop with a knife; then take some shelled walnuts and peeled almonds that have been crushed together, and then incorporate; and add some pepper, saffron, salt, and a half ounce of caviar, mixing everything together; then make two sheets of dough as for the onion torte; and in case you do not have any caviar, use a half ounce of pike roe.[12]

---

11. Compare "Roman broccoli," in the Library of Congress manuscript, page 74.
12. Sturgeon roe—the most prized—was generally used for "caviar."

HOW TO MAKE A LENTEN PAPAL TORTE

Take a libra, or even a libra and a half, of two-day-old, tender sturgeon fish, together with a good pike, and cook with water and salt; when cooked through, remove and make sure that you do not leave the spine in; crush well in a mortar and then remove; then a half libra of peeled almonds and a half libra of pine nuts that have been crushed into a dough like marzipan; then add a half libra of rice that has been well washed with lukewarm water; cook in almond milk, and once cooked, crush with the same things above; then add a half libra of sugar, a half ounce of white ginger, a half ounce of fine cinnamon, a bit of saffron, and a little crushed salt, mixing everything together with two ounces of raw pike roe and four ounces of rose water; pass everything through a stamine; then [. . .] everything together until well incorporated. Note that this torte should not be too tall, but certainly shorter than meat tortes. Then make a crust in a pan like that for meat, and do not cook it any more or any less, being careful that no part of it burns.

HOW TO MAKE A GOOD PAPAL TORTE FOR BREAKFAST

Take a heaping libra of good, fresh, fatty cheese, and crush with butter; then take a half libra of Parmesan cheese, combine all these things, and crush well; then take a good piece of two-day-old tender capon and cook well; once cooked, remove and, if fatty, remove the skin and make a pottage as is described in the previous recipes; if it is lean, do not remove the skin; then take the breasts of all the capons, finely chop, and crush in a mortar; once crushed, then return to the mortar together with the cheese, adding a libra of crushed sugar with the same things above, an ounce of fine cinnamon, a half ounce of white ginger, eight fresh eggs that have been beaten, and a bit of saffron; add more or less a pint of milk; a fatty, well-cooked veal teat that has been well chopped with a knife; mix everything together; then make a thin dough in a well-greased pan; and this torte should be two fingers high with this filling; it should be boiled, making sure that it does not burn, and when it is almost done, take some fine dried lasagne with sugar and crush and sprinkle these two things over the torte, applying heat from above and below; remove and sprinkle with rose water and then top with eight bay leaves; lastly, sprinkle with two ounces of candied pine nuts, and serve following the credence table courses.[13]

HOW TO MAKE FRENCH SOUP

Take some sliced bread with crusts removed, not too thick, or too thin; then put them over a grill until slightly browned but not burned; put everything on a platter; then put it in the best broth, which you will have seasoned with saffron, and let this bread soak with another wide cheese;[14] then take some grated Parmesan cheese and a good amount of marzolino,[15] one and

---

13. Courses served from side tables (i.e., *credences* or *credenze*).
14. Perhaps a scribal error occurred here.
15. *Marzolino*: a sheep's-milk cheese, traditionally made in March; hence the name, from *marzo*.

a half grated, and another half with the grated cheese, cinnamon, ginger, and sugar; then take another platter and put first a layer of one and then a layer of the other; and then a layer of cheese mixed with those spices, and then a layer of bread; repeat until the platters are full; then add a sufficient amount of hot fatty broth to cover; and [. . .] serve immediately, and even better, who [. . .].

HOW TO PREPARE LARGE SKIRRET

Clean well and remove the hard part in the middle; once cooked, dredge well in flour and fry in oil; but when they have been boiled, put them on a cutting board to dry; then make a dough with sifted flour, sugar, and cinnamon, with saffron and rose water;[16] batter in the dough and then fry.[17]

HOW TO MAKE ASPIC IN A CARAFE WITH A LIVE FISH INSIDE

Have a carafe made especially with a spout on the bottom that reaches midway up the carafe; make sure that the spout has a hole large enough for a chickpea to pass through; then make a gelatin as for other [. . .]; make sure that it is very dense; then put a little of the gelatin on the bottom of the carafe, about a finger high; let it congeal thoroughly; then turn the carafe upside-down; close and seal the hole at the end of the spout with some hard dough; then add more gelatin and fill it all the way to the neck of the carafe, or even a little higher; then let the mold set until thoroughly congealed; but when you put it in, be sure that the broth is very cool; when it has completely congealed, add some water slowly through the little hole at the tip of the spout, making sure that it does not overflow; put some small fish inside, as small as the hole, and thus, there will be live fish in the water and you can send it as a gift to anyone you wish.

HOW TO PREPARE A HEN IN A CARAFE

Take a hen that has been butchered the evening before; then pluck without water and burn without breaking the skin; then open and remove the innards; then skin, up to the neck, and then turn the skin inside-out; then take the meat and cook without the skin, and once cooked, take the skin breast,[18] and crush well in a mortar; then put a little Parmesan cheese inside with some good aromatic herbs that have been well chopped with a knife, adding them together with the

---

16.   Text missing here in manuscript.

17.   This version of Martino's skirret recipe offers two preparations, while the Library of Congress manuscript offers only one.

18.   Here the scribe erroneously wrote *skin*, and then, without correcting his error, wrote *breast*; in fact, the skin must remain intact to achieve the desired effect.

breast and crushing again with spices of every sort, with a bit of saffron veal fat, and an egg or two; then make this filling slightly liquid; then take a carafe big enough that a hen or capon will fit inside; the mouth of the carafe must be very wide; then take the raw skin of the hen and sew well where you have skinned it; and as for its neck, it should overflow, because this mixture should fill through the neck and the mouth, but do not fill it too much because [before you add the skin, you must see if the carafe is big enough to hold it; if it is, fill the hen through its neck, which will be sticking out of the neck of the carafe, but do not overfill];[19] then tie the neck and let it lie in the carafe; then skewer it with a stick, slowly, without letting the hen break apart, so that the filling goes up; then fill the carafe with water and add a portion of salt; place the carafe in a cauldron over hot coals and simmer slowly; and thus, it will appear to have been cooked alive in the carafe.

HOW TO MAKE NUT-STUFFED CABBAGE

Take the hazelnuts and some good Piacentine cheese,[20] two cloves of garlic crushed together with the other ingredients, good herbs, well-crushed marjoram, mint, and parsley with walnuts; then take two eggs that have been beaten, finely chopped veal fat with pepper, and saffron, and season generously with pepper; use this paste to make a loaf; then take some cabbage leaves, as they say in Lombardy,[21] and wet this with warm water; then enclose the loaf [. . .] in different parts of the leaves, so that nothing can spill out; then cook with other cabbage leaves and serve as soon as it is done cooking.

---

19. In the Riva del Garda manuscript, the text is illegible here. The text in brackets is taken from the Neapolitan manuscript, which reports this recipe nearly identically.

20. That is, from Piacenza; possibly what is called *grana padano* today—a cow's-milk cheese, produced similarly to Parmigiano Reggiano.

21. *As they say in Lombardy*: in other words, in northern Italy. This gloss is an indication that the scribe hailed from the south.

THE NEAPOLITAN RECIPES

These recipes either are not included in the Library of Congress, Vatican, or Riva del Garda manuscripts or appear there in significantly different versions. — Translator

RICE IN THE ITALIAN STYLE

Take a pot and put some fatty and lean broth in it, and boil. Then take some well-cleaned rice that has been washed repeatedly with lukewarm water, put it inside, and boil, stirring a few times with a spoon so that it does not stick to the pot. When it is done, add some eggs and grated cheese that have been beaten together with a bit of pepper. Serve in bowls.

BROTH FOR A DELICATE MAN

Take some pullets to make broth and put them in a clean pot and fill it with water so it can be well scummed. When it has been scummed, add a little salt-cured meat and immediately cover the pot; this will make the broth turn white. If it does not turn white, take a pullet head and crack it, and once it has been broken, boil well, and when the pullets and salt-cured meat are done, cook the broth until it reduces to one or two bowlfuls.

PORRIDGE FOR A SICK MAN

Take some barley flour and some almond milk and some hen broth, and after passing the flour through a sieve, add it to the milk, and cook thoroughly. Serve in bowls, and when it is almost set, add some fine sugar.

BEANS

Cook the beans in pure water or in good broth; when they are done, take some onions that have been thinly sliced and fry in a pan with good oil and top with the fried onions and with pepper, cinnamon, and saffron; then let them set over hot ashes for a little while. Serve in bowls, topped with good spices.

MUTTON'S HEAD

Take a mutton's head and wash well; then cook well. And if you can remove all the bones, do so. Then cut out all the meat, mince, and place in a pot; when it is almost entirely cooked, take

some parsley root,¹ mint, marjoram, and minced onion, and add together in the pot; then take some spices, eggs, and broth, and bread that has been soaked in broth, and some liver; mix these things together and put them in the pot away from the flame, and simmer until cooked through; then remove from heat and serve in bowls, topped with spices.

PAN-BAKED MEAT IN THE FLORENTINE STYLE

Take some veal meat or other meat with bone; cut it up into pieces the size of your fist and put them in a pan with a little water and a cup of wine and a cup of good verjuice; if your master likes, add a few onion rounds; if not, add parsley, that is, the root, and grapes that have been dried, and salt. Make sure that the meat is not covered with water by more than a finger above, and put in the oven; and when halfway done, add a small amount of cloves, a generous amount of cinnamon, pepper, and a generous amount of saffron; make sure that it tastes really peppery; when halfway, turn it and the remove to a platter topped with spices and sugar or leave it in the pan. You can prepare fish in the same manner, that is, gray mullet or eel, cut into pieces four fingers wide, well washed, and then placed in the pan with a bit of oil. Note that you can make these things sweet or sour as suits your master's tastes.

CANDIED CAPON

Take some fat capons that were butchered two days beforehand; clean well and boil but do not overcook; remove from pot and dry; then take fine sugar as necessary for the desired number of capons to be candied; break up the sugar and dissolve with some rose water, and simmer. Then use the dissolved sugar to top these capons until fully covered; top also with good cinnamon. Serve immediately.

DIFFERENT WAYS TO PREPARE KID

Clean well and roast on a spit with the skewer passing through its nose, but be careful not to burn. And for a sauce, take some parsley and some toasted bread that has been soaked in vinegar with a clove of garlic and pepper; crush everything together and thin with verjuice or with cooked wine must, making it as sour or sweet as you desire.

---

1. The Neapolitan scribe uses two terms for parsley: (1) *petrosillo,* a term used in the Library of Congress, Vatican, and Riva del Garda manuscripts to denote parsley; and (2) *julivert,* a Catalan term that also denotes parsley, from the Latin *lilium viride* ("green lily"). Elsewhere in the text (see the next recipe, "Pan-baked meat in the Florentine style"), when the scribe uses *petrosillo,* he elaborates, "that is, the root." He is probably referring to what today is called Neapolitan parsley: generally larger than other parsley plants, it is consumed like celery in southern Italy. The latter term, *julivert,* is used to denote flat-leaf parsley, also known as Italian parsley or Italian plain-leaf parsley (*Petroselinum crispum*).

HENS OR CAPONS ON A SPIT WITH SAUCE

Once the hens or capons have been well roasted, take five almonds that have been peeled and well crushed with fine sugar,[2] and if you do not have sugar, add honey, and thin with lemon juice until slightly thick; use this to top the hens or serve the sauce in a small bowl, and the hens, hot, on platters.

LEMON SAUCE OVER HENS OR CAPONS

Take some hens, or one hen, or some capons or one capon, or pullets that have been slightly cooked in water; then remove from the water and put on a spit; take some peeled and well-crushed almonds and thin with the hens' cooking water; then take some lemon juice and mix all these things together with good spices and place in a pot; cook for a little while; then use this to top the roasted hen and serve very hot with a little fat.

HEN, PULLET, OR CAPON ON A SPIT WITH LIVER SAUCE

Take some pullets or capons on a spit. Take some pepper, ginger, and saffron, and crush well. Then take the animals' livers and some well-cooked egg yolks, and a bit of onion, if you wish, and crush all these things together; thin with some verjuice or other sweet liquid; then take the hens or capons or pullets, and cut up into pieces and place in a pot together with the above ingredients; stew for a little while, and then arrange on a plate and serve topped with spices.

A PREPARATION FOR SMALL BIRDS

Parboil the birds and then fry with good lard; then take their livers and some egg yolks and toasted bread that has been soaked in verjuice and parboiled parsley; crush all these things together, thinning as well with the birds' cooking water; after the birds have been fried, top with this sauce and put into a pot until cooked through.

SHAKEN SAUCE OVER PARTRIDGES IN THE FRENCH STYLE

Take a half libra of almonds and blanch well, or toast under hot ashes without burning them; then clean well with a cloth and crush; take fifty wafers made with sugar and soak in red wine; add them to be crushed with the other ingredients and thin together with the almonds, adding a generous amount of cinnamon and a sufficient amount of sugar with melegueta pepper and cloves that have all been well crushed; pass all of these things through a stamine with a little

---

2. Most probably "five almonds" per hen or capon.

verjuice. Put everything in a pot, stirring often, with a bit of rendered lard and then use this mixture to top roast partridges, and sprinkle with sugar and cinnamon.[3]

HOW TO MAKE A COW OR SUCKLING CALF OR DEER APPEAR TO BE ALIVE

First butcher the cow or veal as you would usually. Then, beginning between the hooves, skin it, but make sure that the hooves remain attached to the skin and flesh. Once this has been done, lay out the skin. Take some cumin, fennel seeds, cloves, pepper, and salt that have been well crushed until they have a powdery consistency, and sprinkle this powder on the inside of the skin; cut away the haunch downward from the knees; then remove the tripe through the flank.

If you wish to roast capons, pheasants, or other animals, put them inside the body of the cow; if you wish to roast it in the oven, arrange on a rack.

If you wish to roast it over an open flame, take a piece of wood, that is a staff, shaped like a spit, and insert; lard the cow well and cook very slowly so that it does not burn. Then fashion some irons large enough to hold it up standing. When cooked, nail the irons to a large table and tie in such a way that it stands up. Then dress it with its skin as if it were alive. Should there be a spot where the meat is missing, in its place you could use bay leaves, sage, rosemary, and myrtle; then return the skin and seal in such a way that you cannot see the irons. Then pose it as if it were alive.

You can also prepare a doe or a pig sow in this manner, and likewise it can be done with a hen, and with any other animal you wish. Note that in order to prepare animals with such ingenuity, the cook must be neither a madman nor a simpleton, but he must have a great brain.

And note, my master, that if your cook is not sharp enough, he will never prepare anything good, no matter how good it is to begin with.

KID PIE

Take some kid meat and cut up into small pieces; then make a dough with egg yolks and fine oil and use it to make the casing of the pie; put the kid meat in this casing and make a layer of the pieces of meat and a layer of spices, that is, cinnamon, ginger, pepper, and saffron, with a piece of good prosciutto. Cook in the oven, and when done make its sauce: take some egg yolks that have been beaten with rose water, verjuice, sugar, spices, and saffron, and mix together; carefully top the pie with this mixture so that it does not break the crust.

SQUAB PIE OR SQUAB POT PIE

Take some squab and cut up into pieces, with or without the belly; make a casing with eggs, sugar, and rose water; then put in the pieces. Make a layer with the pieces of squab and another layer

---

3. This recipe is called *tremolette* in the original, and is of French origin (as the suffix *-ette* reveals), from the Latin *tremulus*, "shaking," and possibly akin to the Catalan *tremolitja,* a stuffing for seafood. The title of this recipe seems to derive from the mixture of many different ingredients. According to Scully, "No written source, or close parallel, of this recipe is known" (Terence Scully, ed. and trans., *Cuoco Napoletano: The Neapolitan Recipe Collection,* a critical edition [Ann Arbor: University of Michigan Press, 2000], p. 126).

with slices of prosciutto, and a layer of good spices, sugar, and saffron. Then make a sauce with hen and squab livers; crush their meat well, adding some marjoram and sugar, and some egg yolks, verjuice, and rose water to thin the sauce. Serve with this sauce when it is all done.

FISH PIE

Take a fish and cut up into large pieces and cook with salt, wine, and verjuice; the same can be done with every fish that you wish to encase in bread—sardines, shad, mackerel, bass, and mullet, cooked on a spit or on a grill. Serve when it has cooked through; then take some pepper and saffron and vinegar and finely chopped onion, and top the pie with this mixture.

I do not intend to discuss this undesirable dish any further.

DRESSINGS OR FILLINGS

STUFFING FOR A RAM'S SHOULDER

Take a shoulder and boil; then break it open and remove the bone up to the joint; take good spices and salt-cured ram meat and chop; mix all these things together with some eggs and use the mixture to stuff the shoulder. Then take another slice of mutton meat and lay over the entire shoulder, if you wish. Lastly put the shoulder over a grill or over hot coals. When it has cooked through, serve it accompanied by a parsley sauce.

FISH DRESSING

Take ginger, saffron, figs, and apples that have been peeled, and crush all these things together well; then take some good pine nuts and thinly slice and tear open the fish; stuff the fish through its mouth and make sure that you first clean it carefully; pour a drop of oil down its mouth; then put it over a grill with rosemary and make a brine with vinegar, spices, and saffron.

KID DRESSING

Take some boiled kid's pluck and after it has been well cooked, chop until fine; take some raisins, dates, pine nuts, prosciutto, cinnamon, pepper, ginger, and sugar, and chop up all these things together; stuff the kid and then grease with fine oil or with good fat and water and salt, so that it will have a nice crust.

CAPON DRESSING

Take marjoram and parsley root and crush well; then take one or two capon breasts and crush well together; take some Parmesan cheese and two egg yolks and cinnamon, pepper, saffron, and ginger, with a little lard or prosciutto; crush all these things together; and stuff the capon with the mixture. Boil or roast, making a crust with egg yolks and rose water.

VEAL INTESTINE STUFFING

Take some intestines and clean well; scrape and make sure that they are not fatty; take some shelled walnuts and a half clove of garlic, and a little aged Parmesan cheese, fine spices and saffron, and raisins, together with some veal fat that has been chopped as finely as possible but not crushed, and two eggs; mix these things all together and stuff the intestines until filled just over halfway.

This mixture can be used to fill kid, by which I mean boiled quartered kid, as well as capons.

HOW TO MAKE GOOD BOLOGNESE SAUSAGE

Take twenty-five librae of pork meat or veal and remove the thigh nerves and the fat; chop as finely as you can; add fifteen ounces of salt and an ounce and a half of pepper, cracked and whole. Then take some large intestines and clean well and wash, and pack with the meat as tightly as possible; and make each sausage a span's length, in the Bolognese fashion; then smoke to dry.

It was in this manner that a true prince used to make them, and they are even better when two more ounces of salt are added and a half ounce more of white pepper. And of these seventeen ounces of salt, make sure that at least two are pure white salt.

You can also make them fat by using half lean meat and half fatty meat and adding a generous amount of fennel seed. But, as such, they do not keep as well.

ASPIC LIKE A CHESSBOARD

Use a generous amount of feet so that the gelatin will be thicker, and make a white broth with a bit of ginger. Once you have made the broth, take four or five capon or hen wings, and place them on a platter; then take the broth, that is, the strained decoction of the feet, and make sure that it covers the wings by a finger. Once this broth has congealed, cut out and remove one of the squares, so to speak, and put a green square in its place, just as for the colored sections in the recipe for meat aspic. You can make this dish using as many colors as you wish.

ARAGONESE SOPS

Take some chicken livers and boil and crush with a slice of bread that has been moistened in lean broth; pass through a stamine and add some pepper, saffron, and ginger, and then cook the mixture in a pot away from the flame; when done, remove from heat; then take some bread slices and toast over a flame; top with the hot mixture and serve.

CHEESE AND BREAD TORTE

Take some bread and remove the crust, thinly slice, and toast over a flame until browned. Then spread the slices with fresh butter and top with sugar and cinnamon. Take some sliced bread and fatty cheese and place on top of the cheese with more sugar and cinnamon; then put these slices in a covered torte pan over hot ashes, and top the pan with hot coals. As soon as the cheese has melted, serve.

APPLESAUCE

Take some almonds and crush until milky; then take ten or twelve previously cooked apples, crush well, and pass through a sieve; mix with the almond milk and a little rose water and sugar; cook this milk with the apples until it thickens; then remove from heat and serve in bowls.

PLUCK POTTAGE

Take some well-cooked kid pluck and finely chop with parsley and marjoram; put all these things in a pot with good fatty broth and some pepper, saffron, and beaten eggs, with a slice of prosciutto and a little rose water and verjuice and sugar; as soon as it is done, serve in bowls.

DISTILLED HAUNCH

Put the haunch in a pot large enough to accommodate it; make sure that the haunch has been well studded with good cloves and cinnamon; then put a little rose water in the pot and cover the pot.

DISTILLED HAUNCH OR HEN IN A CARAFE

Take a hen and cut up into small pieces and put in a carafe with a little rose water and some cinnamon sticks; put the carafe in a cauldron full of water and boil; make sure that when the cauldron boils the carafe is well secured and covered; put something on top of the carafe to press it down and keep it still in the water. For a sauce, cook a bit of the hen in the water in the cauldron. When it is done cooking, the hen in the carafe will be too. Remove the carafe and the juice and drink it or serve it together with the cooked meat, topped with sugar. This is not something for your mouth, my dear cook![4]

HUNGER KILLER

Take some salt-cured meat, parsley root, marjoram, minced onion, and when the salt-cured meat is done, remove; beat the other ingredients with some eggs, spices, and saffron, and serve.

ALL SORTS OF SAUCES

SAUCE FOR PULLET PIECES

Take marjoram, pullet livers, egg yolks, pepper, and cinnamon, and crush everything together and pass through a stamine with verjuice and a little rose water; and when enough has been passed through for the desired amount, top with a sufficient amount of sugar, or you can put this sauce

---

4. *Not something for your mouth*: It is well known that medieval and Renaissance "distilled" dishes—that is, foods cooked together with rose water (purported to have healing properties) by applying indirect heat—were intended for the ill (see Scully, *Cuoco Napoletano*, pp. 140–41).

over pullets that have been previously cut up and fried in good rendered lard. When you have finished frying them, remove the lard and simmer the sauce with the pullet pieces and serve on platters.

SAUCE FOR HARE

Take a hare, cut up into pieces, and parboil; then fry in good lard with a chopped onion. For a sauce, take the hare's liver, roast and crush; then take a toasted slice of bread and pass everything through a stamine with cooked wine must; after you have done this, add pepper, cinnamon, ginger, cloves, and saffron, and make it tart with verjuice or sweet with sodden wine; top the hare with this sauce.

GOOD SAUCE

Take some strong, sweet pomegranates and extract a jug of their juice; boil with a half libra of sugar and a half ounce of cinnamon. Note that it should be simmered slowly for a long time; serve hot.

LEMON SAUCE

Take almonds, blanch, and crush so as to turn them into milk; then boil the milk, that is, the almond milk, with cinnamon, ginger, and saffron; pass the milk, that is, the almonds, through a stamine with lemon juice or pomegranate and a little verjuice and lean broth; if you wish to make it stronger, add more lemons or other citrus.

SAUCE FOR MARZIPAN

Take four fingers of marzipan and crush with a bit of good ginger; thin with lemon juice or with sweet, strong pomegranate juice, and it will taste good.

SAUCE FOR EVERY TYPE OF WILD BEAST, INCLUDING DEER, BEAR, ROEBUCK, OR OTHER MEAT

Clean the meat thoroughly and roast or boil; then make the sauce as follows: take toasted bread white with a handful of the meat and with pepper and ginger or saffron; crush well together; then thin with some lean broth and verjuice and honey; boil until thick and then serve in bowls.

SARACEN SAUCE

When you cook in the Saracen style, cut the meat up into pieces and wash well with hot water; then put into a pot without its juices, and add fatty lard and vinegar and thinly sliced onion,

parsley, sage, and marjoram, and brown these things with the meat; once you have browned a good piece of the meat and it has cooked through, prepare platters full of the sauce and serve to Saracens.

EVERYDAY SAUCE

Take an ounce and a half of ginger and an ounce of pepper and eight *tornesi*[5] worth of saffron; boil with vinegar, that is, bitter wine, until all of the spices have wholly imparted their flavor to the vinegar.

NORTHERN ITALIAN SAUCE

Take parsley, mint, sage, garlic, pepper, thyme, and a leaf of chard, and toasted bread soaked in vinegar, and crush everything together; then thin with vinegar. If too strong, add some sodden wine or a little broth.

FRENCH-STYLE SAUCE FOR PARTRIDGE, HEN, OR OTHER FOWL

Take pine nuts and almonds and crush well together with good cinnamon, pepper, cloves, ginger, and saffron; thin with some bitter wine or with vinegar or with sweet or bitter pomegranate juice, and serve in bowls.

PAPAL SAUCE

Take some carrots that have been half-cooked under hot coals—as much as a finger of the red part that has been blackened;[6] then take a ginger root that has been crushed, a generous amount of cinnamon, and fine sugar; incorporate all these things together and let set overnight; then strain as you would gelatin and serve in bowls.

REGAL SAUCE

Take some strong white vinegar; then take a ginger root that has been crushed. For twelve servings, take an ounce of good whole cinnamon that has been crushed, not ground, and a half libra of fine sugar; put everything together in a small, clean pot and simmer slowly over hot coals for an hour; then strain through a stamine and serve in bowls, topped with sugar and cinnamon.

FRENCH MUSTARD

It is merely thinned with bitter or sodden wine. This is French mustard—for what it's worth.[7]

---

5. *Tornese* (plural *tornesi*): a coin originally used in Tours, and later in Italy.
6. See note 14, page 110.
7. *For what it's worth*: a note of disdain for inferior French-style mustard, that is, mustard thinned only "with bitter or sodden wine."

CUSTARD PIE IN THE SIENESE STYLE

Take twenty almonds, blanch and crush as finely as possible; take a half libra of sugar, twelve eggs, and a pint of milk, and two *quatrini*[8] worth of cinnamon, a sufficient amount of salt, a half cup of fresh *provatura* that has been crushed as fine as possible; grease a baking pan with butter and then flour and add the mixture. Place the pan or baking pan far from the flame, covered, over moderate heat. Note that in the mixture you can also add a ladleful of lasagne cooked in good broth, and as soon as it is done, top with sugar and rose water.

JULY CUSTARD

Take an ounce of good Parmesan cheese and crush thoroughly; then take twenty eggs and beat well, and a half jug of milk and a half ounce of well-crushed white ginger, a half libra of good butter and a half libra of fine sugar; mix all these things together. Then take a large pan and lay a crust over the bottom; take some grated bread, but first grease the pan with butter; and if you do not care to add this mixture to the bread stuck to the bottom of the pan, use grated cheese or flour in its place; make sure that the pan is well dressed and greased with good butter. Add this mixture to the pan and cook slowly, and top with a generous amount of sugar, as if it were a marzipan, and with rose water. Serve very hot.

This is the best custard of all down at the harbor. It is nice to go down to the harbor, but it is even better when you have this custard in the shade of an elm tree.

SCRAMBLED EGGS IN THE GERMAN STYLE

Take some eggs, beat well, and add a bit of cheese; for ten eggs, add two ounces of sugar and a bit of cinnamon, ginger, saffron, one ounce of rose water, and a little verjuice or orange juice. Cook in good butter: when the butter is hot, add these eggs to the pan, stirring all the while with a spoon so that they will not overcook; serve on a platter, topped with sugar and cinnamon.

APPLE TART IN THE FRENCH STYLE

Cook the apples however you like, in water or in cooked wine must, or in a baking pan, or under hot coals; then take pine nuts that have been soaked overnight in water and make sure they are not rancid; crush well with the apples; then take a generous amount of sugar and a bit of cinnamon, ginger, and saffron, and a cup of well-crushed pike roe that have been passed through a stamine; mix all these things together and pass through a stamine with rose water or other water; then make the dough by taking sugar, flour, oil, water, and salt, and mixing everything together; lay it over the bottom of a short pan; then add no more than a finger of this mixture; cook in the oven or over a flame as for other tortes; when it is almost done, take some wafers and sprinkle them over the tart— the wafers should be made with good sugar. As soon as it is done, top with sugar and rose water.

---

8. *Quatrino* (plural *quatrini*): a coin.

WHITE TART

Take the belly of a good fish that has been boiled, and crush well; take some almond milk, pike roe, sugar, and ginger, and thin all these things with rose water or other water; pass everything through a stamine; then cook as you would other tortes, topping with powdered wafers when it is almost done. When it has cooked through, sprinkle with candied pine nuts but first wet the torte with rose water; then remove from the pan and top with sugar and a little rose water.

Note that you need to add a sufficient amount of salt for everything. Remember that if the cook is not too sharp, all the sweet things that he makes will be either overly salted or too bland. Make sure that the cook is a glutton: not for his sake but rather for his master's.

MAESTRO MARTINO TODAY

FIFTY MODERNIZED RECIPES

Stefania Barzini

WHENEVER A RECIPE TITLE FROM MARTINO'S ORIGINAL HAS BEEN CHANGED,
REFERENCE TO THE ORIGINAL IS NOTED BENEATH THE NEW RECIPE TITLE.

GOLD OF PLEASURE SAUCE

Serve with cold meats, fish, or boiled vegetables like asparagus or artichokes.

SERVES 6

¹/₄ cup raisins
3 slices crusty bread, toasted
1 cup red wine
1 cup verjuice

1 teaspoon ground cinnamon
¹/₄ teaspoon cloves, crushed
¹/₄ teaspoon grated nutmeg
Salt and freshly ground black pepper

Soak the raisins in 1 cup of warm water until soft (about an hour). In the meantime, moisten the bread with ¹/₂ cup of red wine. When the bread has softened, squeeze out the excess wine. In a mortar (or a food processor), mash the bread and the raisins, adding the remaining red wine, the verjuice (if you do not like verjuice or prefer a stronger flavor, you can add cider vinegar instead), cinnamon, cloves, and nutmeg. Season with salt and pepper to taste.

SAUCES

DRIED PRUNE SAUCE

Serve with roasted pork or other roasted meats.

SERVES 6

15 dried prunes
1½ cups red wine
½ cup unblanched almonds
1 slice grilled country bread
3½ tablespoons verjuice
   (or equal parts lemon
   juice and cold water)

1 pinch grated ginger
1 teaspoon ground cinnamon
1 tablespoon sugar
Salt

Soak the dried prunes in the wine for 2 to 3 hours. Strain and reserve the wine, and then pit and mash the prunes.

Grind the almonds in a food processor. Soak the bread in the reserved wine; when it has softened, remove and mash, reserving the wine. In a bowl, combine the prunes, bread, and almonds, and then slowly add the reserved wine and the verjuice until you reach the desired consistency (it should be soft but not too liquid). Add the spices and sugar, strain well, and season with salt to taste.

SAUCES

GREEN SAUCE

Pour over hot or cold meats.

SERVES 6

1 cup finely chopped Swiss chard
2 or 3 fresh garlic fronds
   (or 1 garlic clove, peeled)
1 bunch fresh Italian parsley
2 sprigs fresh thyme
2 sprigs fresh mint

1 pinch freshly ground black
   pepper
1 teaspoon grated ginger
$\frac{1}{4}$ cup good wine vinegar
$\frac{1}{4}$ cup extra-virgin olive oil
Salt

In a mortar, crush the chard and garlic fronds until you obtain a smooth purée. Add the parsley, thyme, mint, pepper, and ginger; continue to mix. Add the vinegar and olive oil, stirring constantly, until you obtain a creamy consistency. Season with salt to taste and pour over the meat. This sauce can also be made by puréeing all the ingredients in a blender.

SAUCES

GRAPE SAUCE

Particularly good with roasted or boiled meats.

SERVES 6

2 slices country bread
½ cup verjuice or vinegar
1 pound black grapes
1 teaspoon grated ginger

1 teaspoon ground cinnamon
2 pinches grated nutmeg
1 pinch freshly ground black pepper
Salt

Soften the bread in half of the verjuice. Purée the softened bread with the grapes in a food processor. Stir in the ginger, cinnamon, nutmeg, and pepper, and gradually pour in the remaining verjuice. Season with salt to taste. Transfer to a saucepan, bring to a boil, and simmer over low heat for about 30 minutes. Stir constantly to prevent the bread from sticking to the pan. Serve warm.

SAUCES

MULBERRY SAUCE

An ideal accompaniment for roast or boiled chicken, and especially for roast goose.

SERVES 6

$^1/_2$ cup peeled almonds
2 slices country bread, crusts
   removed
1 pound mulberries
1 teaspoon grated ginger
$^1/_2$ teaspoon ground cinnamon

$^1/_2$ teaspoon grated nutmeg
Salt
Freshly ground black pepper
3 tablespoons verjuice
   (or 1 tablespoon apple vinegar
   and 2 tablespoons verjuice)

Purée the almonds and bread in a food processor. Add the mulberries and continue to blend for a few minutes (the seeds of the mulberries must also be ground). Transfer to a bowl; add the ginger, cinnamon, and nutmeg, and salt and pepper to taste; add the verjuice, stir well, and serve.

SAUCES

YELLOW PEPPER SAUCE FOR FISH

Perfect for boiled and roast fish.

SERVES 6

2 slices country bread, with crust
³/₄ cup red wine
¹/₄ cup aromatic balsamic vinegar
    (see note below)
¹/₄ teaspoon saffron stigmas,
    infused in 2 tablespoons hot water
    and strained

1 teaspoon freshly ground black pepper,
    plus extra to taste
1 teaspoon ground cinnamon
1 teaspoon grated nutmeg
1 teaspoon grated ginger
Salt

Toast the bread slices in the oven or toaster. In a heavy pot, combine the bread, wine, and balsamic vinegar; bring to a boil, stirring constantly; add the saffron infusion and continue to cook for a few minutes. Transfer to a food processor, add the pepper, cinnamon, nutmeg, and ginger, and purée. Season with salt to taste, and add more pepper, if desired.

Note: Two types of balsamic vinegar are available today in North America: "aromatic" balsamic vinegar, easy to find in most supermarkets and gourmet stores, and "traditional" balsamic vinegar from Modena (which bears the mark of the Consorzio Produttori Aceto Balsamico Tradizionale di Modena). Be sure not to use the latter for this recipe, which would make it too syrupy (and much too expensive!).

SAUCES

WHITE GARLIC SAUCE

This sauce is ideal with boiled chicken but also goes well with steamed vegetables (especially asparagus and artichokes).

SERVES 6

3 ounces ($^3/_4$ cup) blanched almonds
2 garlic cloves, peeled
2 slices white bread, crusts removed,
    roughly chopped

2 cups well-strained chicken
    stock, hot
Salt and freshly ground black
    pepper

Crush the almonds in a mortar, add the garlic cloves, and continue to work. Soak the bread in 1 cup of the hot stock and crush until you obtain a smooth purée; add the garlic and almonds to the crushed bread. Mix well and add the remaining stock in a thin, even stream, working constantly to obtain the desired consistency. Season with salt and pepper to taste.

SAUCES

VIOLET GARLIC SAUCE

This sauce has a very distinct taste, and it should be served with strongly flavored dishes like boiled beef or roast pork. The fruit juice makes it sweeter than the previous sauce.

SERVES 6

1 pound red grapes (or 1 pound black cherries)

3 ounces ($^3/_4$ cup) blanched almonds

2 garlic cloves, peeled

2 slices white bread, crusts removed and roughly chopped

Salt and freshly ground black pepper

To obtain the grape juice, wash and crush the grapes, and pass through a food mill so as to eliminate the seeds (if you use cherries, remove their pits beforehand). Reduce the juice over medium heat in a saucepan for 15 minutes until you obtain a syrupy consistency. Crush or purée the almonds; add the garlic cloves and continue to crush. Soak the bread in part of the grape juice and crush well until you obtain a creamy purée; add the garlic and almonds to the bread, working constantly. Thin the mixture with the remaining grape juice until you obtain the desired consistency. Season generously with salt and pepper.

SOUPS AND PASTA IN BROTH

BLANCMANGE OVER CAPON

(SEE "FIRST: HOW TO MAKE A BLANCMANGE OVER CAPON," PAGE 62)

SERVES 6

1 capon (about 3 pounds)
1 stalk celery, chopped
1 large carrot, chopped
1 large onion, chopped
1 large potato, finely diced
1/2 fennel bulb, finely diced
1 bunch Italian parsley,
    finely chopped
1 sprig rosemary, finely chopped
2 fresh sage leaves, torn
1 bay leaf
Coarse salt

2 large slices country bread, crusts
    removed
1 cup blanched almonds
1 tablespoon grated ginger
1/2 cup verjuice
1/4 teaspoon saffron stigmas, infused
    in 2 tablespoons hot water and
    strained
2 egg yolks, beaten
Freshly ground black pepper
2 ounces freshly grated Parmigiano
    Reggiano (optional)

Place the capon in a large pot together with the celery, carrot, onion, potato, and fennel. Add water to cover. Add the parsley, rosemary, sage, and bay leaf, and salt to taste. Cover the pot and bring to a boil. Boil over high heat for 5 minutes and then simmer for 2 hours.

When the stock is ready, remove the capon from the pot; discard the skin and bones, and reserve the meat.

Soak the bread in 1 cup of the stock. Crush or purée the almonds; cube the capon breast (reserving the other meat), and add the bread and capon breast to the almonds; continue to work for about a minute. Transfer the mixture to a large bowl and slowly add the remaining stock; continue to work. Add the ginger and verjuice and transfer to a large pot; simmer for about 20 minutes, stirring occasionally. Slice and add the remaining capon meat and the saffron infusion. Continue cooking for about 10 minutes. Remove from heat and add the egg yolks. Season with salt and pepper to taste. Add the Parmigiano Reggiano, if desired, and serve immediately.

SOUPS AND PASTA IN BROTH

CONSOMMÉ

(SEE "HOW TO MAKE CONSOMMÉ WITH CAPON, PHEASANT,
PARTRIDGE, ROEBUCK, SQUAB, OR WILD SQUAB," PAGE 63)

This excellent broth has remarkable restorative properties: it is meant to be served to the ill and to persons with weak constitutions. Until a decade ago, it was often prescribed for children recovering from common childhood illnesses. This practice continues even today in the Italian countryside.

SERVES 2

2 squabs, cleaned, rinsed, bones crushed, and fat removed
3/4 pound lean beef, cubed
1 onion, finely chopped
1 garlic clove, finely chopped
1 carrot, finely chopped
1 celery stalk, finely chopped

6 fresh sage leaves
1 sprig rosemary
2 fresh bay leaves
1 small cinnamon stick
3 or 4 cloves
20 to 30 black peppercorns
4 tablespoons red wine

Put the squab and the beef in a saucepan. Add cold water to cover. Add the vegetables, herbs, and spices, and simmer over low heat for 3½ hours. Ten minutes before it is done, add the red wine. The consommé should be very thick and does not need to be seasoned with salt: the meat and vegetables are sufficiently salty.

SOUPS AND PASTA IN BROTH

ZANZARELLI

(SEE "HOW TO MAKE *ZANZARELLI*," PAGE 64)

This soup is the ancestor of the famous dish stracciatella, *still enjoyed throughout Italy today. The modern name means "little rags": when you drop in the eggs, they turn into streaks that resemble very thin torn rags. It is an ideal dish for children and the elderly.*

SERVES 6

1 chicken (about 3 pounds)
1 stalk celery, chopped
1 large carrot, chopped
1 large onion, chopped
1 large potato, finely diced
½ fennel bulb, finely diced
1 bunch Italian parsley, finely chopped
1 sprig rosemary, finely chopped
2 fresh sage leaves, torn
1 bay leaf

Coarse salt
¼ teaspoon saffron stigmas, infused in 2 tablespoons hot water and strained
5 eggs
¾ cup freshly grated Parmigiano Reggiano
¾ cup grated stale (or slightly toasted) bread
1½ teaspoons mixed spices (pepper, cinnamon, nutmeg, ginger, and cloves)

Place the chicken in a large pot together with the celery, carrot, onion, potato, and fennel. Add water to cover. Add the parsley, rosemary, sage, and bay leaf, and coarse salt to taste. Cover the pot and bring to a boil. Boil over high heat for 5 minutes and then simmer for 2 hours; strain. You should obtain roughly 8 to 9 cups of stock.

Bring the stock to a boil and add the saffron infusion. Beat the eggs together with the Parmigiano and the grated bread until you obtain a smooth purée. When the saffron infusion has fully imparted its color to the stock, add the egg mixture, stir well, and continue to simmer for a few moments until the egg mixture has taken (that is, has formed into streaks). Remove from heat, season with salt to taste, and add the spices. Serve hot.

SOUPS AND PASTA IN BROTH

FARRO WITH CHICKEN,
CAPON, OR OTHER MEAT STOCK

(SEE "FARRO WITH CAPON BROTH OR OTHER MEAT BROTH," PAGES 64–65)

A classic, heavy winter soup. Farro is sometimes referred to as emmer wheat.

SERVES 6

3 tablespoons extra-virgin olive oil
1 onion, finely chopped
1 celery stalk, finely chopped
1 carrot, finely chopped
1 potato, peeled and diced
1/2 pound farro, hulled
1/4 teaspoon saffron stigmas, infused in
    2 tablespoons hot water and strained

8 cups chicken, capon, or other meat stock
    (prepare as above for *zanzarelli,* page
    151), hot
1 bunch Italian parsley, finely chopped
Freshly ground black pepper
3 egg yolks
1/2 cup freshly grated Parmigiano Reggiano
Salt

Heat the oil in a pot (preferably earthenware); add the onion, celery, carrot, and potato. When the onion has become translucent, add the farro and toast for a few minutes, stirring well. Add the saffron infusion to the stock and then add the stock to the pot. Cover and simmer for 40 minutes or until it becomes creamy and the farro has softened. Remove from heat; add the parsley and pepper. Beat the egg yolks with the Parmigiano and add to the pot. Season with salt to taste and serve hot.

SOUPS AND PASTA IN BROTH

RAVIOLI FOR NON-LENTEN TIMES
SERVES 6

For the pasta:
2¼ cups flour, plus extra for dusting
3 eggs
1 tablespoon extra-virgin olive oil
Pinch of salt

For the filling:
¾ pound fresh ricotta
¾ cup freshly grated Parmigiano Reggiano
4 ounces prosciutto, finely chopped
1 whole egg
1 egg yolk
1 bunch Italian parsley, finely chopped

Grated zest of 1 lemon
Salt and freshly ground black pepper
1 teaspoon grated nutmeg
½ teaspoon ground cinnamon
2 or 3 cloves, crushed

For the broth:
8 cups chicken, capon, or other meat stock
    (prepare as above for *zanzarelli*, page
    151), hot
¼ teaspoon saffron stigmas, infused in
    2 tablespoons hot water and strained
Freshly grated Parmigiano Reggiano

Make the pasta by first placing the flour in a food processor. Start the motor, add the eggs one at a time, and then add the olive oil and salt. Continue to work for about 10 seconds. Remove the dough to a well-floured surface and knead until entirely smooth (as smooth "as a baby's bottom"); transfer to a bowl, cover with a kitchen towel, and let set for 30 minutes in a cool, dry place.

In the meantime, make the filling by incorporating all the ingredients in a bowl.

On a well-floured surface, roll the pasta out into very thin sheets (for best results, use a pasta machine). Distribute teaspoon-sized portions of the filling across half of each sheet, about 3 inches apart. Then fold the other half of each sheet over the filling; use a knife or pasta wheel to cut out the ravioli, and pinch around the edges to seal.

Bring the stock to a boil, and add the saffron infusion. Lower the heat and let the broth simmer gently. Carefully drop the ravioli into the simmering broth and cook for about 5 minutes or until *al dente*. Remove the ravioli with a slotted spoon and transfer to a soup tureen; add the broth and top with Parmigiano.

SOUPS AND PASTA IN BROTH

POTTAGE OF GREENS

Use only fresh vegetables for this soup. One or two crostini—toasted slices of yesterday's bread—can be placed in the bottom of each serving bowl before adding the soup or served on the side.

SERVES 6

3 tablespoons extra-virgin olive oil
1 clove garlic, peeled
1 pound Swiss chard, stems removed, roughly chopped
1 pound borage, stems removed, roughly chopped
8 cups beef broth (prepare as above for consommé, page 150, omitting the squab and using twice the amount of beef)
1 bunch Italian parsley, finely chopped
½ bunch fresh mint, finely chopped
Grated zest of 1 lemon
Salt and freshly ground black pepper

Heat the olive oil in a large pot and add the garlic. Remove the garlic as soon as it begins to brown (make sure that it does not burn because it will give a bitter taste to the olive oil). Add the chard and borage to the pot, and when the greens have wilted, add the broth and cook uncovered over low heat for 15 minutes. Transfer to a food processor and purée until you obtain a smooth, liquid consistency. Return to the pot, bring to a boil, and cook for 5 minutes. A few moments before removing from heat, add the parsley, mint, and lemon zest, and season with salt and pepper to taste. Serve hot.

SOUPS AND PASTA IN BROTH

RED CHICKPEA BROTH

This ancient recipe is still very popular in central and southern Italy. It was a classic dish of the Etruscans, who were crazy about it and used to add long, broad noodles to it—fresh lagane *or* lasagnette.

SERVES 6

3 tablespoons (plus a little more) extra-virgin olive oil
1 clove garlic, peeled
¼ pound smoked pancetta, diced
1 pound dried chickpeas, soaked overnight in cool water with a pinch of baking powder, and strained and rinsed
1 bunch rosemary

1 bunch sage
1 teaspoon black peppercorns, or more to taste
½ teaspoon ground cinnamon
Small bunch Italian parsley, finely chopped
Salt
½ pound spaghetti, broken into large pieces (optional)

Heat the oil in a pot (preferably earthenware); add the garlic and pancetta. When the garlic has begun to brown, add the chickpeas, cook for a few minutes, and then add cool water to cover. Add the rosemary, sage, peppercorns, and cinnamon; cover and cook for 2 hours over very low heat until the chickpeas have become very tender. At this point, strain half of the chickpeas (returning the strained liquid back to the pot), pass through a food mill or purée in a food processor, and return to the pot. Continue to cook for a few minutes before adding the parsley. Season with salt to taste, add 2 or 3 tablespoons of olive oil, and serve hot.

For those who prefer a heartier and tastier dish, spaghetti that has been broken into large pieces can be added while the soup is still boiling. Continue to cook over low heat until the pasta is *al dente,* stirring all the while so that it does not stick to the bottom. The starch in the pasta will give the soup a creamier consistency. Remove from heat, drizzle with olive oil, and before serving top with freshly grated Parmigiano Reggiano, if desired.

SOUPS AND PASTA IN BROTH

FRESH FAVA BEANS WITH MEAT BROTH

SERVES 6

3 tablespoons (plus a little more)
    extra-virgin olive oil
1 onion, thinly sliced
12 ounces smoked pancetta, diced
3 pounds fresh fava beans, removed
    from their pods and peeled

8 cups chicken or beef stock (prepare
    as above for *zanzarelli*, page 151), hot
1 bunch basil leaves
1 bunch Italian parsley, finely chopped
Salt
Freshly ground black pepper

Heat the oil in a pot (preferably earthenware); add the onion and pancetta. When they begin to brown, add the fava beans and cook for a few moments; then add the stock and simmer for 30 minutes uncovered (the beans should be tender). At this point, strain half of the fava beans (returning the strained liquid back to the pot), pass through a food mill or purée in a food processor, and return to the pot. Continue to cook for about 10 minutes. A few moments before removing from heat, add the herbs (the basil leaves should be left whole) and season with salt and pepper to taste. Serve hot, drizzled with olive oil.

SOUPS AND PASTA IN BROTH

WINTER SQUASH SOUP

(SEE "COOKING SQUASH," PAGE 72)

Serve this pumpkin soup with crostini *in the bottom of each bowl or on the side.*

SERVES 6

3 tablespoons extra-virgin olive oil

1 onion, thinly sliced

1 medium-sized pumpkin (about 4 pounds), peeled, seeds and fibers removed, and cut up into 1-inch-thick cubes or slices

3 tablespoons verjuice, or 2 tablespoons aromatized balsamic vinegar mixed with 1 tablespoon room temperature water

8 to 9 cups chicken or beef stock (prepare as above for *zanzarelli,* page 151), hot

$\frac{1}{4}$ teaspoon saffron stigmas, infused in 2 tablespoons hot water and strained

Salt

3 egg yolks

2 ounces freshly grated Parmigiano Reggiano

Freshly ground black pepper

1 teaspoon ground cinnamon

1 teaspoon grated nutmeg

1 teaspoon freshly grated ginger

Heat the oil in a pot (preferably earthenware); add the onion. When the onion has begun to brown, add the pumpkin and cook over high heat for a few minutes. Then add the verjuice or balsamic-vinegar-and-water mixture. Lower heat, cover, and simmer for about 5 minutes. Add the stock and the saffron infusion, season with salt to taste, and simmer for about 20 minutes (or until the pulp has become very tender). Remove from heat and pass the soup through a food mill or purée in a food processor until you obtain a creamy consistency. Allow the soup to cool. Beat the egg yolks with the Parmigiano and the pepper and then add to the soup. Add the cinnamon, nutmeg, and ginger, stir well, and serve at room temperature.

SOUPS AND PASTA IN BROTH

ROMAN-STYLE MACARONI

This recipe is an ancient version of one of Rome's most famous dishes: cacio e pepe, *long noodles with sheep's milk cheese and freshly cracked pepper. The shepherds of the Roman countryside prepared their meals with the ingredients at hand, just cheese and pepper. Maestro Martino adds sweet spices: in this modernized version, nutmeg helps to refine the flavor.*

SERVES 6

1½ tablespoons salt
1¼ pounds spaghetti
1½ cups freshly grated
   pecorino romano,
   plus extra if desired

1 teaspoon freshly
   grated nutmeg
Freshly ground
   black pepper

Bring 4 quarts of water to a boil and add the salt. Add the spaghetti and cook until *al dente*. Reserve ½ cup of the pasta's cooking water; strain spaghetti and transfer to a warm tureen. Add the cheese, nutmeg, pepper, and reserved cooking water. Toss and serve immediately.

SOUPS AND PASTA IN BROTH

FINE BROTH OF BREAD, EGG, AND CHEESE

(SEE "HOW TO MAKE A FINE BROTH OF BREAD, EGG, AND CHEESE," PAGE 65)

SERVES 6

8 cups beef stock (prepare as above for *zanzarelli*, page 151)

¼ teaspoon saffron stigmas, infused in 2 tablespoons hot water and strained

4 large slices crusty stale bread, in 1-inch cubes

5 egg yolks, beaten

1 cup freshly grated Parmigiano Reggiano

Salt and freshly ground black pepper

Bring the stock to a boil; reduce to a simmer and add the saffron infusion. Add the bread and continue to cook for 15 to 20 minutes, until an even, dense consistency has been obtained. Let the soup cool. Beat the egg yolks with the Parmigiano and salt and pepper to taste. Fold into the soup and serve at room temperature.

SOUPS AND PASTA IN BROTH

ROMAN BROCCOLI

Martino's Roman broccoli is the famous green cauliflower, distinguished by its color and its pointed florets. It is cultivated almost exclusively in Latium. You can use common white cauliflower in its place.

SERVES 6

3 tablespoons extra-virgin olive oil
1 clove garlic, peeled
1 spicy red pepper *(peperoncino)*, seeds removed, finely chopped
4 ounces pancetta, diced
7 or 8 cherry tomatoes, sliced in half

1 large head cauliflower (about 2 pounds), cut up into large florets
Salt
½ pound spaghetti, broken into large pieces (optional)

Heat the oil in a pot (preferably earthenware); add the garlic and red pepper. When the garlic begins to brown, add the pancetta and brown for a few moments. Add the tomatoes and cook over high heat for 3 or 4 minutes. Add the cauliflower, stir well, and then add 8 cups cold water. Cover and bring to a boil. Reduce to a simmer and cook for 30 minutes. Pass through a food mill or purée in a food processor. Season with salt to taste. If desired, return to the pot, bring to a gentle simmer, add the spaghetti, and cook until *al dente*. Serve hot.

SOUPS AND PASTA IN BROTH

BLANCMANGE IN THE CATALAN STYLE

Blancmange is a classic dish of medieval cuisine, still prepared today, although modern versions vary greatly from the original recipes. The name itself indicates its characteristics: bianco mangiare *in Italian, or "white food." It is composed of entirely white ingredients: rice, blanched almonds, and chicken breast.*

Refreshing and light as it was, this ubiquitous pittance was also considered an ideal dish for the ill and convalescent. It was typically flavored with spices and sugar, although Martino omits the sweetening agent.

The present recipe follows Martino's preparation almost to the letter so as to allow diners to taste its true essence. The addition of salt to the rose water and spices imparts a sweet-and-sour flavor.

SERVES 6

1½ pounds blanched almonds, ground in a food processor (not overly fine)

2 tablespoons rice flour

8 cups chicken stock (prepare as above for *zanzarelli,* page 151)

1 boiled chicken breast, white only (use the meat from the stock), puréed in a food processor

Salt

½ cup rose water

1 teaspoon grated nutmeg

1 teaspoon ground cinnamon

3 or 4 cloves, crushed

Freshly ground black pepper

¼ teaspoon saffron stigmas, infused in 2 tablespoons hot water and strained (optional)

Combine the ground almonds and rice flour in a pot; stirring constantly, add 4 cups of stock in a thin, even stream. Then add the chicken breast and remaining stock; season with salt, cover, and simmer until the mixture thickens into a thick, creamy consistency. Remove from heat, add the rose water, and fold in the nutmeg, cinnamon, and cloves. Season with pepper to taste; serve hot. (If desired, the saffron infusion can be added to make a "yellow" blancmange.)

ROASTS AND STEWED MEATS

CIVET WITH GAME

(SEE "HOW TO PREPARE CIVET WITH GAME," PAGES 51–52)

Traditionally, recipes for civet call for the meat to be boiled in its own juices, thus retaining all of the animal's fat. Not only does Martino boil the meat, he then roasts it. In the present recipe, the meat is simply roasted, thus making it more tender, less heavy, and less stringy.

SERVES 6

6 ounces good lard, diced
I medium-sized pheasant (about
    4½ pounds) or 2 smaller ones,
    cut up into pieces
I cup wine vinegar
Black peppercorns
2 cups red wine
Salt

I½ cups chicken stock (prepare as above
    for *zanzarelli,* page 151)
3 large slices crusty bread, slightly toasted
3 ounces almonds, unpeeled
4 ounces raisins
I teaspoon ground cinnamon
I teaspoon freshly grated ginger
I large onion, thinly sliced

In a large sauté pan, heat half of the lard over medium heat until it liquefies; add the pheasant. When it has browned, add the vinegar, peppercorns, and half of the wine. Season with salt and cook for a few moments over high heat; add the stock, cover, and continue to cook over low heat for 45 minutes, until very tender. In the meantime, soak the bread in the remaining wine. In a food processor, grind the almonds together with the raisins, cinnamon, and ginger until you obtain a fine paste. In another pan, cook the onion in the remaining lard; add the almond-and-raisin paste to the pan, and simmer for a few moments. Distribute the pheasant on a serving platter, top with the cooked almond paste, and serve immediately.

ROASTS AND STEWED MEATS

HOW TO DRESS A ROAST SUCKLING PIG

Maestro Martino's recipe calls for a suckling pig, cleaned of its innards, turned inside out, and then stuffed. These days, it is not so easy to find a whole suckling pig, nor is it common to find a butcher who knows how to perform the necessary incision. The present version is much simpler but just as tasty.

SERVES 6

3 eggs

6 ounces pork livers, finely chopped

1/3 pound smoked pancetta, finely chopped

2 garlic cloves, peeled and finely chopped

1/2 cup mixture of finely chopped Italian parsley, fresh mint, dill, and marjoram

3/4 cup freshly grated Parmigiano Reggiano

Salt

1/4 teaspoon saffron stigmas, infused in 2 tablespoons hot water and strained

1 pork shoulder (about 3 1/2 pounds), well pounded

1/3 cup (plus a little more) extra-virgin olive oil

1 sprig fresh bay leaves, finely chopped

1 sprig rosemary, finely chopped

Black peppercorns

1 cup red wine

In a bowl, beat the eggs and add the livers, pancetta, garlic, herb mixture, and Parmigiano. Season with salt and add the saffron infusion. Rub this mixture over the pork shoulder and then fold the shoulder over itself and tie with butcher's string.

In another bowl, beat the olive oil together with the bay leaves, rosemary, peppercorns, and more salt. Grease a large sauté pan with olive oil, place the pork shoulder in the pan, put over high heat, and brown the pork shoulder on all sides. Add the wine, and when it has evaporated, lower the heat and continue to cook for about an hour, brushing the meat every so often with the oil and herb emulsion. When the meat has become very tender, remove from heat, let cool, slice, and serve immediately.

ROASTS AND STEWED MEATS

ROAST CHICKEN

(SEE "HOW TO PREPARE ROAST PULLET," PAGE 55)

Maestro Martino's recipe for roast chicken is still perfectly viable today—save for the fact that chickens were probably much smaller in his day. He used the juice of bitter oranges and added sugar. The present version does exactly the opposite: it uses sweet oranges and salt. The result is a particularly delicious formula for sweet-and-sour chicken.

SERVES 6

One 3½-pound (or larger) free-range
   chicken, plucked and cleaned
1 whole lemon, well washed and dried
2 or 3 fresh bay leaves
1 sprig rosemary
2 or 3 sage leaves

Black peppercorns
2 or 3 tablespoons extra-virgin olive oil
Salt
Juice of 3 sweet oranges combined with
   ½ cup verjuice and 1 tablespoon rose
   water, at room temperature

Preheat the oven to 400°F. Stuff the chicken with the whole lemon, bay leaves, rosemary, sage, and peppercorns. Rub well with the olive oil and season with salt. Arrange in a roasting pan on a rack, place in the preheated oven, and roast for about 1 hour (more for larger birds) or until the thickest part of the haunch exudes its juices when pierced with a fork. Baste with its own juices so that it does not dry out. After about 45 minutes, pour the orange juice, verjuice, and rose water over the bird. When done roasting, season with salt and serve.

ROASTS AND STEWED MEATS

ROMAN-STYLE *COPPIETTE*

(SEE "HOW TO PREPARE ROMAN-STYLE *COPPIETTE*," PAGE 56)

The present recipe differs slightly from that proposed by Maestro Martino, whose coppiette *were a sort of shish kebab.*

SERVES 6

6 thick slices beef fillet
Fennel seeds
Coriander seeds

6 thin slices pancetta
Salt and freshly ground
   black pepper

Cut each slice of beef in its middle so that it is divided neatly into 2 pieces but remains attached by a thin piece (these are the *coppiette,* or "little couples"); pound well with a meat tenderizer. Sprinkle the surface of the meat with the fennel and coriander seeds, and then lay a slice of pancetta on each piece. Place the assembled *coppiette* on a heated and lightly greased ridged steak pan and cook for about 10 minutes (or less if desired rare), turning just once. Before removing from heat, season with salt and pepper. Serve hot.

ROASTS AND STEWED MEATS

KID WITH GARLIC

(SEE "HOW TO COOK A QUARTER OF KID WITH GARLIC," PAGES 57–58)

This tasty dish has a particularly modern flavor. While Maestro Martino uses verjuice, the present recipe calls for lemon juice, thus giving a less bitter taste.

SERVES 6

1 kid haunch
2 garlic cloves, peeled and finely chopped
2 ounces pancetta, finely diced
3 egg yolks
Juice of 1 lemon
1 teaspoon freshly ground black pepper
Salt

¼ teaspoon saffron stigmas, infused in
   2 tablespoons hot water and strained
½ cup beef stock (prepare as above for
   zanzarelli, page 151)
3 tablespoons extra-virgin olive oil
2 heaping tablespoons finely chopped
   Italian parsley

Preheat the oven to 400°F. Lard the haunch by making incisions all over and inserting the garlic and pancetta. Gently beat the egg yolks with the lemon juice, pepper, salt, saffron infusion, and stock. Brush meat well with this emulsion, reserving the remainder for basting. Grease a roasting pan with the olive oil, put the haunch in the pan, and place in the preheated oven for about an hour. Baste often using the remaining lemon emulsion. A few minutes before the kid is done, pour the remaining emulsion over it and sprinkle with parsley. Before removing, make sure that the lemon emulsion has become creamy but has not overly thickened. Serve hot.

ROASTS AND STEWED MEATS

HOW TO PREPARE THE LIVERS OF FOWL, PULLET, PORK, OR OTHER ANIMALS

The present recipe calls for pig livers because they are perhaps the most flavorful, although you can use any type of liver that you like.

Maestro Martino reminds us not to cook them too long. He's perfectly right, especially when you consider that in his time the tendency was to overcook all types of meat. This is just another example of the extraordinary modernity in Martino's technique. Liver in general should be cooked only briefly, so that the inside remains pink; otherwise it becomes hard and stringy.

SERVES 6

½ cup extra-virgin olive oil
Freshly ground black pepper
1 teaspoon grated nutmeg
1 teaspoon ground cinnamon
1 teaspoon fennel seeds

9 pork livers, membranes removed,
   well washed
½ pound caul fat
8 thin slices smoked pancetta
½ cup red wine

In a mixing bowl, combine the olive oil with the pepper, nutmeg, cinnamon, and fennel seeds. Add the pork livers and let them marinate for 1 hour. When the livers are done marinating, put the caul fat in a separate bowl and add lukewarm water to cover; soak for 10 minutes. Wrap each liver first in a slice of pancetta and then in the caul fat; cook on a preheated ridged steak pan. After a few minutes, brush with the wine and turn, making sure they cook well on both sides. Serve hot.

ROASTS AND STEWED MEATS

RASHERS

(SEE "HOW TO PREPARE RASHERS," PAGE 58)

Martino's rashers, or carbonata *in his Italian, bring to mind* straccetti, *a popular dish of central Italy: thinly sliced beef cooked in olive oil (*straccetti *literally means "little rags"). He preferred marbled salt-cured pork for his rashers, but beef will make it less heavy and thus easier to digest. Of course, you can also use prosciutto or cooked ham.*

SERVES 6

2 pounds beef fillet, sliced paper thin
3 tablespoons extra-virgin olive oil
1 garlic clove, peeled
2 or 3 fresh bay leaves
1 sprig rosemary
4 tablespoons aromatic balsamic
   vinegar

Juice of 1 lemon
Juice of 1 orange
Freshly ground black pepper
1 teaspoon ground cinnamon
1 tablespoon finely chopped
   Italian parsley
Salt

Cut each slice of beef into 3 or 4 pieces. In a frying pan large enough to accommodate all of the meat, heat the olive oil; add the garlic and cook over low heat for a few minutes (do not allow the garlic to brown). Add the beef, together with the bay leaves, rosemary, vinegar, lemon and orange juice, pepper, cinnamon, and parsley; sauté 6 or 7 minutes over high heat (be careful not to overcook). When the liquid has reduced, season with salt and serve hot.

VEGETABLES

CRUSHED FAVA BEANS

This fava bean purée is a classic of southern Italian cuisine. In Apulia, it is accompanied by chicory, first boiled and then sautéed with olive oil, garlic, and red chili pepper. It can also be spread over toasted slices of crusty bread that have been rubbed with garlic and drizzled with olive oil.

SERVES 6

4½ pounds fresh fava beans, removed from their pods
Salt
1 spring onion

Extra-virgin olive oil, as needed
1 teaspoon cumin
Freshly ground black pepper

Boil the fava beans in salted water until tender; strain, reserving 1 cup of the cooking water. Chop roughly half of the spring onion and pass through a vegetable mill together with the favas, and transfer to a mixing bowl. Add the olive oil to the purée in a thin, even stream until you obtain the desired consistency (if too thick, add the reserved cooking water). Fold in the cumin. Thinly slice the remaining spring onion and sprinkle over the purée; top with freshly ground pepper, drizzle with olive oil, and serve.

VEGETABLES

MUSHROOMS

(SEE "HOW TO COOK MUSHROOMS," PAGE 68)

Fresh porcini mushrooms are difficult to find in the United States and they tend to be very expensive. Some retailers like Urbani in New York bring them in fresh from Italy (in spring and fall), and they also "flash-freeze" them so that they are available nearly all year round. While dried porcini are acceptable in risotto and with pasta, never use reconstituted dried porcini for this dish.

Generally, the fresh porcini sold in this country have already been cleaned. If they have not, use a damp cloth to wipe away any dirt (never wash them, because they will lose their flavor and become spongy). If a little dirt remains, it certainly will not hurt you. As they say in Italy, Quel che non strozza ingrassa, *"If it doesn't make you choke, it can only be good for you."*

SERVES 6

6 large porcini mushrooms
3 tablespoons extra-virgin
   olive oil

2 garlic cloves, peeled and minced
1 bunch Italian parsley, finely chopped
Salt and freshly ground black pepper

Slice off the tips of the porcini stems and then slice the mushrooms in half lengthwise. In a bowl, combine the olive oil, garlic, parsley, salt, and pepper, and then rub this emulsion gently over the mushrooms. Cook on a hot griddle, turning once, about 5 minutes per side. Serve hot.

VEGETABLES

FRIED SQUASH

This dish can be prepared a day in advance.

SERVES 6

1 small pumpkin (about 2 pounds), peeled, seeds and fibers removed, and very thinly sliced (no more than $1/10$ inch thick)
Salt
Flour for dredging
1 large slice crusty bread with crust removed, puréed in a food processor

2 garlic cloves, peeled and minced
1 tablespoon fennel seeds, crushed
$1/4$ teaspoon powdered saffron
1 cup verjuice, or $1/2$ cup aromatized balsamic vinegar mixed with $1/2$ cup wine vinegar
Extra-virgin olive oil for frying
Freshly ground black pepper

Parboil the pumpkin slices in boiling salted water (about 2 minutes), strain, and dry with a kitchen towel. Dredge in the flour. In a bowl combine the bread white, garlic, fennel seeds, saffron, and the verjuice or vinegar mixture; this is the sauce. In a frying pan, heat 3 inches of olive oil to 375°F and fry the pumpkin slices; remove and put on paper towels to drain off the excess oil. Arrange the pumpkin slices on a serving platter, pour the sauce over them, cover, and allow to macerate at room temperature for 2 or 3 hours. Before serving, season with salt and pepper to taste.

SAVORY PIES

NEAPOLITAN RUSTIC TORTE

(SEE "WHITE TORTE," PAGE 80)

Maestro Martino's white torte calls to mind this Neapolitan torta rustica *and many other southern Italian tortes. In Naples, salami or prosciutto is added to the filling for seasoning, but in this recipe only sweet spices are used to evoke the flavors of medieval cuisine.*

SERVES 6

For the crust:
2$^1/_2$ cups flour, plus extra
    for dusting
$^3/_4$ cup sugar
1 teaspoon freshly grated ginger
Salt
8 tablespoons butter, softened,
    plus extra for greasing
    the pan
3 egg yolks

For the filling:
1$^1/_2$ pounds ricotta
4 eggs
$^3/_4$ cup freshly grated Parmigiano Reggiano
$^1/_3$ pound mozzarella, diced
$^1/_3$ pound smoked provola, diced
1 tablespoon finely chopped Italian parsley
1 teaspoon ground cinnamon
1 teaspoon grated nutmeg
Salt and freshly ground black pepper

Make the crust by combining the flour, sugar, ginger, and salt in a well on a well-dusted surface; place the butter and egg yolks in the center of the well, and then use a fork to beat the eggs; slowly incorporate the flour, beginning with the inside (without breaking the wall of the well); when you have obtained a firm mixture, begin to work it with the tips of your fingers and continue until all the ingredients are combined (short crusts like this one should be worked as little as possible so that they do not lose their flakiness); shape the dough into a ball, and let it rest for 30 minutes, covered, in a cool place. Preheat the oven to 400°F.

In the meantime, make the filling. In a mixing bowl, crush the ricotta with a fork, and then add the eggs and mix until you obtain a creamy consistency; add the Parmigiano, mozzarella, provola, parsley, cinnamon, and nutmeg, and season with salt and pepper to taste.

Next assemble the torte. Grease with butter a 9-inch tart or quiche pan with 2-inch walls; divide the dough in half and roll out each half into disks with a diameter of about 11 inches; place one of the disks in the pan, add the filling, top with the remaining disk, remove the excess dough, and pinch to seal around the edges; season the crust with salt.

Bake the torte in the preheated oven for about an hour or until the crust has become golden brown. This torte can be served hot, but it is best served at room temperature.

SAVORY PIES

BOLOGNESE TORTE

Maestro Martino's Bolognese torte is the ancestor of the famous dish of Emilia-Romagna, scarpazzone (also called erbazzone in certain areas). Over the centuries, this torte has become richer through the addition of pancetta, garlic, and onion.

SERVES 6

For the crust:
3½ cups flour
4 tablespoons extra-virgin olive oil

For the filling:
3 pounds Swiss chard, well washed
1 pound smoked pancetta, finely chopped
4 spring onions, peeled and finely chopped
2 garlic cloves, peeled and finely chopped
3 ounces extra-virgin olive oil

¾ cup freshly grated Parmigiano
  Reggiano
1 bunch Italian parsley, finely chopped
1 heaping tablespoon freshly chopped
  marjoram
Salt and freshly ground black pepper
1 egg yolk
¼ teaspoon saffron stigmas, infused in
  2 tablespoons hot water and strained

Preheat the oven to 400°F. Make a pie crust by combining the flour, olive oil, and about ½ cup water. Work the dough vigorously and then divide in half and roll out each half into a disk with a diameter of about 11 inches; grease a 9-inch tart or quiche pan with olive oil, and arrange one of the disks in the pan.

Then make the filling. Wilt the chard, with the water clinging to the leaves after being washed, adding a handful of salt. Drain the chard in a colander, pressing on it with the back of a large spoon to remove as much water as possible; finely chop. Sauté the pancetta, spring onions, and garlic in the olive oil; add the chard and continue to cook for a few minutes.

In a bowl, combine the Parmigiano, parsley, marjoram, and the chard, pancetta, and onion mixture; season with salt and pepper to taste. Distribute the filling in the pan, top with the remaining disk, and pinch around the edges to seal. Beat the egg yolk with the saffron infusion and some warm water; brush the crust with this egg wash. Bake the torte in the preheated oven for about an hour, or until golden brown.

SAVORY PIES

SQUASH TORTE

(SEE "HOW TO MAKE SQUASH TORTE," PAGE 81)

Maestro Martino's squash torte is both sweet and savory, combining a generous amount of cheese and pork. The filling is encased in a crust without a "cover."

The present version omits the meat and substitutes sugar with crumbled amaretti (the famous almond macaroons used to sweeten the filling for pumpkin ravioli). Of course, sweet spices are mandatory.

SERVES 6

For the crust:
3 cups flour
8 tablespoons butter, cut into ¼-inch
    pieces, plus extra for greasing the pan
1 egg

For the filling:
1 medium-sized pumpkin (about 2
    pounds), peeled, seeds and fibers

removed, and cut up into 1-inch-thick
    slices
1 cup crumbled amaretti
1 cup freshly grated Parmigiano Reggiano
1 cup freshly grated Gruyère
1 teaspoon ground cinnamon
1 teaspoon freshly grated ginger
Salt and freshly ground black pepper

Use the flour to make a well on a well-dusted pastry board. Sprinkle with salt and put the butter in the center of the well; work the butter into the flour until you obtain a somewhat lumpy mixture; then add the egg and a few tablespoons of cold water; work quickly and vigorously until all the ingredients have been fully incorporated; cover in plastic wrap and let the dough set for 30 minutes in a cool place.

In the meantime, boil the pumpkin in salted water for 10 minutes, drain, and thinly slice. Preheat the oven to 375°F.

Use ⅔ of the dough to make a disk about 11 inches in diameter and arrange on the bottom of a 10-inch tart or quiche pan previously greased with butter, covering the edges of the pan with the dough (roll out the remaining dough and reserve). Sprinkle the crumbled amaretti on the bottom and then cover with a layer of pumpkin slices; combine the Parmigiano and Gruyère, and top the pumpkin slices with a layer of this cheese mix. Add another layer of pumpkin and then a layer of cheese, repeating these steps until you use up the ingredients. Top with the remaining crumbled amaretti. Sprinkle with the cinnamon and ginger, season with salt and pepper to taste, and use the remaining dough to make a lattice top.

Bake in the preheated oven for about 50 minutes. Serve at room temperature.

SAVORY PIES

MIGLIACCIO

(SEE "HOW TO MAKE *MIGLIACCIO*," PAGE 82)

Migliaccio *is a descendant of* farinata, *a type of flatbread common among the Etruscans and the Romans, and is mentioned in* Apicius. *Originally,* migliaccio *was made with millet flour or farro (emmer wheat). The present version combines elements of Maestro Martino's recipe (a sweet dish) and the modern ingredients used in classic Neapolitan* migliaccio *(see note 2, page 82).*

SERVES 6

4 cups water
Salt
2½ cups cornmeal
1 cup freshly grated Parmigiano Reggiano
1 cup freshly grated sharp provolone

1 bunch Italian parsley, finely chopped
1 teaspoon ground cinnamon
1 teaspoon grated nutmeg
Freshly ground black pepper
Butter or rendered lard for greasing the pan

Bring the water to a boil in a large pot and add salt. Slowly add the cornmeal in a thin, even stream, stirring constantly. Lower heat and simmer for 45 minutes, stirring constantly. Remove from heat and fold in the Parmigiano, provolone, parsley, cinnamon, nutmeg, and pepper. Grease a frying pan with butter or lard and heat the pan well before pouring the mixture into it. Brown on one side and then flip to brown on the other. Turn out onto a serving platter and serve immediately.

SAVORY PIES

EEL TORTE

This is one of the more difficult recipes to prepare, but the delicious result will certainly justify the effort. If you cannot find fresh eel at your local fishmonger (Asian fishmongers are more likely to carry it), you can use any type of fish you like, although strongly flavored fish, such as fresh sardines or anchovies, are best.

SERVES 6

For the crust:
2½ cups flour
8 tablespoons butter, softened
Salt

For the filling:
3 fresh eels (about 1¾ pounds), peeled,
    cleaned, and cut into 1-inch to
    1½-inch pieces
1 bunch mint, finely chopped
1 bunch Italian parsley, finely chopped
1 teaspoon ground cinnamon
Freshly ground black pepper
1 teaspoon freshly grated ginger

3 or 4 cloves, finely crushed
2 dried figs, diced
⅓ cup raisins
2 egg yolks
¼ teaspoon saffron stigmas, infused in
    2 tablespoons hot water and strained
⅔ cup blanched almonds
1 cup verjuice, or 1 cup aromatic balsamic
    vinegar mixed with 4 tablespoons water
Extra-virgin olive oil
Salt
⅓ cup heavy cream
¼ cup pine nuts

Use the flour to make a well on a well-dusted pastry board. Put the butter and salt in the middle of the well and use your hands to mix the ingredients, adding water a little bit at a time, as needed, until you obtain the right consistency for a short pastry dough or pie crust. Cover the dough with a kitchen towel and let it set for at least 30 minutes.

Preheat the oven to 375°F. In a bowl, combine the eel, mint, parsley, cinnamon, pepper, ginger, cloves, figs, and raisins. In a separate bowl, beat the egg yolks with the saffron infusion; purée the almonds in a food processor together with the egg yolks, saffron infusion, and verjuice.

Work the dough vigorously and roll out into a disk with a diameter of about 11 inches; grease a 9-inch tart or quiche pan with olive oil, and arrange the disk in the pan. Add the eel mixture, season with salt, and drizzle with olive oil; cook for 20 minutes in the preheated oven. In the meantime, add the cream to the puréed almonds and mix well. Remove the torte from the oven, pour the almond purée over the eel, sprinkle with the pine nuts, and return to the oven for about 25 minutes, or until done. Serve hot.

SAVORY PIES

DRIED PIES MADE WITH WHOLE FISH

If you do not wish to use the timballo-style crust in this recipe, make a regular pie dough or use frozen pie dough.

SERVES 6

For the crust:
3½ cups flour
4 tablespoons butter,
    softened
4 egg yolks
4 tablespoons dry Marsala
Salt

For the filling:
6 fresh trout (or trout in brine),
    washed and cleaned
1 teaspoon grated nutmeg
1 teaspoon freshly grated ginger
3 or 4 cloves, well crushed
Salt and freshly ground black pepper

Make the crust by combining all the ingredients, adding water as needed, until you obtain an even, elastic dough. Work well, cover, and let set for about 1 hour.

Preheat the oven to 375°F. After washing and cleaning the trout, dry well on a double layer of paper towels. Use a sharp knife to make long incisions on both sides of the trout, and then sprinkle inside and out with nutmeg, ginger, cloves, salt, and pepper.

Divide the dough into 6 balls and roll out into relatively thick sheets, each about an inch longer than the fish. Wrap each trout in the dough and then shape one end of the dough to resemble a fish head and the other end a fish tail, leaving a hole on either end. Arrange the fish on parchment paper and bake in the preheated oven until golden brown.

EGGS AND FRITTERS

SAGE FRITTERS

Maestro Martino's recipe has endured unchanged for more than five centuries. Fried sage is still served today as a decadent, savory appetizer. Always fry in extra-virgin olive oil: the result will invariably be more healthy and more tasty. Serve accompanied by prosciutto.

SERVES 6

1⅓ cups flour
1 egg
½ cup dry white wine
¼ teaspoon saffron stigmas, infused in
    2 tablespoons hot water and strained

1 teaspoon ground cinnamon
Salt
1 tablespoon extra-virgin olive oil,
    plus more for frying
1 large bunch sage

In a bowl, combine the flour, egg, wine, saffron infusion, cinnamon, salt, and the tablespoon of olive oil. Work the batter with a whisk, adding water as needed, until you obtain a thick, even mixture. Remove the sage leaves from the sprigs, wash, and dry well. Heat the olive oil in a frying pan to 375°F. Dip the leaves in the batter and then fry until golden brown; be careful not to overcrowd the pan (depending on the size of the pan, it may be best to fry the leaves in batches). Drain on a double layer of paper towels. Serve hot.

EGGS AND FRITTERS

FRITTATA

No matter which herbs and vegetables you use to make Maestro Martino's classic frittata, the result will be great.

SERVES 6

$^1/_3$ pound Swiss chard
$^1/_3$ pound spinach
Salt
2 tablespoons butter
1 garlic clove, peeled
1 bunch Italian parsley, finely chopped
1 bunch marjoram, finely chopped

1 bunch mint, finely chopped
10 fresh sage leaves, finely chopped
6 fresh eggs
3 tablespoons freshly grated
    Parmigiano Reggiano
$^1/_2$ cup milk
Freshly ground black pepper

Wilt the chard and spinach, using the water that clings to their leaves after they have been washed and a pinch of salt. Squeeze well and finely chop. Melt the butter in a pan. Add the garlic clove, and when it has browned, remove. Add the chard and spinach to the pan, together with the parsley, marjoram, mint, and sage. In a bowl, beat the eggs with the Parmigiano, milk, salt, and pepper; pour the egg mixture into the pan and allow it to cook through without burning the bottom (you can cover the pan when it is almost done cooking, if the top of the frittata is still liquid). Turn out onto a serving platter.

EGGS AND FRITTERS

POACHED EGGS

(SEE "EGGS POACHED IN WATER," PAGE 96)

In Italian, poached eggs are called uova in camicia, *literally "eggs wrapped in a shirt," in the same way that certain English and American dishes are prepared "in a blanket." The trick is to wrap the yolk with the white, giving it the appearance of being snugly wrapped in a white lining.*

SERVES 6

Salt
2 tablespoons aromatic
   balsamic vinegar
6 eggs

6 tablespoons freshly grated Parmigiano
   Reggiano
1 teaspoon grated nutmeg
1 teaspoon ground cinnamon
Freshly ground black pepper

Fill a pan with water; add salt and half the balsamic vinegar. Heat the water, and when it begins to boil, gently break the eggs into it. As the whites begin to solidify, gently wrap the whites around the yolks with the spoon. Remove with a slotted spoon, transfer to a serving platter, sprinkle with the Parmigiano, nutmeg, cinnamon, salt, and pepper, and then top with a few drops of the reserved balsamic vinegar. Serve hot.

EGGS AND FRITTERS

EGGS IN THE SHAPE OF RAVIOLI

This dish is reminiscent of the traditional Tunisian brick, *a recipe that definitely tests one's ability in the kitchen: it requires that you break an egg in a thin sheet of pastry and then fry it—true culinary gymnastics! Martino's recipe is sweet; the present recipe is savory in keeping with modern tastes.*

SERVES 6

For the pastry:
2½ cups flour
1 tablespoon extra-virgin
    olive oil
Salt

For the filling:
6 eggs
1 teaspoon ground cinnamon
1 teaspoon grated nutmeg
3 or 4 cloves, crushed
Salt and freshly ground black pepper
Extra-virgin olive oil for frying

Make a pastry dough by combining the flour, olive oil, and a pinch of salt; add water as needed to obtain an elastic dough. Shape the dough into a ball and let set covered in a cool place for 30 minutes. Then divide the dough into 6 pieces and roll out to a thickness of about ¹/₁₀ of an inch.

Use the 6 pieces of dough to line 6 coffee cups and then break an egg into each one of the cups. Sprinkle with cinnamon, nutmeg, and cloves, and season with salt and pepper; brush the edges of the dough with water, carefully seal each "raviolo," and fry in the olive oil just until the eggs have cooked inside. Drain on 2 layers of paper towels and serve hot.

SEAFOOD

SOLE

This nouvelle cuisine recipe is another one that bears testimony to Maestro Martino's great modernity.

SERVES 6

6 sole fillets	Juice of 2 oranges
Salt	Juice of 1 lemon
Flour for dredging	3 teaspoons finely chopped Italian parsley
2 tablespoons butter	Freshly ground black pepper

Season the sole fillets with salt and dredge in the flour. Melt the butter in a pan, and brown the sole fillets on either side (about 3 or 4 minutes per side). Lower heat and add the orange and lemon juice. Remove to a warm platter, sprinkle with parsley, and season with pepper. Serve hot.

SEAFOOD

OYSTERS

(SEE "HOW TO COOK OYSTERS," PAGE 102)

Maestro Martino's recipe is relatively simple: oysters cooked over hot coals. Unfortunately, wood-fired stoves are rare in today's world. Inspired by the original, the present recipe for oven-baked oysters is just as tasty.

SERVES 6

36 oysters
Coarse salt, as needed
Extra-virgin olive oil

Lemon juice
Freshly ground
   black pepper

Preheat the oven to 375°F. Clean the oysters well with a brush, cover the bottom of a roasting pan with about $1/3$ inch of salt, and arrange the oysters on the bed of salt. Place in the broiler of the oven for about 15 minutes. Remove from oven, open the oysters, discard the top shell, and then arrange on a serving platter. Dress with the olive oil, lemon juice, and pepper, and serve immediately.

SEAFOOD

MARINATED SALMON

(SEE "FRYING TROUT LIKE CARP," PAGE 112)

In the original, Martino gives a recipe for cooking trout like carp, that is, by marinating the fish beforehand. The substitution of salmon for trout makes for a richer and tastier dish.

SERVES 6

6 salmon steaks
3 tablespoons sea salt
$1/2$ cup aromatic balsamic vinegar

$1/2$ cup red wine vinegar
3 tablespoons extra-virgin olive oil
Freshly ground black pepper

Use a small, sharp knife to make small incisions in the salmon. Combine a cup of water, the salt, and the vinegars, and marinate the salmon for 3 hours. Drain the salmon of its marinade and then place it in a press for 2 hours: in other words, cover in plastic wrap and then place something heavy (like a brick, weighing at least 2 pounds) on top of it. Heat the olive oil in a pan and brown the salmon on either side (about 4 minutes per side). Sprinkle with pepper and serve hot. This dish can also be served cold.

DESSERTS

RICOTTA PIE

(SEE "COMMON TORTE," PAGE 83)

Maestro Martino includes this recipe among his savory tortes (in fact, he uses meat broth in the preparation). This new version is similar to the white torte (page 80); it is made sweet by using ricotta and raisins and by eliminating the broth and spices.

SERVES 6

For the crust:
2½ cups flour
8 tablespoons butter, softened,
 plus extra for greasing pie tin
¾ cup sugar
2 egg yolks
Grated zest of 1 lemon

For the filling:
1 pound ricotta
2 eggs
½ cup sugar
2 tablespoons raisins
1 teaspoon ground cinnamon
Grated zest of ½ orange

Make a short crust by combining the flour, butter, sugar, egg yolks, and lemon zest. Work the dough vigorously, cover, and let set in a cool place for 30 minutes.

Preheat the oven to 375°F. Push the ricotta through a sieve and then combine with eggs, sugar, raisins, cinnamon, and orange zest. Divide the dough into 2 pieces, roll out, and use one sheet to line a pie tin that has been greased with butter. Fill the pan with the ricotta, use the remaining dough to make a lattice crust for the top, and bake for 40 minutes.

DESERTS

CHERRY PIE

(SEE "HOW TO MAKE A RED CHERRY AND ROSE TORTE," PAGE 84)

This pie is a classic dessert of Jewish-Roman cuisine. Nowhere is it made better than in the pastry shops of Rome's Jewish quarter.

SERVES 6

For the crust:
See the previous recipe

For the filling:
⅔ pound ricotta
2 eggs
1 cup sugar

1 teaspoon ground cinnamon
1 teaspoon freshly grated ginger
1 tablespoon rose water
⅔ pound sour cherries,
    pitted and chopped
Butter for greasing pie tin

Preheat the oven to 275°F. Prepare a short-crust dough as above for the other pie. Pass the ricotta through a sieve and then combine with the eggs, sugar, cinnamon, ginger, rose water, and lastly the cherries. Divide the dough into 2 pieces, roll out, and use one sheet to line a pie tin that has been greased with butter. Add the filling, level off, and use the remaining dough to make a lattice top. Bake in the preheated oven for 45 minutes. Cool before serving.

DESSERTS

MARZIPAN

(SEE "HOW TO MAKE TEN SERVINGS OF MARZIPAN," PAGE 119, AND
"HOW TO MAKE FOUR OR FIVE SERVINGS OF MARZIPAN," PAGE 120)

This ancient recipe has remained unaltered literally for millennia. It is still served in Sicily today, generally accompanied by small, painted marzipan "fruits." Marzipan is simple to make and keeps for a long time.

SERVES 6

$^3/_4$ pound almonds 1 teaspoon ground cinnamon
$^3/_4$ pound sugar Rose water

Blanch the almonds by parboiling and peeling, and then crush in a mortar or food processor. Add the sugar, cinnamon, and a dash of rose water. Allow it to set before serving.

DESSERTS

CALZONES

(SEE "HOW TO MAKE CALZONES," PAGE 88)

Although today calzones are generally stuffed with savory fillings, in Sicily they are still served stuffed with marzipan.

SERVES 6

For the pastry: 8 tablespoons butter, softened
3 cups flour   1 teaspoon vanilla
4 egg yolks   *For the filling:*
³⁄₄ cup sugar   Marzipan (prepare as in
                             the previous recipe)

Preheat the oven to 375°F. Make the dough by combining all the ingredients; work vigorously and then roll out into 6 thin sheets. Prepare the marzipan, and then place a spoonful of it on each of the 6 pastry sheets; seal well. Use a fork to make small holes in each calzone, and then bake on parchment paper in the preheated oven until golden brown.

DESSERTS

CUSTARD PIE

(SEE "CUSTARD," PAGE 90)

SERVES 6

For the crust:
Prepare as above for eel torte
   (page 176)
Dried beans,
   for blind baking

For the filling:
6 egg yolks
$2^{1}/_{3}$ cups sugar
4 cups milk
1 tablespoon ground cinnamon
Rose water

Prepare the pie dough and let it rest in a dry place for 1 or 2 hours. Preheat the oven to 375°F. Roll the dough out and line a quiche pan that has been greased with butter. "Blind bake" the crust: top with dried beans and bake for 20 minutes.

    In a bowl, whisk the egg yolks together with the sugar, adding the milk a bit at a time; fold in the cinnamon. Fill the crust with the custard and return to the oven: if the custard begins to brown, cover with aluminum foil. When the custard has solidified, remove and top with a few drops of rose water. Cool and serve.

DESSERTS

FRENCH TOAST

(SEE "GOLDEN SOPS," PAGE 91)

Maestro Martino's golden sops are the answer to one of the world's most ancient questions: what do you do with stale bread?

SERVES 6

6 eggs
3 heaping tablespoons sugar
4 tablespoons rose water
6 slices stale country bread, crust
    removed, cubed and toasted

8 tablespoons butter
$\frac{1}{4}$ teaspoon saffron stigmas,
    infused in 2 tablespoons
    hot water and strained

Beat the eggs together with 2 tablespoons of the sugar, add half the rose water, and mix well. Soak the bread in the eggs for 10 minutes. Melt the butter in a pan and brown the bread. Once browned, sprinkle with the remaining rose water mixed with the saffron infusion. Serve immediately, sprinkled with the remaining sugar.

DESSERTS

PUFF FRITTERS

(SEE "WIND-FILLED FRITTERS," PAGE 95)

Maestro Martino called these "wind-filled fritters" because when they are fried, they puff up. In modern-day Naples, these puff fritters are called pizzelle, *literally, "little pizzas," and they are generally served as a savory dish. The present recipe is a sweet version.*

SERVES 6

2½ cups flour   Olive oil for frying
Pinch of salt   Sugar

Combine the flour, salt, and enough water as needed to obtain an even, elastic dough. Work for 30 minutes and then let set for 1 hour. Roll out into a thin sheet and use a glass to cut into disks. Fry the disks in the olive oil until golden brown, drain on 2 layers of paper towels, sprinkle generously with sugar, and serve.

TEXTUAL NOTE

Jeremy Parzen

THE CORPUS OF RECIPES ATTRIBUTED to Martino (as well as many pseudo-Martinian recipes) is represented by five manuscripts—all of which were probably composed in peninsular Italy during the second half of the fifteenth century or the early sixteenth century. Of these, four have been transcribed and published in recent years:

1. Library of Congress, Washington, D.C., Medieval Manuscript no. 153
2. Biblioteca Apostolica, Vatican City, Rome, Manuscript Urbinate Latino no. 1203
3. Archivio storico, Riva del Garda (Trento), Italy, *Martino de Rubeis [ricettario]*
4. Pierpont Morgan Library, New York, Manuscript Bühler no. 19

See Claudio Benporat's *Cucina italiana del Quattrocento,* in which the Vatican, Riva del Garda, and Morgan manuscripts are reported; and Emilio Faccioli's *L'arte della cucina in Italia,* in which the Library of Congress manuscript is transcribed. See also *Cuoco Napoletano: The Neapolitan Recipe Collection,* translated, edited, and annotated by Terence Scully, in which the Morgan manuscript is transcribed. Lastly, see the *Libro di cucina del Maestro Martino de Rossi,* edited by Aldo Bertoluzza: the modern adaptation of the recipes and glossary is laden with gross errors, but the photographic reproduction of the manuscript is highly valuable.

The fifth manuscript belongs to an as-yet-unidentified private collection, and unfortunately no transcription is currently available to scholars. According to at least one scholar, Claudio Benporat, it is probably similar to the Washington and Vatican manuscripts, which are generally held to be the most faithful codices with respect to the genuine Martinian tradition. The most recent description of the manuscript was reported on the occasion of its sale at auction at Christie's of London, on November 13, 1974. Bruno Laurioux, the eminent scholar of medieval and Renaissance culinary texts, had limited access to the manuscript before its sale, and he reports that it is a beautifully decorated book on vellum, and he even proposes—although without any substantiation—that the hand can be ascribed to Bartolomeo Sanvito, the great fifteenth-century scribe from the town of San Daniele in Friuli. This copy was probably a "privileged" manuscript intended for an illustrious reader, and it is regrettable that its whereabouts are unknown. Laurioux maintains that this could be an earlier manuscript because it reports "Maestro Martino, cook to Cardinal Trevisan," instead of "Maestro Martino, once cook to Cardinal Trevisan," as reported in the Washington manuscript. But he does not take into account a very simple fact that makes such conjecture moot, however enticing it may be: the rubrics could

have been added at any time—even after the main texts of the manuscripts had been copied. The inherent nature of philology defies exact dates, despite human nature's impulse to assign them.

Laurioux's attitude is indicative of the many highly qualified scholars who have written about these manuscripts and who have tried desperately—and at times ingenuously—to ascribe to them an exact or nearly exact date.

Claudio Benporat, for example, has published numerous articles in which he tries to date this manuscript tradition, and in particular, he has attempted to ascribe a *terminus post quem* (i.e., a date after which it was composed) to the Riva del Garda manuscript. The whereabouts of the last eleven pages of this manuscript were unknown until they were discovered in 1973 by a Milanese dealer of rare books among the pages of a prayer book. (See Claudio Benporat, "Un frammento inedito di Maestro Martino," *Appunti di gastronomia* 26 [1998]: 109–21.) In 1994 Benporat was allowed access to the missing folios by the current owner, a Milanese collector, and he used them to propose a date: either 1501 or 1503, in accordance with the date ascribed by various scholars for the wedding of Nicolò Trivulzio (Gian Giacomo's son; for more on Gian Giacomo Trivulzio, see the introduction to the present volume, page 17, and page 41, note 69) and Paola di Rodolfo Gonzaga, whose wedding feast—Benporat maintains—is described in these final pages of the manuscript. Benporat admits that his thesis is tenuous at best, and despite his intense study of this handwritten book, it seems unlikely that anyone will be able to date it with certainty.

The script of the manuscript would seem to indicate that it could be dated no later than 1527 (i.e., the year of the sack of Rome by Charles V, and the year considered by paleographers to mark roughly the disappearance of the hybrid script such as that adopted in the Riva del Garda manuscript—somewhere between the demise of Gothic script and the birth of humanist cursive scripts) and no earlier than the late 1400s. In other words, the Riva del Garda manuscript, like the others, almost certainly belongs to that period of handwritten books that were still unaffected by the appearance and rapidly growing popularity of printed books (1470–1527).

Although a precise date for the manuscript would be useful and indeed is an alluring—however elusive—conundrum, the fact remains that the Riva del Garda manuscript is among the least "fair" in the tradition of Martino manuscripts.

It is important to remember that none of the extant manuscripts are autographs (nor is there any indication that any of them are idiographs, i.e., a semiautograph or a transcription overseen and authorized by the author). Platina speaks of Martino's "book," but it is unlikely that Martino possessed the skills of an amanuensis. It is also possible that he dictated the text to a copyist (in fact, there are many instances where the text reads "I say" or "I mean to say," etc.).

The possibility that the Riva del Garda was the earliest of the manuscripts, as some would maintain, has little philological bearing on the hierarchy of the manuscript tradition: the textual tradition of the Library of Congress and Vatican manuscripts is clearly the source for the Riva del Garda manuscript, because of these manuscripts' uniformity in transcription and the

homogeneity of their terminology. When, where, or how the Riva del Garda scribe had contact with the alpha manuscript (i.e., the original text that was dictated or perhaps transcribed by Martino himself) is nearly impossible to determine; there easily could have been other manuscripts circulating at the time.

Aside from a few variants (cited by Benporat in the preface to his transcriptions of the Vatican, Riva del Garda, and Morgan manuscripts: see the bibliography, *Cucina italiana del Quattrocento*), the Vatican and Library of Congress manuscripts are fundamentally identical, and it is likely that the text was transcribed for an elite or privileged readership: the fact that the recipes were transcribed by a humanist scribe indicates that these were privileged formulas intended for a select audience of Renaissance culinary enthusiasts, perhaps centered around the papal court, and of whom Platina may be considered an indicative, if not directly related, representative.

The Library of Congress manuscript has generally been considered to be the most faithful—although not necessarily the earliest or the primary source—of the Martino tradition, and this manuscript is the one that was used for the present translation. The Vatican manuscript was used for the Washington manuscript lacunae (including recipe titles: brackets, "[ ]," are used to denote the Vatican manuscript).

Although it lacks a number of recipes found in both the Library of Congress and Vatican manuscripts, the Riva del Garda manuscript also contains a significant number of extravagant recipes: these recipes are "extravagant" in the philological sense of the word; that is to say, they are recipes most probably not part of the alpha tradition of Martino's book and were transcribed from other sources. It was not uncommon for scribes to indiscriminately collect texts from extraneous sources (in the same way that "extravagant" Petrarchan ballads, sonnets, and songs, composed by other poets, were often included by scribes in songbooks comprising mostly Petrarch's compositions).

While many scholars (Benporat among them, albeit with some reservation) have attributed these formulas to Martino, the heterogeneous nature of the Riva del Garda recipes would seem to suggest that they cannot be unequivocally ascribed to Martino, and that their provenance in fact is more probably identifiable with an unrelated tradition to which the scribe had access in some form (perhaps it was even transmitted to him orally).

The terminology, style, and ingredients of the Riva del Garda manuscript vary greatly from those of the Library of Congress and Vatican manuscripts. For example, *provatura* (a plastic cow's-milk cheese, belonging to the same family as mozzarella and provolone, both specifically native to southern Italy) and eggplant (yet another southern ingredient, most probably unknown to northern chefs at that time) are entirely absent in both the Library of Congress and Vatican manuscripts.

Moreover, many of the extravagant Riva del Garda recipes are specifically regional, that is, they are referred to as "after the Genoese style" or "after the Lombard style" (these recipes also include ingredients foreign to the privileged Martinian tradition). This is an element almost entirely absent in the Library of Congress and Vatican manuscripts, where some reference is

made to the French and Catalan traditions, but no peninsular (that is, no regional Italian) reference is made.

Another indication of their probably extravagant provenance is that the Riva del Garda recipes tend to be grouped at the end of sections that loosely reflect the order of the Library of Congress and Vatican manuscripts, as if the scribe had added these recipes after completing a section of transcription.

In light of these elements, the Riva del Garda recipe collection is less akin to our modern concept of the cookery book (a homogeneous compendium of recipes that reflect a national or regional tradition or an individual's knowledge and experience) than it is similar to the Renaissance concept of miscellanea, in which the formulas or various texts were gathered from widely varied sources.

The extravagant recipes of the Neapolitan manuscript are reported in the final chapter of the Martino text in this book. Most modern scholars concur that they are not ascribable to Martino, and both Benporat and Terence Scully have dealt at length with this question.

But as Scully asserts in the preface to his transcription and translation, they reflect a culinary tradition of which Martino was undoubtedly the primary figure. Although Martino may have never deemed such recipes worthy of or pertinent to his own gastronomic ideology, he certainly would have appreciated the spirit with which they were gathered and conserved for posterity. Like the extravagant recipes in the Riva del Garda manuscript, they should be considered to be "in the Martinian school" or "after the Martinian fashion," the way an eighteenth-century *veduta* may be attributed to the school of Francesco Guardi although it is not by the great Venetian *vedutista* himself.

SELECTED BIBLIOGRAPHY

Benporat, Claudio. *Cucina italiana del Quattrocento.* Florence: Olschki, 1996.

——. "Un frammento inedito di Maestro Martino." *Appunti di gastronomia* 26 (1998): 109–21.

——. "Maestro Martino e i suoi ricettari." *Appunti di gastronomia* 14 (1994): 5–13.

——. "Il ricettario di Martino de Rubeis nel contesto della cucina rinascimentale italiana." *Appunti di gastronomia* 13 (1994): 5–14.

Bertoluzza, Aldo, ed. *Libro di cucina del Maestro Martino de Rossi.* Trento: Edizioni U.C.T., 1993.

Faccioli, Emilio. *L'arte della cucina in Italia.* 1987. Reprint, Turin: Einaudi, 1992.

Laurioux, Bruno. "I libri di cucina italiana alla fine del medioevo: Un nuovo bilancio." *Archivio Storico Italiano* 154 (1996): 45–54.

Martino da Como [Maestro Martino]. *Libro de arte coquinaria.* Ed. Emilio Montorfano. Facsimile of the Library of Congress manuscript 153. Milan: Terziaria, 1990.

——. *Libro de arte coquinaria: Copia anastatica dell'incunabolo stampato a Cividale da Gerardo di Fiandra nel 1480 e conservato al Museo Archeologico Nazionale di Cividale del Friuli.* Udine: Società Filologica Friulana and Arti Grafiche Friulane, 1994.

Milham, Mary Ella. "Martino and His *De Re Coquinaria*." In *Medieval Food and Drink* 21 (1995): 62–66. Binghamton, N.Y.: Center for Medieval and Early Renaissance Studies.

——, ed. and trans. *On Right Pleasure and Good Health.* A critical edition of *De honesta voluptate et valetudine.* Tempe, Ariz.: Medieval and Renaissance Texts and Studies, 1998.

——. "Platina and Martino's *Libro de Arte Coquinaria*." In *Acta conventus neo-latini hafniensis,* ed. A. Moss et al., 669–73. Binghamton, N.Y.: MRTS, 1994.

Scully, Terence, trans. and ed. *Cuoco Napoletano: The Neapolitan Recipe Collection.* An annotated critical edition. Ann Arbor: University of Michigan Press, 2000.

Spadaro di Passantello, Carmelo. "Il codice Bühler 19 della Pierpont Morgan Library di New York." *Appunti di gastronomia* 9 (1992): 9–14.

——. "Relazioni tra il *Libro di arte coquinaria* di Maestro Martino e i ricettari italiani rinascimentali." *Appunti di gastronomia* 14 (1994): 119–204.

Vehling, Joseph Dommers. "Martino and Platina: Exponents of Renaissance Cookery." *Hotel Bulletin and the Nation's Chefs* (October 1932): 192–95.

——. *Platina and the Rebirth of Man.* Chicago: W. M. Hill, 1941.

INDEX

Page numbers in italics indicate this book's modernized versions of Martino's original recipes.

TEXT:
Requiem Text Roman
DISPLAY:
Requiem HTF
DESIGNER:
Jessica Grunwald
COMPOSITOR:
Integrated Composition Systems
PRINTER AND BINDER:
Friesens Corporation